Perched: Jürgen Klopp's Liverpool FC – Champions Of Everything

Paul Tomkins

For Mike Hajialexandrou and Peter Verinder

Paul Tomkins is the author of over a dozen football books, an academic paper on the role football finances play in success, and the novel *The Girl on the Pier*. In addition, he was a columnist on the official Liverpool website between 2005 and 2012. In 2009 he set up the website *The Tomkins Times*.

www.TomkinsTimes.com

Contents

Introduction

And so it was done – 30 years of some close-but-no-cigars, but about 25 never-even-closes. With seven games still to go, Liverpool secured a 19th league title; breaking the record for the quickest-ever title success by two full games (beating Manchester United's record from 1907/08, shared by three other teams including Pep Guardiola's Manchester City), to make for both the earliest league title confirmation and also the *latest*, given that it occurred on June 25th. Liverpool is in England, and England is in Europe, and Europe is in the world – and on that date, Liverpool were reigning champions of *everywhere*.

When Jürgen Klopp arrived at Liverpool Football Club in October 2015 the team were 10th in the table and ranked a lowly 34th in Europe. Four years later they were ranked the 4th-best in team *in football history*, above every other English side, and behind only the best-ever vintages of Barcelona (2012), Bayern Munich (2014) and Real Madrid (2014), and just ahead of the great 1961 Real Madrid team. When Fenway Sports Group bought Liverpool the club were in a relegation battle, managed by Roy Hodgson, and pinning their hopes on Paul Konchesky, Joe Cole, Jay Spearing, Sotirios Kyrgiakos, Milan Jovanović, Jonjo Shelvey, David N'gog and Christian Poulsen.

As with all progress, it's easy to forget how far you've come; you acclimatise to the improvements along the way, and perhaps forget just how dire things were in decades past.

For a while, as Covid-19 swept the country and ravaged the globe, it looked like Liverpool's unprecedented lead could be nulled and voided; a quarter of the season left, and some – with intentions purely humanitarian, it has to be noted, such as those NHS key workers and *Médecins Sans Frontières* volunteers who own and run West Ham United – wanted to end it there and then, no prizes, and completely coincidentally (for you must appreciate the goodness of their souls), *no relegations*. The last time the league title was decided in June was way back in 1947, when a harsh winter saw 55 consecutive days of snow; the subsequent postponements meaning it was June 14th when some plucky outsiders were finally crowned champions. The club? Liverpool. Coincidentally, 1947 was also the only other time the Reds had won a league title on a day that they were not playing.

If you told me in 2015, a few games into the season that had just started with Brendan Rodgers still at the helm, that by 2020 Liverpool would be European champions, world champions, win the Premier League after having just finished 2nd with 97 points, and rise to be ranked *the 4th-best team in history of football* by a long-established sporting statistical methodology – all with a net spend of just c.£75m in those five years – then I'd have called you insane. The only way that would be even remotely possible would be to go out and get Jürgen Klopp – but as I wrote in the summer of 2015, when seeing him as an obvious candidate to rejuvenate the club if Rodgers were to be sacked, why would Klopp join an increasingly mediocre outfit like Liverpool? The club was in a far better position than when Fenway Sports Group (then NESV) bought it five years earlier, but one in a period of regression, on the pitch at least, after an unlikely title challenge in 2013/14.

There's a narrative that FSG lucked out when they got Klopp. But *Fenway Sports Group got Klopp*. You can argue that any club gets lucky when they make an appointment or sign a player that works out. Did Liverpool get *lucky* when they signed Fernando Torres in 2007? Did Chelsea get *unlucky* when they signed Fernando Torres in 2011? Klopp had previously been approached by Manchester United, but he found their sales pitch tacky. Other big clubs wanted him; he didn't want them. Even so, why go to Liverpool at that juncture? The squad, despite some promising players, was a bit of a mess, and pretty much all the key men of 2014 were gone by 2015.

Liverpool had no Champions League to offer, but the new driving force of the FSG-Liverpool axis, Mike Gordon, was both convincing and believable to Klopp. Such was their lust for a winner, FSG would even have taken Jose Mourinho in 2015 had they failed to lure the German, but Mourinho's toxicity – even before his failed stint at Manchester United – was starting to become increasingly clear, obscuring the winning value he might bring; and in that sense, Klopp united all sections of the club – analytical, scouting, medical, commercial, ownership – in a way someone like Mourinho never could. "Winners" *may* win with a scorched earth policy, but who cleans up afterwards? And if they *don't* win, the mess is even more costly.

So FSG *did* get lucky, to a degree, in that Klopp was a multiplier of talents, not a reducer of abilities; they got lucky in that *Klopp was even better than they expected*. (Just as Klopp had initially preferred the idea of signing Julian Brandt to Mo Salah, but was talked around by Michael Edwards and co., and Salah *was even better than anyone expected*.)

But from that point on, FSG worked with Klopp, sharing his vision and enabling his plans for success; and in 2016 everyone, Klopp included, agreed that Edwards should be made Sporting Director, as the club moved from the petty infighting of the Rodgers' reign to the unified aims of every single person rowing in the same direction. (Prior to Klopp's arrival, many weren't even in the same rowing boat. Others were in the boat, but doing interpretative jazz dance, or making origami pterodactyls.) Gordon, upon working with the German, claimed he could be an elite leader in *any* industry, if not football. Edwards, in an office within Melwood, was absolutely thrilled at the collegiality and transparency of the new manager, after the previous one plotted against his transfer committee. Gordon, Tom Werner and John W. Henry had found a manager who would lead from the front, and not alarm them behind the scenes with mixed messages and undermining briefings to the press. No players would be publicly thrown under the bus. Liverpool Football Club was whole again. Indeed, in the bid to regain their perch, it was, of all ironies, *united*.

Flashover
Until October 2017, Klopp's tenure wasn't quite catching light. Pockets were burning brightly – the addition of Sadio Mané, the development of Philippe Coutinho into a more regular goalscorer, the instant impact of Mohamed Salah, the raw promise of Trent Alexander-Arnold – but the defence, and its goalkeeper, was extinguishing the power of the attack, like a self-sabotaging firetruck that sprayed kerosene instead of foam (after all, the idea of a defence is to put out fires, not create them).

But then, after the 4-1 defeat at Spurs that represented the nadir – the proverbial bucket of cold water – things started to turn around, and the heat was gradually ramped up. More areas of the team entered combustion – lukewarm turning hot, hot turning red-hot. It was as if Klopp had lit a fire under all the players and, one by one, they were reaching the required temperature, with a satisfying crackle and pop. They were still separate fires, but some were joining, merging; others still catching up, but burning brightly.

Then, at the start of 2018/19, the team reached *flashover:* superheated, it was no longer a collection of fires *but the whole damn team had ignited* (although this blazing metaphor would like to stress that there was no thermal decomposition, nor were there the releases of flammable toxic gases. Also, it's fair to say that the only backdraft was experienced, from 2019 onwards, at the Etihad, as they saw their chief rivals race ahead like a rocket-powered projectile painted with the giant white smile of Bobby Firmino).

Once it caught light, Klopp was like a psychotic pyromaniac – a firestarter, a twisted firestarter – splashing the metaphorical football petrol in all directions from the touchline, and tossing a smouldering cigarette butt to see it light the sky orange and gold. Sadio Mané was a one-man inferno; Mo Salah a flying flamethrower; Bobby Firmino, with that smile, nuclear fusion. So much emotion, so much passion; the kind that saw the Anfield night sky lit red with flares on the 25th of June, as fans defied an easing lockdown (which itself had been defied by government advisers, politicians, and various others who saw themselves as above the rest), and let off their pyrotechnics, as people in passing cars honked horns and sang *You'll Never Walk Alone*.

And yet conversely combustible, in amongst all this heat, Liverpool were also the acknowledged world leaders in data, in analytics. And these pursuits are cold and, in terms of decision-making, largely emotionless; ice-cool, composed and calculating. (Not *robotic*, but certainly not all about passion.) As such, they are diametrically opposed to Klopp at his most combustable; the polar opposite of his emotional – but emotionally intelligent – style of man-management.

And yet that is what makes the marriage so devastating: Klopp *humanises* the data. He takes all the information and uses it in a way everyone understands; in a way that someone with a PhD in astrophysics could never hope to convey to a bunch of 6ft ripped athletes overflowing with adrenaline, biceps and fighting spirit.

If someone like Unai Emery was in charge of this Liverpool side then his own lack of a spark – his technocratic, attention-to-details style and his dour personality – might make the swathes of new data more deadening, sending it crashing into deaf ears. And whilst Klopp represents the passion that can never be found in pure numbers, he is not *opposed* to information. On the contrary. He is the conduit, the facilitator of knowledge; he knows that information is power, provided it can be understood. And he is not just a passionate person, but a man capable of quiet reflection and self improvement; a man of *science*, not just belief.

Perched!

In the end, it needed a small favour from Chelsea of all clubs – and a slip by a Man City player, as ironies rained down on ironies – but after 28 wins, two draws and one defeat in 31 games, it was hardly like Liverpool hadn't earned it. Champions in March … and yet it happened on a Thursday night in *June,* in subtropical conditions, in an empty stadium in London. It was just over 12 months since

Manchester City players sang a derogatory song about Liverpool after clinching the 2019 title.

Three decades earlier, Liverpool had knocked themselves off their own perch. In 1991, as the team aged after the horrors of Hillsborough (and Kenny Dalglish, suffering in the aftermath, lost his ruthless edge in replacing them), the decline began – and was hastened as one Scot replaced another (sound familiar?). The Reds were starting to regularly finish outside the top five when Alex Ferguson claimed he'd knocked Liverpool "off their fucking perch" in 1993. But Manchester United did become the dominant force – it was now *their* perch – and Liverpool would only hit 80 points, which only gave an outside chance of the title, roughly once every five years; and in those seasons it usually turned out to be 90 points that were required. Now Liverpool, after 97 points in 2018/19, were already on 86, with 21 points left to play for; and City, 23 points behind, would only be able to amass 21 further points if they failed to beat Chelsea. For a while it looked like they may manage that after equalising at Stamford Bridge, but the home side tore through the City defence time and again in the remainder of the match, and won with a late penalty.

In a weird shift that wasn't even possible in 1990, Liverpool would become champions of Europe not once but twice before regaining the domestic crown; Istanbul at the exact halfway point between the Dalglish side of 1990 and the Klopp champions of 2020. As such, it hasn't been such a bad journey to endure, for all the talk of decades of 'hurt'.

Having looked like they may limp over the line following a tepid encounter at Goodison Park upon Project Restart, the Reds' utter crushing of Crystal Palace a few days later – and 24 hours before the title was sealed by City's defeat – was a fitting way to become champions, even if it wasn't confirmed at the full-time whistle. A thumping 9-0 home win against Palace in 1989/90 was followed 30 years later with an equally dominant display, if not the same scoreline. That said, at least that old Palace side got out of their own half. As Opta noted after Klopp's side ran out 4-0 winners, "Crystal Palace failed to record a single touch in the opposition box against Liverpool, the first side to do so in a Premier League match since Opta have full data for this statistic (2008-09)".

Roy Hodgson, who had overseen the Reds' lowest point in the three decades, reminded us of what watching his teams at Anfield could be like. Indeed, there were usually plenty of empty seats towards the end of his reign; so he should have been used to the mass of spaces in the stadium.

So, Jürgen Klopp succeeded where Graeme Souness, Roy Evans, Gérard Houllier, Rafa Benítez, Hodgson, Dalglish (second time around) and Brendan Rodgers failed; some narrowly, some by a great distance. Think of all the top-class and world-class players who failed to win the league – Steven Gerrard, Robbie Fowler, Luis Suarez, Xabi Alonso, Fernando Torres, Javier Mascherano, Steve McManaman, Jamie Carragher, Pepe Reina, Michael Owen, Sami Hyypia, and others – and you realise that sometimes it's all about timing; players who could have won the title but for quirks of fate, just as Djimi Traoré won a European Cup and the incomparable John Barnes didn't.

Every title near-miss was painful, but it all just added to the joy in 2020. Plus, Liverpool have not dethroned weak champions, nor have they won the title with a low points tally. This has been won in style, by some distance.

Klopp has now achieved a mix of the greatest feats of Bill Shankly and Bob Paisley, albeit their greatness was also in repeating those feats for the length of time that Klopp hasn't yet had the chance to experience; he is only at the halfway point of Paisley's tenure, and a third of Shankly's. He has built the club up from outsiders to champions, in the way that Shankly did, if not from such a low starting point (but in an era where it's harder to claw back deficits); and he took the team to the European pinnacle, just like Paisley. He even added the new honour of World Champions. In addition, Klopp has broken all kinds of club records, and several English football records too.

These are the times you will tell your grandchildren about, and perhaps one day they will tell theirs, too.

A Quick Word About This Book
While I don't quote anyone directly, over the years I have spoken to various people connected to the running of Liverpool Football Club and the operations behind the scenes. As an independent Liverpool writer and 'football analyst' who has run his own website for 11 years and been covering the club for 20, I do not operate like a journalist; it is not my aim to make contacts within the game or to break stories. But since 2009 I have been contacted by more than one incumbent Liverpool manager, more than one of the current owners, as well as people in charge of the football operations whose contributions will be discussed in this book. As such, I have *some* insight, but I never sought contact with any of these people (not least as I never saw it to be my place). I may occasionally ask a question, if they open the lines of communication. On the whole I find it's better to operate at some kind of distance, so as to be as clear-eyed as possible, although this means

fewer tidbits and less insider-info, and that's fine by me. As such, I may draw erroneous conclusions from the facts at hand, as I don't have *all* the facts at hand; but a certain group of *proper* journalists seem to be well informed about the club, and some of their reporting is quoted in this book.

Also, I wasn't expecting to write a book like this so soon after writing a book about how Liverpool became European champions. While it felt that Liverpool could build on the amazing consistency of 2018/19, there was also the chance that they'd just given their best shot; just as 2008/09 and 2013/14 saw Liverpool give everything, and have nothing left a season later (albeit in part due to internal divisions, outbound transfers and other factors).

Mentality Monsters was not the *full story* of how Liverpool became European champions, and the same applies to this and the league title. There will be other books and different stories, that offer alternative insights. And while this book looks in depth at various factors behind the club's 19th title, that previous book deals more with the transition from Brendan Rodgers' Liverpool to Klopp's Liverpool. It covers more of the recruitment, and the move from slow, small players to faster, taller players who also happen to have more skill, to play faster, better football. It looks at transfer spending in more detail than this book; whereas in 2019/20 there was actually very little transfer activity to add to what had preceded it.

Like *Mentality Monsters*, this book is a mix of action and data, facts and football, analysis and opinion. As with that book, I have been ably assisted by Daniel Rhodes and Andrew Beasley, two stalwarts of *The Tomkins Times* since the dark days of Hodgson and co. – from the time we live-blogged the takeover court case in 2010 as if it was a European final. I'd also like to acknowledge the assistance of Chris Rowland (who also helped put together the subscribers-only companion book), Mick Thomas and Tricia Hill in the editing stage, and as ever, Daniel Marshall for the superb design. Finally, a huge thanks to the subscribers and benefactors of *The Tomkins Times*, and the numerous other people who write for it – all are owed a huge debt of gratitude.

Part One

Picking Up Where They Left Off: Why Reds in 2019 Were The Best-Ever European Champions

A start often follows an end, and for Liverpool the 2019/20 season began on the back of a quite remarkable achievement that I first detailed in the summer of 2019. There was, after all, still talk of "bottling" the title, even though the Reds won their final nine league games of the season, and finished with the third-best points tally in English football history; losing just once, and drawing just seven games, with a staggering 30 victories.

While Liverpool won *only* the Champions League, the overall body of work in 2018/19 was simply stellar, and its significance – as part of the rapid rise of the Reds – will be outlined in this chapter; in part to act as context for what was to follow. (For those of a slower disposition, or who have just arrived from Mars, I'm talking about becoming *champions of everything*.)

It remains a bold claim – that Liverpool in 2019 were the best-*ever* European champions. But bear with me. Let's be clear: this is not some arcane stat that I dug up by going back through the history books, but something *truly significant* – relating to what Liverpool achieved in 2018/19 – that didn't seem to get any attention elsewhere. This is not subjective: this is an *objective* measure of greatness, even if no argument on who is the greatest can ever be tested, due to the as-yet undiscovered powers of time travel.

Prior to Liverpool in 2018/19 only *four* of the other 64 European Cup/Champions League winners were able to match this incredible achievement, and only one of those occurred after 1973; and if you take into account some added difficulties Liverpool faced that those other teams did not, and use them to weight the data (with just a little jiggery-pokery that I will explain), then *no single team since 1955 achieved what Jürgen Klopp's Liverpool managed to do*.

That major statistical achievement by Liverpool in 2018/19? – that no other European champion since the competition's introduction in

1955 won as many points in their domestic league (97) whilst *simultaneously* undergoing the rigours of actually winning Europe's top prize. And yes, that is with all games converted to three points for a win; something that was introduced in the early 1980s in England but which other major leagues took more than a decade longer to implement. In contrast to all of the winners prior to 1991 (when you *had* to have won it to enter), and many since, Liverpool did not win the league to qualify for the Champions League they ended up winning; but unlike Liverpool after 2004/05, Inter Milan after 2009/10, Chelsea following 2011/12 and Real Madrid after winning in Kiev, Liverpool were more than merely challenging for their domestic title *the year after*. In the end, they blew the bloody doors off that thing. Liverpool's potential greatness in 2019/20 could be foretold by looking at just how unique the achievement of 2018/19 was; and while you can never be sure that a great team won't have a bad year, the proof was clear that Liverpool *were a great team*.

The truth is that a lot of domestic champions have fairly mediocre league seasons – by their exalted standards – whilst successfully fighting to win the European Cup/Champions League (for instance, Borussia Dortmund in 1996/97 won the Champions League when also finishing 3rd in the *Bundesliga*, in a season in which they drew six and lost nine). This is because it's doubly tough to *simultaneously* fight for both. It seems few people think about the difficulties of doing it this way around, but teams often fight for the league, then *the next season* ease off domestically as they fight for the Champions League; Liverpool were fighting tooth-and-nail for the league – to the very last day, amassing a near-record points tally – whilst trying to win the Champions League, which they succeeded in doing. The simultaneous challenge is the greatest of all; and while Liverpool could not maintain a dual challenge in 2019/20 (going out by the narrowest of margins to Atlético Madrid, in that the Reds were ahead in extra-time in the second leg), their league form, with little scope to improve, then improved *to record levels*, securing the title a full two games before any other team in English history. Irrespective of what the final points tally would be (99, one short of the all-time record), Klopp's team took the record of winning the league with five remaining games – achieved four times in 132 years of history – and blew it up to *seven* remaining games. As I pointed out in the summer of 2019 when referring to these stats about how Liverpool's Premier League points tally of 97 *allied* to becoming champions of Europe, there was something statistically very special about the team that wasn't always getting appreciated; lo and behold, more records were broken in the next 12 months, with a world title thrown in too. Even now, in the summer of 2020, I still keep hearing that "yes, but Manchester City are better", as if aesthetics and attacking flair are the only two things that make a team both great and successful. When City lost at Southampton in early July, it was their *ninth* league defeat of the season; almost a third of their games. (And their supposed defensive saviour, Aymeric Laporte, now fit and well, played in more league defeats in ten days than Joe Gomez had in two years.) Add the four defeats of the season before and, with 2019/20 not quite over, it stood at 13 league defeats; in the same time, Liverpool had lost three (and two of the three were *at City*: one unluckily so in 2018/19, when the Reds were the better team, and the other a bit of a hammering – albeit seven days after Klopp's team were crowned champions, and therefore, presumably, unlikely to be as fervently fired up for it as would normally be expected, and in some cases, looking like they'd spent the week on the ale).

The average number of domestic league points for the 64 European champions up to 2019 – in the season in which Klopp's mentality monsters achieved that *European* success (rather than the preceding season which saw the teams qualify) – is just 79, a massive 18 below what Jürgen Klopp's men posted in 2018/19. So, most clubs winning Europe's biggest prize posted unremarkable league tallies that same season.

Those 64 teams averaged a fairly hefty six league defeats apiece. By contrast, Liverpool rank joint-top in European history, along with just three other teams, when it comes to the fewest league defeats while conquering Europe: one. One measly top-league domestic defeat, whilst successfully fighting to be crowned kings of Europe. While it could be argued that bigger points tallies are now easier due to the age of the Superclub, it's worth noting that Liverpool ranked as low as 4th on current English financial might in 2018/19. Liverpool essentially only became a Superclub once more during 2018/19; it wasn't that being a Superclub made life easier. The finances improved markedly as a result of European success and rapid domestic improvement.

Okay, Now For The Caveat
Now, admittedly for Liverpool's 2018/19 achievement to rank top in European history it does need a caveat – a *slight* finagling of the figures (but which can be partially justified) – to exclude just over half of the other winners since 1955: and that caveat is to apply a *minimum* of 38 league games played.

If that seems arbitrary, then at least consider that the more domestic games you play the greater the likelihood of burnout – which is kind of my point with this whole angle; while obviously English clubs did not have the bonus of a midwinter break, and the league is notoriously attritional. Teams who play fewer domestic games can obviously find themselves with more fuel left in the tank to try to conquer Europe. Indeed, leagues in other countries even help with the arrangement of fixtures, to make life easier for their teams.

This caveat mostly cuts out a lot of the early winners, who played in leagues with between just 26 and 30 games in a campaign; albeit a bit more problematically, admittedly, it therefore also excludes all the Dutch and German champions, with their regular 34-game seasons (and here I'm finagling furiously, like a man desperately trying to hide a browser tab that may just happen to contain something he doesn't want the world to see; and no, I don't mean the Sean Dundee fan appreciation page I created). Despite that, 34-game league campaigns are obviously more than 10% "easier" in terms of matches played; so there is *some* justification to exclude them, even if it's also a little unfair in other ways to write off the great Ajax and Bayern Munich sides, whose achievements helped to redefine football. They will have had different challenges to overcome, but all the same, they certainly played fewer league games than Liverpool had in 2018/19.

That leaves 28 eligible winners since 1955 spread across England, Italy, Spain and France, although due to Italy and Spain originally having smaller top divisions (they both had 30-game league seasons for a while), just two of the 28 are from Italy and one is from France; 13 are from England and 12 from Spain, with the early Real Madrid domination also erased from the equation.

However, even if you include the great Ajax and Bayern Munich sides, and the Real Madrid of the 1950s, then, out of the 64 champions since 1955, the Reds in 2018/19 would rank an impressive 5th for pro rata league points tallies; although Benfica only played 26 league games in 1960/61, and unlike 34 games, that seems *far* too low to be taken seriously (as it needs a 12-game extrapolation of the points per game to take them to 99). And of the four teams from "fewer-matches leagues" that would rank ahead of the Reds, only one (Bayern in 2012/13) dates after 1973.

And that, I'd argue, is *hugely* significant.

Following the success in Madrid last June, I made the point that no *English* winner of the Champions League/European Cup had won as many league points; but closer inspection also shows that the next-fewest amount of league defeats was three, by Manchester United (1999) and Nottingham Forest (1979); and that Liverpool in 2018/19 finished a full ten league points ahead of England's next-best European

Champions: Manchester United from 2007/08, who finished the season of their third European crowning with 87 league points (and as with Liverpool in 2018/19, the league went down to the final game of the season).

All of Liverpool's first four European Cups came from 42-game seasons, which made it even tougher in many ways; and in 1977 the Reds also won the league and reached the FA Cup final at a time when that cup was far more vigorously contested, with seemingly ceaseless replays on boggy pitches. So every era has its own drawbacks, but also, its own advantages. For instance, Liverpool were able to buy very expensive players in the '70s and '80s, in a more meritocratic and egalitarian era, in contrast to the way that, in the 2010s, the club found themselves – due to changes that occurred in the '90s – far adrift of the biggest spenders (Chelsea, Manchester United and Manchester City). Money has always played a role in football, but the modern era has seen the stakes raised by the super-rich owners of rival clubs.

Now, I would accept the grounds for arguments that some of the European champions – such as Pep Guardiola's Barcelona, the great Ajax and Bayern sides previously mentioned, the Reds in 1977 and 1984 and Manchester United in 1999 and 2008, amongst others – may be deemed superior on aesthetic terms (particularly Barça), or on overall dominance of a season, with a domestic crown too. But of course, Liverpool posted a better league total than *any* of those clubs in a "minimum 38-game season" in which the European crown was collected, which is kind of my point: Liverpool only failed to win the league almost on a technicality (that City were unfeasibly good, albeit when failing again in Europe). By all measures prior to 2018, 97 points would *guarantee* you the league title; and usually by a country mile.

You could obviously argue that Manchester City were better than Liverpool in 2018/19, but yet again City bowed out of the Champions League before the final three games, which are obviously the ones that take the most out of players – not just *afterwards*, but often beforehand, when the mind starts pondering the need to avoid injuries and fatigue. Indeed, it was a bruising encounter with Newcastle a few days before the return leg against Barcelona in May 2019 that saw Mo Salah join Roberto Firmino in missing that momentous 4-0 comeback. Liverpool defeated the odds in despatching the Catalans in May, but the physical toll of those league games was clear.

So my point – originally made in the aftermath of Madrid – is that, while *obviously* no one has celebrated Klopp's team as being the best in the history of European football (and these things usually take time to be fully appreciated), it could be argued that they were *not that far off.* Remember, the Reds also faced an incredible level of opposition on the way to the final: PSG, Napoli, Bayern Munich, Barcelona and a strong Spurs side who should have been freed up by the underdog tag, but who instead seemed to freeze. In single games, Liverpool put three past PSG and Bayern (away), and four past Barcelona.

The season before those crazy celebrations in Madrid – 2017/18 – saw the Reds break the all-time scoring record for the Champions League/European Cup, scoring close to 50 goals. But that led only to a losing final. A year later Klopp had a better, more experienced all-round team, but it wasn't quite as *blitzy*. Therefore it was a bit easier to write off as not that special. And yet "this" Liverpool – with virtually the same players, and definitely the same front three – also retain that 2018 scoring record as a further indicator of their brilliance; it just needed a bit of time, and a couple more additions, to take it to the next level as an overall team. (Plus, some better luck in Kiev could have seen Klopp's men crowned European champions a year earlier.) So, the barnstorming run to the final in 2018 was also part of this same team's body of work, just as Guardiola's City posted 100 and then 98 points in consecutive league seasons (whilst not getting past the quarter-finals in Europe).

Again, I stated all this a year ago more as a way of pointing out the Reds' underrated overall qualities, rather than arguing with a totally straight face that Liverpool last season were the best side seen in the history of European football. However, subsequent data – discussed later in the book – suggests that even this claim has more validity; albeit it needed a lot of games in 2019/20 to achieve. It ranked Liverpool as one of *the four best sides of all time.*

Let Battle Commence!

Given that preseason was a mixed bag for the Reds, due to the chaotic nature of the international tournaments, my hopes were not the highest come August. It was clear that Liverpool had a team *capable* of great things, but such was the disruption of the summer schedule that I feared a slow start to the season – which, given the pace Man City had set over the previous two seasons, could prove costly. (It seems increasingly true that titles are won in the early part of the season, although it obviously always needs to be backed up in the second half of the campaign.)

In August I wrote that: "… it's hard to look ready when your players only finished their competitive club season in June (three weeks later than every other English club bar Spurs, and the first time since forming in 1892 that the Reds had a competitive game in that particular month), followed by a host of players going to the Nations League (four first-XI players and an impact sub), the Copa América (two first-XI players) and the African Nations Cup (three first-XI players and a borderline first-XI player), whilst others were out injured.

"… Liverpool have to play the Community Shield, the European Super Cup and then, before the turn of the year, the World Club Cup. That will make this season more challenging than last season in that it's three additional 'competitions' (no matter how brief and relatively unimportant they are in the grand scheme of things), and yet this is a team that I believe will improve due to time spent together, and the way it can mature from one of the youngest teams in the Premier League last season to a mid-spectrum average age this time around. Long-term, the future looks incredibly bright; short-term there may be some bumps in the road, simply because the road ahead is full of potholes."

It seems my pessimism, whilst logical, was misplaced. The big positive was that, actually, the Reds' players were all fitter and sharper *because they had highly competitive summers* – but of course, that posed risks for the second half of the season, and potential burnout (not least with the Club World Cup jammed in), in that time before Covid-19 even existed. And of course, Man City's players also had a fairly busy summer; just not as busy as Liverpool's.

The Community Shield was the least important of Liverpool's additional games, and Sadio Mané wasn't even on the bench after firing Senegal to the final of the African Cup of Nations, which his country lost to Riyad Mahrez's Algeria; the City player also absent from the game at Wembley. City ended up winning the game on penalties, although the Reds played some great football and were unlucky not to win the game in normal time.

Norwich Whirlwind
The league season started on a Friday night with the visit of newly promoted Norwich City, and the game was over as a contest well before half-time. As part of what would become a theme for the season, the Reds' opening goal – just seven minutes into the match – started deep in their own half; and even more pertinently, it was from a *throw-in*. As

Daniel Farke's side tried to block all options for a Trent Alexander-Arnold throw, the young full-back launched the ball 30 yards infield, over the four-strong "box them in" brigade, who were instantly taken out of the game. Virgil van Dijk helped it on to Andy Robertson, who advanced over the halfway line on the left, and played in Divock Origi, whose previous touch (more-or-less) in competitive football in a Liverpool shirt was to steer the ball into Spurs' net in Madrid. Here he turned the Norwich defence one way, then another, and eventually fired in a low cross that Grant Hanley – with a foot like a traction engine – half slashed, half sliced, into his own goal.

In fairness to the visitors they created some promising openings, with Liverpool looking a little disjointed at times, perhaps as a result of the summer; while no notable fitness was lost, the late returns of the front three to preseason training meant they were not quite operating at the optimum rhythm. Mané and Firmino made it all the way to the finals of their respective competitions, with Firmino returning to England with yet another medal. (Mané would have to wait a few months to be crowned African Footballer of the Year). Another Liverpool player – Alisson Becker – had starred at the Copa América, although his Liverpool season got off to a terrible start – perhaps due to the lack of a proper preseason – when he injured his calf taking a goal-kick, and was ruled out for a couple of months (he too was later voted Brazilian Footballer of the Year, a rare honour for a keeper).

On came Adrián San Miguel del Castillo – or Adrián, for short – snaffled from West Ham on a Bosman transfer, having seen his contract ebb away. As West Ham fans celebrated the loss of this 'liability', Liverpool generally only had good experiences with the new shotstopper – at least during Alisson's early-season injury layoff; whilst, ironically, the Hammers would face all kinds of goalkeeping catastrophes as the season unfolded. (Adrián would fare less well as the campaign progressed, but he played a key role in setting the early-season pace.)

Norwich were blown away well before half-time. Mo Salah added the second, and Virgil van Dijk the third, from a corner, before an Origi header from a beautiful deep cross by Trent Alexander-Arnold. The opening game was a wonderful showcase of what was to follow in 2019/20: a mixture of super-fast intricate passing moves and rapid breaks, allied to some great dead-ball goals and chances created with long, sweeping laser-guided passes. Such was the lead at the interval that the Reds could coast the second half, just a few days after the Community Shield against Manchester City, and just a few days before facing Chelsea in Istanbul for the European Super Cup, which itself was scheduled just a few days before a trip to Southampton. Teemu Pukki snatched a deserved second-half consolation goal for the Canaries on his Premier League debut, but by then the Reds had gone into power conservation mode.

Klopp told the BBC's *Match of the Day*: "For 60 minutes we looked very sharp, then we have to control the game a bit more. Norwich have all my respect – they stayed cheeky, they enjoyed their football. At the start of the second half we could have scored a fifth or sixth goal, then Norwich scored. After that we were never in danger but had to work hard to keep the score what it was.

"The players had a break [over the summer]. For the body it was long enough, nobody [from the squad] asked for longer, so they didn't lose a lot of their physical standards. We have to be a bit smart for the next two games, we have to make a few decisions and try to win both of those games, which will be difficult."

Back In Istanbul As Champions of Europe
Fourteen years after lifting a fifth European Cup the Reds were back in Istanbul, months after lifting their sixth. Only now, the stakes were much lower. The game finished 2-2, with goals from Roberto Firmino and Sadio Mané – meaning a penalty shootout would follow. As with the Community Shield, there was just one penalty missed, although this time the Reds scored all five of theirs, courtesy of Firmino, Fabinho, Origi, Alexander-Arnold and Salah. Adrián saved Tammy Abraham's penalty, and off the keeper ran – albeit after first collecting his yellow towel from the back of the net – and slid to his knees as the squad charged towards him in celebration.

The Super Cup, though not especially relevant, had the almost unbearable drama of penalties, which makes defeat feel like a kick in the guts, and victory feel like the biggest of surprises. Whatever the stakes, the urge for everyone to run onto the pitch and celebrate with the goalkeeper or winning penalty taker seems natural. "Adrian!" bellowed the Reds' boss in the post-match interview, referencing Rocky Balboa from the 1976 movie – a tale of the underdog boxer overcoming the odds that Klopp had previously used in team-talks as a motivational tool; and now he had his own hero whose name – minus the Spanish accent – was famously shouted by Sylvester Stallone's character in the ring after a gruelling fight.

A fortnight earlier, Adrián did not even have a team. Liverpool had sold Simon Mignolet and sent the promising young Pole Kamil Grabara on loan to Huddersfield in the Championship, to gain valuable experience (which, alas, later involved a stay in hospital after a serious injury which involved bleeding on the brain). With yet more transfer brilliance, the Reds managed to bag Adrián for free, whilst collecting £6.4m for Mignolet – and also lowering the wage bill in the process. Not only that, but – initially, at least – Adrián had none of the mental baggage accrued by Mignolet during some difficult times at Anfield.

In outlining the new keeper's stats for TTT upon the Reds' latest free signing, Andrew Beasley wrote: "By this measure [save percentage], Adrián's worst season at West Ham was broadly in line with Mignolet's best at Liverpool. Notice too that in 2013/14, the Reds' new goalkeeper wasn't far shy of what Alisson delivered in his debut campaign (76.5% vs 77.8%). Adrián's record on this front has dipped a little over the years, but he still had the fourth-best save percentage in the Premier League in 2017/18, the last time he featured in the competition, having been benched for Łukasz Fabiański the following season."

After leaving West Ham in the summer of 2019, Adrián was training in his home city of Seville. "One month ago I was training by myself in Spain with my goalkeeper coach and friends helping me with the training," he later told *Liverpoolfc.com* amid the celebrations at Beşiktaş Park. "Two weeks ago I really didn't know who I was going to sign for, whether in Spain or another league. But Liverpool came to me and asked me. It's the best decision I've taken in my life now.

"I knew the moment was going to come but obviously not as quick as it has. I'm really happy to be here and really proud for the players to help me from the beginning. They opened their arms to make me feel like a great friend. It was a magnificent night."

Ings Can Only Get Better
After 120 minutes on the Wednesday night, played in stifling heat on the edge of Asia, Liverpool were back in England, on the south coast, for a Saturday match against high-energy Southampton – managed by the Klopp-lite Ralph Hasenhüttl – and complete with Danny Ings, a popular player at Melwood.

Given that it was early in the season, with the extra-time in Turkey, in addition to the travelling, even a point at St Mary's might have been seen as a good result. Instead, the Reds extended their run of consecutive league wins to 11, dating back to March 2019.

Almost as if Istanbul had turned Adrián into pomp-years Peter Schmeichel, the new keeper somehow saved point-blank from a first-half Maya Yoshida header from an inswinging corner. It provided the platform from which Liverpool could later go and take the lead.

Sadio Mané then opened the scoring with a sumptuous curler into the far corner on the stroke of half-time, before Roberto Firmino sealed the points. There was just enough time for Adrián to gift Ings a goal, before the former Liverpool striker missed a big chance at the death.

The Reds' manager was naturally delighted to see his side hang on for the win. "A lot of times in my life I had sensational players always [but] not world-class players," Klopp told *Liverpoolfc.com*. "Now, thank God I have them and they make the difference. We don't have to talk about that. Sadio Mané, Bobby Firmino, Mo Salah – these guys in the last situation are really outstanding. They were a constant threat, however tired they are. That's brilliant and, of course, made the difference."

Both of the Reds' goals also highlighted the work of Thomas Grønnemark, the Danish throw-in coach, who had been working with the Liverpool players one week every month since the autumn of 2018, and whose attention to detail focuses not just on Liverpool's own throws – which have become staggeringly more effective – but the opposition's, too. This was therefore a perfect game, as Liverpool scored from each. In an interview the following month, Grønnemark told James Pearce of *The Athletic*, the secrets are "… about technique but also body language, relations between players, precision, the mentality of the thrower. Sometimes it's really good to throw it fast, sometimes it's really bad. Sometimes you need the patience to wait for the space to be created by the runs we work on.

"It's not a coincidence that we scored those two goals at Southampton and it's satisfying to see. I'm not saying we only scored those two goals because of having a throw-in coach but it's like a big puzzle and throw-ins are part of that. Right now, Liverpool's puzzle is almost perfect but you can always improve.

"It's difficult to measure exactly how many goals have come from throw-ins as sometimes we've scored 20 seconds later. It's about seven or eight but for me it's just as satisfying to see the movements and see us keeping possession."

Having already played Manchester City and Chelsea, Arsenal were up next, in the Reds' first big league game of the nascent season.

Arsenal and David Luiz, The Gift That Keeps On Giving
To counter the Reds' narrow front three, Arsenal boss Unai Emery elected against three central defenders – a common reaction by managers to try and nullify Sadio Mané, Mo Salah and Roberto Firmino – and opted instead to deploy a midfield diamond formation at Anfield, which essentially allowed the Reds the freedom of the flanks – another strong area – but condensed the space in the box; countering one strong point, but enabling another. With most of their team

packing the box, and leaving little room for the Reds' clever passes and accurate crosses to fall *just right* – it looked like Arsenal would hold out until half-time. Trent Alexander-Arnold's high and long corner was fairly standard fare, but Arsenal's generally short players failed to deal with the tallest man on the pitch: Joël Matip, 6'5", heading relatively easily into the Kop-end net, four minutes before the interval.

David Luiz then essentially wrapped the game up for the Reds when Roberto Firmino's glorious first-time layoff from a fast Alexander-Arnold infield pass put Salah in on goal, only for the Brazilian defender to pull his shirt so hard that even Mancunian referee Anthony Taylor – who had denied Salah protection via the red card Vincent Kompany's wild lunge merited at the Etihad eight months earlier – had no choice but to award Liverpool a rare Anfield penalty. Even though the relatively new rule stated that there was no double-jeopardy of the red card for defenders conceding penalties, the new legislation was intended for genuine attempts at playing the ball; as such, this should have also been a red card for Luiz (although perhaps Taylor felt Arsenal would be more handicapped if the Brazilian stayed on? Anyway, Luiz was sent off later in the season at Manchester City, by Taylor, for a similar offence).

Salah took the spot-kick himself and fizzed it into the top corner. As the commentators like to say, *they could have had two goalkeepers and they wouldn't have saved it.* Arsenal had a chance of pulling a goal back when Pierre-Emerick Aubameyang broke through on goal, but Matip recovered as the Gunners' no.14 took too long to pick an option. One piece of trivia from the match was that Nicolas Pépé became the first player to successfully dribble past Virgil van Dijk in the Dutch defender's last 50 appearances for the Reds, since Mikel Merino in March 2018 for Newcastle; a statistic that was remarkable, but which was also gaining undue attention, to the point where it was almost a relief when it was put to rest.

Liverpool's third – to kill the game – came from an Arsenal attack, as Mattéo Guendouzi played a low ball into the channel for Pépé to get in behind van Dijk. (A foolish idea!) The Dutchman mopped up with ease, laying the ball back to Adrián, who, as Pépé closed in, nonchalantly dinked a pass out to Alexander-Arnold. He moved the ball infield, and, first time, Fabinho curled a sweet 40-yard pass to Mo Salah's feet. Salah, in the Arsenal half but a good 45 yards out and with his back to goal – level with the edge of the centre circle – took a neat first touch. When Luiz tried to charge into the Egyptian – a split second after the Liverpool man took possession – the walking Brazilian disaster zone ended up bodychecking thin air; Salah was gone, ducking past the challenge with another touch that took him close to the touchline, from which point, with Luiz sat eating a pie in the Lower Sir Kenny Dalglish Stand, he headed to goal at a perfect 45° angle; Nacho Monreal, aged 33, was clearly thinking "I need to get out of this club ASAP", as he valiantly tried to chase a man twice as quick. Now just inside the area, Salah curled a trademark left-footed finish past Leno, and the game was as good as over.

Arsenal grabbed a late consolation through Lucas Torreira, and the game ended with Arsenal having a respectable nine shots, but conceding a catastrophic 25, on the way to a 3-1 defeat. In the process, Liverpool equalled a club record of 12 league wins in succession.

Afterwards, Klopp was buzzing. "It was a performance full of power, energy, greed and passion, which I think you need against a team like Arsenal" he told *Sky Sports*. "… We were completely in charge of the game.

"We are not Disneyland, we do not need to excite everyone in every second."

The use of the term Disneyland was interesting, as this was the exact phrase that, five years earlier, Ed Woodward had used to describe Old Trafford when trying to lure Klopp to Manchester from Borussia Dortmund. The future Liverpool manager told a friend back in 2014 that the image was distinctly "unsexy", and the German's Spidey senses were proven correct: he bided his time, and joined a club whose atmosphere more closely resembled a mosh-pit at a Metallica concert than a tea waltz with Mickey Mouse.

Burly Burnley Beaten
Burnley away hasn't always been the easiest fixture for Jürgen Klopp's Reds, with a 2-0 defeat coming earlier in his reign, despite total domination of the ball. In 2017/18 it required a last-gasp Ragnar Klavan goal to restore a win that looked to have been denied by Jóhann Berg Guðmundsson's 87th-minute equaliser. And in 2018/19, the Reds lost Joe Gomez to a broken leg, and went 1-0 down in the second half, before goals from James Milner and Roberto Firmino gave Klopp's men a slight advantage that, into injury time, Alisson Becker helped protect, with some excellent goalkeeping – before launching an attack that allowed Xherdan Shaqiri to seal the victory.

By contrast, this was a walk in the park, on the way to the Reds breaking their club record for most consecutive league wins, moving from 12 to 13 at Turf Moor. Goals from Mané and Salah – who would share the headlines for different reasons – followed an opening goal from a deflected deep Alexander-Arnold cross. The result – a comfortable 3-0 win – was therefore a kind of symbol of how far Liverpool had come under Klopp: from those early nightmares of facing this brand of direct football with two giant strikers, and unable to get past their low defensive blocks, to being able to tame the likes of Ashley Barnes and Chris Wood, and despatch them with relative ease. Not only could Liverpool now *physically* match such teams, they had gone from bossing possession without being able to score, to being able to pull such defences apart.

Klopp saw something close to perfection from the Reds in the uglier side of the game: "It was pretty much the best second-ball game we've played since I have been together with the boys. We were really there, we won pretty much all of the first balls, which is difficult enough against Barnes and Wood because they do really well there. Then being around, they have a good formation for the second balls. It was just amazing, [we were] using the space for immediate passing, trying to be quick in our decision-making, we wanted to have direction immediately. It was really good. It is not the only thing that Burnley do obviously, they have these early crosses, they play three, four or five passes to prepare an early cross and you have to be there as well. Then they chip the balls in behind from different positions from the last line; I don't know how often today Burnley were offside. It was brilliant how we did that, how we adapted in these situations.

"Against a 4-4-2 system, it is really difficult if you are not quick, if your passes have no real direction, then you play their cards pretty much because the formation is good, the full-back is under pressure from the winger, the No.6 can close the gap and stuff like this. Immediately, you have no real situation which can create kind of a momentum. In the first half, we were completely in a kind of fluent [way], as much as you can without creating massively."

But the game also sparked controversy, with Mané furious at being substituted, with his anger seeming to stem from an occasion where Salah failed to pass the ball to his better-placed team-mate. Indeed, it was one of two incidents in the game where the Egyptian seemed to take a necessary greediness for goals beyond the point of footballing virtue and into the realms of avarice; the other occasion being when Firmino was in even more space than Mané. Even Firmino's decisive goal came from Salah arguably overplaying, and it's a side of the little no.11's game that can occasionally get out of balance, albeit something that is usually soon brought back into line.

Klopp said of Mané: "He was upset, that was obvious. You cannot hide his emotions like that. We spoke about it, everything is fine. We are individuals, we are emotional. It was a situation in a game obviously, what else could happen? It's not a phone call. It was a situation in the game he wasn't happy about and then that's completely fine. Would he do it in exactly the same manner again? Probably not, but it happens … Thank God we are now away for a week, so if you write something about it, we will not read it anyway. And after a week, nobody can remember anymore, so it's a really cool moment to do it. But it is all good really, all fine."

Behind the scenes there would need to be a bit of patching up, as American journalist Grant Wahl explained in *Sports Illustrated* in January 2020, having spent some time with Klopp at the end of 2019. Both players, Klopp explained to Wahl, were brought into his office – separately – and the matter discussed.

"In the world of football, it looks so big; it's like, 'Oh, my god, how can you do it?'" Klopp told Wahl. "But I just spoke to them."

Simple.

While the world's media hummed and buzzed with the thrill of some kind of shocking disharmony at Liverpool – the cracks finally starting to show! – Klopp simply dealt with the issue; everyone had his say, and everyone moved on. The truth is, far from being easy, the job of managing highly competitive players who are under intense pressure and scrutiny is a high-wire act. Klopp makes this kind of thing *look* easy; in part because, to him, in many ways it actually *is* easy. His people skills are such that he can defuse virtually any difficult situation that will arise in a dressing room – a remarkable ability that few others can match. And while his management skills encompass a whole spectrum of abilities, that will be analysed in this book, what marks him out as one of the best the game has ever seen is just how incredibly well he relates to other human beings.

Marginal Gains and Throwing A Game

One of the most prominent marginal gains made by Liverpool came via the work of much-mocked Thomas Grønnemark, the Danish throw-in coach.

At the time of the appointment, former Everton striker Andy Gray had Grønnemark in his sights, giving him both barrels. Speaking on *beIN Sports*, the hoary dinosaur sniped: "I'm sorry, a throw-in coach? I know how you can take advantage of a situation, throw it to one of your own players. That would be No.1 ... No.2. Keep hold of the ball. Maybe we are going to see Andy Robertson do a headstand and take it. Here is a lesson. Here's the ball, pick it up with both hands, take it behind your head and throw it with both feet on the ground."

Gray added, "I've got a new one for you, I want to be the first kick-off coach."

(This might actually be a good idea, because any club dumb enough to employ Gray would really be in dire straits, and likely conceding ten goals a game. As such, kick-offs could be their only chance to build an attack.)

In February 2020, after Liverpool had scored yet another vital goal from a throw-in, the erudite football philosopher Tim Sherwood stated "... Yes, Liverpool are flying at the top of the league because they have a throw-in coach [laughs], and if Klopp said to me – and I tell you these players have a lot more patience than me – we are having 30 minutes on throw-ins, I'd be like 'no chance I'm not doing this!' It is nonsense. Absolute nonsense!"

Yes, creating and scoring goals from hitherto undervalued situations is indeed absolute nonsense. (Liverpool players, with all that inexplicable patience, are also picking up a lot of winners' medals, and a ton of success-related bonus payments.)

It would be one thing if, for all the talk of Grønnemark's addition to the coaching ranks, Liverpool still constantly wasted possession from throw-ins, and were not finding any benefit. But by the time of the Covid-19 shutdown, Liverpool had scored a staggering *fifteen* goals in the season from throw-in situations in the major competitions (excluding the domestic cups). Not only that, they came against major opposition or in important situations: Red Bull Salzburg, KRC Genk (two throw-in goals), Tottenham Hotspur, Manchester City, Everton, Monterrey, Leicester City, Wolves (H), Tottenham Hotspur and Wolves (A). All of those games were won, as were the games against Norwich City, Southampton (two throw-in goals) and Aston Villa, in which the other four goals were scored. Of the 15, two were from opposition throws that were cleverly closed down.

Of course, Liverpool were winning virtually every game *anyway*, but the throw-in goals mostly came in big games, and/or at big *moments*. Many proved to be the vital goal. Now, all teams score some goals where, at some point, the move can be traced back to a throw-in, but in these cases with Liverpool there is often a specific design that can be identified.

On eight occasions the Reds' opening goal was via a throw-in, with a further four scored as their second goal in a game. Twice it was the third goal, and one of those – against Manchester City – was vital in killing the game, helping to see off a late revival from the visitors at Anfield. The only goal that wasn't really necessary – a 'junk' goal, as it were – was the fourth against Leicester in the 4-0 victory, albeit a work of beauty that capped a sensational display. On the four occasions when a throw-in led to Liverpool's second goal of a game, twice it proved to be the crucial winner; one of them away at Wolves, with time running out. The home game against Wolves, and the away win at Spurs, were 1-0 wins sealed by goals that stemmed from throws. Hardly any of the goals came from a simple unpressurised throw; almost all had an element of the opposition trying to mark Liverpool players, as the Reds moved to create space to release the ball at just the right moment. None was a ball just thrown thoughtlessly down the line, for both teams to contest.

A key man was Roberto Firmino, whose late movements – often dropping deep and wide to receive the ball – created space for vital goals against Manchester City, Spurs and Wolves, as well as the cake-icer at Leicester.

Now, all of the examples are prone to some outcome bias. Liverpool had scored those 15 goals, but were they *because* of the throw-in? Also, what about all the throw-in chances that weren't scored? After all, they could have been from even smarter routines, that are wiped from the memory as, moments later, the striker put the ball over the bar or straight at the keeper.

Even so, if any cleverly worked and pre-planned situation leads to a goal, it is worthy of note. It doesn't mean that there has to be one precise move that has to be followed to a tee; but if certain options are worked on, players can intuit what to do, and success can follow. In the four big goals in which his movements played a key role, Firmino didn't even touch the ball in one of them: a dummied header at Wolves, where he ducked just under the flight of the ball to allow it through to Mo Salah.

German football analysis site *Spielverlagerung* noted in January 2020 that, "throw-in strategies are often neglected, even though some simple guidelines could easily help to utilise them better. A great example for that is Liverpool, who even hired a throw-in coach, Thomas Grønnemark, in order to increase their effectiveness in this part of the game. Since [then] Liverpool has a very high success rate (around 70%

or maybe even more) in maintaining possession after a throw-in (just to put that into context, usually the average is around 50% at best)."

Of course, the aim of the throw-in is not necessarily to score; especially as, unlike at some of his other clubs, Grønnemark doesn't really focus on the extra-long throw in his work with the Reds. The only player at the club who can do that is Joe Gomez, and he plays centre-back these days, which isn't the ideal position to be a thrower. And Liverpool don't exactly have the tall players to aim a long throw at, unless it's a hail-Mary towards the end of the game (and even then, it may not be resorted to). Grønnemark has helped Liverpool players improve their throwing distances, but simply to *beat the press* as the opposition gathers close to the thrower. The aim is often to retain possession, and from then, when the space opens up, move towards the opposition goal. (Or just to keep the ball, to take the sting out of the game, rather than ceding possession).

Trent Alexander-Arnold was initially a real ditherer with his throws, as if scared to concede possession. In addition, he couldn't get any great distance. But now that he can throw further he can find midfielders nearer to the centre of the pitch – with the longer infield throw – rather than just hoping to toss it, with no great danger, down the line, into the crowd of smaller Liverpool players and bigger opposition defenders. On the other flank, Andy Robertson has increased his throwing distance by more than 50%, to now be able to throw the ball 30 metres, up from 19 metres, which on an infield throw would almost take the ball to the Anfield centre-circle, given that the pitch is 68 metres wide. (Gomez can throw the ball almost 40 metres.)

In 2017/18, before Grønnemark was approached by Klopp, the Reds retained possession just 45.4% of the time from their throws, ranking only above sides that have since been relegated. In other words, a Liverpool throw-in was basically a chance to give the ball back to the opposition. Klopp realised this.

As Caoimhe O'Neill of *The Liverpool Echo* wrote early in the 2019/20 season, "Statistics from the 2018/19 campaign – highlighted by *Tifo Football* – show that the Reds have gone from rivalling relegation bound clubs to becoming the most productive team at retaining possession from throws in Europe's top five leagues. Liverpool went from being the third worst throw-in takers in the Premier League to winning the ball back from throws taken under pressure 68.4% of the time. The only club repping a better percentage in Europe is FC Midtjylland. Interestingly, the two-time Danish champions – who boast a 70.2% possession retainment rate – are also coached by the 43-year-old."

When an article with Grønnemark and his work with the Danish analytics pioneers appeared in the German press in 2018, Liverpool and RB Leipzig quickly contacted him, and in addition he now works with Ajax (amongst others), who have returned to fostering youth and smart ideas in order to keep up with clubs in richer leagues.

In January 2020 Grønnemark spoke to Adam Bate of *Sky Sports*. "It is a culture," he told Bate. "Football started, what, 140 years ago. I am 44 and for as long as I can remember nobody has talked about throw-ins. You can watch a match on your TV and a team will lose a ball from a throw-in, and that happens a lot for most teams, and the commentators don't say anything at all. You watch them. They don't say a word.

"Then if the same player loses the ball seconds later when passing it with his feet, they will say: 'Ooh, that was a bad pass'. When he does it twice, they will say that he's not having a good game. If he does it three times then they will say that he doesn't belong in the team. That's just football culture. From my point of view, it is totally weird."

It's no accident that Grønnemark works for Liverpool, Ajax, Leipzig and Midtjylland, and four other clubs (but no two clubs in the same country). "They get in touch," he told *Sky Sports*, "because they are innovative and they are open-minded. They are clubs that are always thinking of new ways to improve and they are willing to give things time … It was the same thing that Jürgen Klopp said to me when he called me in July 2018. He said to me: 'We had a good season in 2017/18. Fourth in the Premier League and a Champions League final. But we lost the ball all the time from throw-ins.'"

Working with Klopp changed not only Liverpool's throw-in success rate, but also people's perceptions of the specialist coach, and indeed, what he is asked to do.

"A lot of people think that my work is just about long throw-ins. Of course it is about long throw-ins. I can coach that too. FC Midtjylland scored 35 goals in four seasons that way. You can do that if you have the right team. But what I found is that teams only wanted my knowledge on the long throws. You could measure that.

"My big breakthrough came when Jürgen Klopp called me. This year I am coaching eight different professional teams around the world, spending most of my time with Liverpool and Ajax. But I can say that if Jürgen had not called me I would still be a little bit frustrated as a throw-in coach because all the teams just wanted the long throw-ins.

"With Liverpool and Ajax, the long throw-ins are not their style so I am also focusing on the fast and clever throw-ins that I first started working on around 2007. That is all about possession. How can we keep possession when we are taking a throw-in under pressure? How can we create chances and score goals from those throw-in situations?"

Grønnemark talked about how the idea with throw-ins throughout his lifetime had always been the same: launch it down the line. Whilst seen as 50-50 situations, he likened them more to 20-80; which fits with the notion that defenders are often taller than attacking players, and so it favours the defensive side. (Also, a defensive team is likely to have more players back, whilst an attacking team cannot commit too many players ahead of the ball.) If the side with the throw pushed its taller players into high, wide positions, to improve its odds, it would destabilise the team: for example, Fabinho going down the line to contest the throw would leave the midfield open to be counterattacked. And even then, Fabinho would only be in a 50-50 situation with equally tall opposition defenders, and if he wins the header, where does the ball go? – further down the line, into a crowded space. Flick-ons are a way to concede possession, as it's hard to do so with control and accuracy (in part as defenders, by contrast, only have to head the ball in the direction they are facing rather than find a teammate), and if one occurs on the flank, it's not even the case that the randomness could equate to an immediate goalscoring chance, in contrast to a centre-forward winning a flick-on on the edge of the box in a central position (which will also more frequently than not concede possession, but where the occasional reward is a clear attempt at goal).

In terms of the percentage game of throwing the ball down the line, Grønnemark said, "Some might say that it is better to lose it 30 yards down the line than to lose it here. That's right. But you have the ball. Why not try to keep it or create a chance from this situation?"

It's analogous to the recent revolution of playing out from the back, and the way the goalkeeper at a top club – rather than the previous requirement of it being an optional skillset (as goalkeepers have long been 'sweeper keepers') – *has* to be able to pass accurately, and deal with the ball at his feet, especially when under pressure. It's no accident that all the successful teams now do this, because it's more efficient, in terms of winning games, than having a keeper boot the ball 70 yards upfield, especially if they are not aiming at tall centre-forwards. There may still be times the keeper must hoof it, but having it as a common fall-back response is not a way to prosper in terms of winning the major trophies. If controlling the ball – rather than contesting 50-50s – makes you more effective as an elite team, then you have to find ways to get the ball under control in all situations, and reduce the low percentage situations.

"You cannot have enough specialists around you," Klopp said, when referring to the appointment of Grønnemark. "I must always be the guy who makes the decisions on when we use all these specialists but you cannot have enough. We have the fitness, medical department, we have the nutrition, and now we have somebody for throw-ins."

Warning: May Include An Excessive Number of Wins

Following the international break, which saw English football resume in mid-September, Newcastle United – who had replaced Champions League and double *La Liga* winner Rafa Benítez with Steve Bruce (if only managerial brilliance was linked to *head size*) – were the next team to try and halt the mighty Red Jürgennaut. The visitors took a shock lead at Anfield in the 7th minute, but that was as good as it got for Bruce's men, who were on the receiving end of some sumptuous football, which resulted in two goals by Sadio Mané before half-time. But the stunning *coup de grâce* came after the break.

It started with Salah winning the ball high on the right. A dozen Liverpool passes saw the ball moved from the right flank to the left, where Mané tried to find a killer pass, but it didn't come off, and so the ball was recycled back to the centre, to Fabinho. He helped it across to the inside-right channel, to Salah, who, surrounded by Jonjo Shelvey and Christian Atsu, played a short forward pass along the floor to Roberto Firmino. In a split second there was movement in all directions; although Shelvey just stood and stared, while Atsu moved to cover the wrong area, as Salah ran towards the Newcastle box. As two players lunged in at Firmino he balletically pivoted and pirouetted, *à la* Zinedine Zidane – not so much stopping time as *reversing* it – and when he clicked his fingers the Newcastle players came out of their trances with Salah bearing down on goal. The Egyptian's run – and the pass to him – was so perfect that all Schär could do was fall over, head-first like a Swiss Phil Jones, into his path; but by then Salah had taken another touch and steered the ball into the far corner, past the helpless Dúbravka. (At the point when Salah shot, Shelvey had not moved a single inch from his position; an apt example of why such a talented player could never make it at a top club – given that talent is only half the equation.)

All The Fives

The 3-1 victory meant Liverpool ended matchweek five with the biggest lead seen in the Premier League era (a full five points) – all with no first-XI signings, and achieved without the best goalkeeper in the league for all but a few minutes, after Alisson limped off in the first half against Norwich; as well as lacking its most dynamic midfielder (*potentially*, at least – based on Naby Keïta at his best).

A lot was made about Manchester City losing Aymeric Laporte for several months after a serious injury picked up in the 4-0 win over Brighton; after which they promptly lost 3-2 at Norwich – to enable the Reds to open up that five-point gap – having previously dropped two points at home to Spurs. In a rare lapse, the usually eminently sensible Ken Early noted on the *Second Captains'* podcast – in what was becoming a widespread narrative – that Man City were without two key players, and if Virgil van Dijk and Sadio Mané – compared here to the long-term absences of Leroy Sané and Laporte – were out in the same manner the title would be "all over" for Liverpool; but let's be clear: the Reds hadn't had Alisson, who everyone said made a huge difference in 2018/19 (when the narrative was all about the addition of van Dijk *and* Alisson), and instead had West Ham's old reserve keeper in goal (a player that West Ham fans suggested would increase Liverpool's odds of relegation, no less).

Had you asked before the five wins from five how Liverpool would do in all those games – and in the European Super Cup – with *Adrián* in goal, you would have seen people saying they would worry for the Reds. After all, goalkeeper is the one specialist position in football, with Liverpool having not been such a good team with Simon Mignolet or Loris Karius in goal. Even when van Dijk arrived, the defence was not suddenly watertight.

Additionally, Alisson, as a *regular*, is indubitably more important to Liverpool than Sané was to City; the winger a non-guaranteed starter, who was due to have been sold before his injury in the Community Shield (and was indeed subsequently sold to Bayern Munich before playing again). Laporte, by contrast to Sané, is obviously more vital to City, especially after they let go of their main leader, Vincent Kompany, but the wisdom in not replacing Kompany is a demerit to City and nothing to do with Liverpool; indeed, the success of Adrián earlier in the season was nothing but further evidence of excellent planning by the Reds. In 2018/19 Kompany returned to the side to help steady their defensive ship – they didn't lose a single league game in which he played, in contrast to Laporte's four defeats, three of which came during a December collapse before the big Belgian was recalled. But when Kompany left in the summer they chose not to replace him, going into the season with just three senior centre-backs, two of whom Guardiola didn't seem to trust. They also retained a short, injury-prone 36-year-old goalkeeper, who patently wasn't even good enough when he was 33, as their main reserve. They did still find the money for yet more full-backs, with two arriving for a combined £70m; the £10m one bought back, after being sold a year earlier (but then loaned out six months on), and the £60m one left on the bench early in the season, and reportedly available to leave in the summer.

This narrative would run for months and months, well into the second half of the season; and yet when Fabinho – another key new addition in 2018/19 – was out injured for a dozen or so games (not starting a league match between late November and early February), few seemed to mention it as any hardship, not least because Liverpool continued to win every week. Yet if ever Fernandinho was out for City – as a fellow elite Brazilian defensive midfielder – it was used as a reason for City failing, if they didn't win the game. Meanwhile, the superbly gifted Kevin De Bruyne only played half of 2018/19; the world was told how much more amazing City would have been had he been fit. Well, he was fit throughout 2019/20, and Guardiola's team ended up having a far worse league season.

In October, after victory against Spurs, Mark Critchley wrote of Fabinho in the *Independent:* "Of the 29 league games he has started during his Anfield career, Liverpool have won 25, drawn five and lost none. [We can forgive his maths here.] He was only a second-half substitute at the Etihad in January, when Manchester City inflicted the only defeat that Klopp's side would suffer all season"; penned in an article titled *Colossal Fabinho Everywhere and Everything in Liverpool Win.* Then later, when the Brazilian was injured, people just seemed to ignore the fact.

Of course, it's easier to say a team didn't miss someone when they keep winning; but that ignores the jobs the understudies performed, and that similar hurdles had to be overcome.

Keïta, meanwhile, seemed to get injured every time he hit peak form, but again, little was mentioned about one of the Reds' true goalscoring threats from midfield. At the Club World Cup, Klopp had to play Jordan Henderson at centre-back, alongside Joe Gomez, due to injuries to van Dijk, Matip and Lovren; yet when Man City played Fernandinho there – because of just *one* injured centre-back – it was a sign of how unlucky the Mancunians were. In January 2020 Stuart Brennan of the *Manchester Evening News* wrote, with a straight face (presumably) but crooked logic, that Liverpool would win the league "regardless of some curious luck with both VAR decisions and injuries".

(What is 'curious luck' with injuries, by the way? Liverpool had eight senior players out injured when he wrote that odd statement, with Klopp forced into placing three rookie teenagers on the bench.)

None of which is to say City didn't have some bad luck with injuries too (although they still lost games once Laporte returned after the coronavirus lockdown). But people like Brennan simply chose to ignore Liverpool's injuries, perhaps because Jürgen Klopp did not make a great deal of fuss; instead, choosing to put faith in understudies rather than undermine them by talking as if they were not fit to replace more established stars.

That said, Jonathan Wilson, writing in the *Guardian* in January 2020, after Liverpool had beaten Manchester United 2-0, noted "United are without their two best central midfielders and their best forward. That would destabilise any side. But then Liverpool had been without their first-choice holding midfielder from the end of November until eight minutes from time on Sunday – and their response to that has been 11 clean sheets in 15 games (and two of the games when they conceded came within 24 hours of each other). Their first-choice goalkeeper missed 11 games with a calf injury. Good teams with well-constructed squads overcome misfortune; weaker ones wallow in it."

VARce

The Newcastle game was also notable in that VAR – the video assistant referee – failed to award an absolutely stonewall penalty to the Reds, that was as clear as day on the video replays. Again, as with bad refereeing and VAR decisions, Liverpool tended to win games anyway, allowing oxygen to the narrative that they were lucky on those occasions the decisions went their way, without the redress of all the decisions that went against Jürgen Klopp's team.

Joël Matip, rushing in to head home a corner, was wrestled to the ground, six yards from goal; held in a headlock by Jamaal Lascelles – at the Kop end. As such, it seems like a good time to discuss a *major* issue, that almost defined the season for many observers (and certainly caused rival fans to go all conspiratorial), before the spread of Covid-19 – itself rife with conspiracies – made VAR look like a mere footnote on the season.

Apparently, Liverpool got all the luck in the world with VAR, despite few of the facts bearing this out; although the technology was used to correct some bad decisions that went against the Reds (whilst also cancelling out goals they scored).

At this point in time – September 2019 – the Reds had received just one Kop-end league penalty since May 2017, a period of over two years; and that initial penalty – against Southampton – also happened to be the last handball penalty Liverpool would receive in the league until December 2019, a full two-and-a-half years later (should anyone think Liverpool get these kinds of decisions *all the time*).

Lascelles was the same player who, with Salah through on goal at the Kop end in his debut season, kicked the Liverpool man up in the air with as cynical and crude a red-card challenge as you will ever see; it was both a red card for the tackle and a red card for the last-man intervention. Yet the officials gave nothing. As I've been pointing out for three years now, the Kop end is where big decisions go to die; the belief that Liverpool get too many decisions is some kind of archaic bias – rooted in 1970s mythology – that gets regurgitated on an almost weekly basis by ex-players and old-school managers. Liverpool get a below-average number of penalties *overall* for a dominant team and, unlike all the other Big Six clubs, get a lower than average number of their penalties at home; ergo, Liverpool win a decent amount of penalties away from home, but a strangely low number at home; and those home penalties are much rarer at the Kop end.

Also, an opposition player hasn't been sent off against Liverpool at Anfield since September 2016 against Hull, and for those who think Liverpool get all the decisions home *and* away, the red-card totals for opponents during Klopp's tenure – despite the Reds often winning the league's fair-play award – number just four (including the one against Hull) in almost five seasons, while in the same time (since October 2015) the Reds have had James Milner, Brad Smith, Sadio Mané, Jordan Henderson, Milner again and Alisson dismissed. While it's hard to argue with most of those decisions, it still doesn't explain why Liverpool get more players sent off at Anfield than the entire combination of visiting teams, given that Liverpool are almost always bossing the game and the ball. Not all games at Anfield will see opponents get away with what should be red card offences – lots of games have no penalty shouts and no red card offences – but that doesn't mean there have been none in that entire period. Far from it.

In almost 50 halves of football – during which time the Reds were unbeatable at home – Klopp's men won fewer Kop-end Premier League penalties than Spurs managed in just two visits. (Liverpool would later get a second Kop-end penalty when Spurs' Serge Aurier – somewhat ironically – clattered Mané, in October 2019, to allow the Reds to merely equal Spurs' record at Anfield; over 50 halves of football for Liverpool, versus three for Spurs.)

One of the reasons I supported the introduction of VAR was because of the number of decisions referees weren't giving the club. Based on a ton of data, the anomalies struck me as two-fold: the erroneous notion or prejudice that Liverpool get too many penalties at Anfield (and specifically at the Kop end), which had led to a kind of reverse bias – or fear – from referees who, in the social media/phone-in age, are almost constantly branded as biased for the big clubs, or for one *specific* big club; and the fact that, based on the previous seven seasons' worth of data (and the makeup of Liverpool's team), British players win more penalties than they should rightfully expect based on the percentage of Premier League minutes played. (This applies to Liverpool in a separate study I did on just the Reds' decisions from 2002-2019, where the more British players in the team, the more penalties they tended to win).

Perhaps more tellingly, foreign players concede an incredibly inflated number of spot-kicks pro rata, to the point where someone as exceptional as Virgil van Dijk had conceded three penalties in recent seasons, but Phil Jones and Ashley Young – despite clear penalty fouls by two near-incompetent defenders (Young committed two clear penalty offences against Liverpool two seasons ago in one single game, and two against Man City around the same time, and yet walked away from all four) – were never punished. Also, the most prolific penalty winners in the recent Premier League era are all English (or English-raised) players who have only really had half a career in the top-flight due to still being fairly young, or being late arrivals: Jamie Vardy, Raheem Sterling and Wilfried Zaha. (In January 2019 Opta Joe tweeted "Since the start of the 2015-16 season, only Jamie Vardy (12) and Wilfried Zaha (12) have won more penalties in the Premier League than Raheem Sterling (11)")

Sadio Mané has still won fewer penalties in the past few years than Glenn Murray, a largely inert veteran English striker.

There is certainly some kind of conscious or subconscious bias on the part of officials, that VAR can help to quell, if not totally dispel. Instead, particularly early on in 2019/20, the referees didn't refer things to VAR and VAR did not step in, as the officials in Stockley Park chose to look away rather than overrule their colleagues; and it took until January 2020 for the pitch-side monitors to be used, with Michael Oliver – pretty much the only reliable referee in the land – being the one to *finally* take the initiative. (Oliver just happens to be the referee most likely to give Liverpool a penalty, particularly at Anfield, but only because the others are almost all too scared to do so; without Oliver the quota of Anfield penalties for the Reds would be even more ridiculously below the levels expected than it already is. By contrast, extrapolating based on his games with Liverpool since 2017, if the Reds had Martin Atkinson as referee for every match in a 38-game season – and this is a ref who has ruled out Liverpool goals in 2019/20 both as a referee and as the VAR – then the Reds would win just two penalties a season, which is fewer than a relegated side could on average expect to receive.)

On something as obvious as the foul on Matip by Lascelles, it seemed VAR could only benefit the Reds – and yet it was somehow not deemed worthy of a spot-kick.

Klopp was baffled. "The fourth official told me they did it [a VAR check]. Was I surprised that it was still not a penalty? Yes, but that doesn't help obviously in situations like this being surprised. For me, it was a clear penalty but as long as you win then it's not that issue. If we would sit here and then we had lost 1-0 then we would speak differently about the penalty. But it's a penalty, we cannot fight like this for a ball – Joël Matip, it's a wrestling situation, he turns him in the air."

Overall, VAR was not helping Liverpool – it was costing the Reds goals as well as saving the Reds goals. And yet the Reds became known on social media as Li*VAR*pool. This was ironic, as the introduction of VAR in the summer of 2019 was actually celebrated by fans of rival clubs who were certain – due to confirmation bias and "feelings" – that Liverpool got too many dodgy decisions from referees and would suffer heavily once technology was used; never mind, for instance, that technology ruled out a Liverpool goal in the crucial game at Manchester City in January 2019, by mere millimetres (the ball did not fully cross the line, so it was not a goal). The data I collated and studied told me that if referees actually looked objectively at decisions then the Reds would *have* to benefit – at least, when based on decisions in the past few seasons.

This is the great power of data: it separates truth from intuition. The data still needs to be mined, poked, prodded, tested and tested again. But with help in collecting all the penalty data from 2012 to 2019 – with a total of around 600 penalties awarded to all teams across seven Premier League seasons – I had no doubt that Liverpool, on average, were getting fewer beneficial decisions than their play merited.

Manchester United won a record 14 Premier League penalties, to add to their 12 the season before. In that time Liverpool won just five and seven respectively, despite being 65 points better off in that two-season sample. (In other words, in amassing 196 points in two seasons, Liverpool got fewer penalties in those two campaigns combined – 12 – as United got whilst amassing 66 points in 2019/20.) While many of the penalties United won in 2019/20 looked legitimate enough (bar a couple of iffy exceptions), the issue was therefore 'where were Liverpool's missing penalties?', as it had been since Jürgen Klopp arrived in 2015. Liverpool attacked more, and had far more touches in the opposition box, than United. Virgil van Dijk was constantly fouled by two or three opposition players at corners, Salah was dragged, grappled and tripped, and Mané was taken out in the box on numerous occasions, and only five times it resulted in a spot-kick. For all my obvious Liverpool bias, it always looks odd when there's a glaring statistical anomaly.

The Champions League Resumes

The Champions League resumed away at Napoli, and the Reds fell foul of an issue of semantics between the referee and the VAR, which ultimately swung the game away from a dominant Liverpool; in this case, hinging on a clear communication error. Andy Robertson was adjudged to have fouled José Callejón, but the referee asked the VAR "Was there contact?" This was another example of why referees should go and check the monitors, as *of course* there was contact; it just happened to have been instigated by Callejón. Robertson went to play the ball, but quickly pulled his foot back; and once his foot was fully back the Napoli player – still thinking, or hoping, that the contact was coming – then dived *into* Robertson, colliding with his hip.

Klopp added: "It's a decision made by human beings. The rules say if it is not a clear mistake and it's still humans who decide if it's a mistake. I think it [VAR] will help in the long-term but as long as human beings make the decision there is still potential for failure. We are all like this. What can I say?"

Having scored the late penalty, Napoli added a second just before full-time, to make for a much harsher defeat than a year earlier, when the Reds were leggy after playing days earlier at Chelsea (where they had just made a staggering 154 sprints in trying to rescue a point, which they eventually did through Daniel Sturridge's late equaliser). This time they had all the energy in Naples, but couldn't find the finishes. And this time, a trip to Stamford Bridge came days *after* the game in Italy, rather than days before.

Stamford Bridge Is Falling Down*   (*Not factually correct)

As Liverpool flitted successfully between fast-flowing open play goals and deadly set-pieces, this was a game won by work on the training ground. The match was as good as over by the 30-minute mark, although Chelsea's gung-ho late response made for a slightly nervy finale. Liverpool opened the scoring after winning a free-kick on the edge of the Chelsea box, to the left of centre. It looked ideal for a direct right-foot shot by Jordan Henderson or, preferably, Trent Alexander-Arnold. However, Mo Salah ran at a 90° angle to the ball and, in taking the free-kick, backheeled it to a more central position – which, in that instant, served to take eight players in blue out of the equation, leaving just two, plus the goalkeeper, now able to block the shot. The notion of blocking the shot, however, was purely *hypothetical*; the way the Reds' no.66 struck it, there could be no hope of intervention, as it curled with maximum power, like a heat-seeking missile, into the top corner.

Chelsea had a huge chance to equalise when Tammy Abraham was clean through against Adrián, but the Reds' keeper continued his heroics against the striker – having saved his penalty to win the European Super Cup shootout – by again denying him with an outstretched leg. Adrián's overall save percentage in his spell of games covering for the injured (and briefly suspended) Alisson was nothing remarkable, but he pulled off some huge saves at key moments in games.

Chelsea thought they'd equalised when, after another impressive Adrián save, César Azpilicueta tucked home the rebound. But the decision went to VAR, and the goal was ruled out for a narrow – but significant enough – offside earlier in the move. It could be argued that the Reds had chances to clear the ball, which made the goal a second-phase issue, but it simply deflected off defenders in red as it bounced around in the area, rather than them ever having a proper chance to clear.

Liverpool then went 2-0 up on the half-hour mark, when they won another free-kick on the edge of the box, albeit in a wide position. Alexander-Arnold was the one who backheeled the ball this time: moving the ball nearer to the byline, giving Andy Robertson a tighter angle to cross from – but with the two-man wall effectively bypassed. He curled in a beautiful ball that Roberto Firmino rose high to head home, as it dropped perfectly in between three Chelsea defenders.

In the second half, Kepa Arrizabalaga produced a wonderful reflex save to deny Firmino, and then the home team pulled a goal back when N'Golo Kanté just seemed to amble around with the ball outside the box; obviously, given his limited ability on the ball, the priority was to mark the attackers he would surely pass to, but this allowed the little French midfielder to stroll through and curl a perfect finish into the corner. By the time the Reds' defence realised he was going to shoot – and with Fabinho, uncharacteristically, too slow to cover – it was too late.

After the game, Klopp explained that only one of the free-kick routines came from the training ground. "The Robbo one is from the training ground, the Trent one I really think the boys have the best view on the pitch. It is their job to see the best opportunity to score. It was a direct free-kick, so we could have shot with that, but this little move changed the whole angle, changed the view and made it pretty impossible for Kepa to make a save. It was a brilliant goal, yes. I have said it before and it is no problem to say it [again] – Pete Krawietz and the analysts do a really brilliant job around set-pieces, but especially corner kicks and stuff like that."

Liverpool then edged past Sheffield United with a solitary goal at Bramall Lane – scored by Gini Wijnaldum with 20 minutes to go. Manchester United goalkeeper Dean Henderson, on loan at the Blades, fumbled the shot and it crept over the line – although the result was still largely merited.

Oktoberfest
October began with a metaphorical festival of football, and an introduction to Takumi Minamino – a player I found myself googling on the way home from Anfield, as someone who stood out as one of the best visiting players I've ever seen in the flesh – as part of a Red Bull Salzburg team that played some amazing football, albeit mostly only after going 3-0 down. Somehow the Austrians pulled it back to 3-3 – Minamino firing in the second and assisting the third – before Mo Salah quickly restored the Reds' lead, and with it, a sense of sanity.

But after winning the Champions League months earlier, and having reached the final the season before, it just felt that the league was now the main focus for the fans. While the European Cup has always had a special place in the Reds' hearts, that had been ticked off on the checklist, just like it had in 2005.

Leicester – themselves sharing a bit of Salzburg's canny transfer dealings in finding young, obscure potential world-beaters – were the visitors to Anfield a few days later, as Brendan Rodgers made his first return to the stadium where he managed almost 100 times, with a mixture of brilliance, mediocrity and, at times, a lack of ideas.

While no one was yet tipping Leicester as title contenders in 2019/20 – that would only happen later in the year, before their run of eight successive league wins petered out in late December and early January (in part when Liverpool hammered them at the King Power Stadium, and in part from the increased frequency of games, which was always an issue for Rodgers at Liverpool) – they did still arrive in third place, with four wins from their previous five league games, including a victory against Spurs.

While the scoreline ended as a narrow 2-1 win to the Reds, this was one of the most one-sided games you could ever see. Indeed, statistically it was more one-sided than 99.1% of all 14,000 matches in *FiveThirtyEight's* expected goals database, according to TTT stalwart Andrew Beasley, who noted that "This game is ranked 36th [out of those 14,000] for a team most deserving to win."

As such, when Rodgers said he felt his team deserved more, it's hard to know what he was talking about.

"I thought we deserved more than that," he said. "It's cruel to concede so late. I am very proud of the team. We're playing against the European champions and we looked like we could get goals. We were always a threat in the game, we had the confidence to pass the ball. We are showing our personality in how we played."

Whilst Leicester had a couple of late corners, this perhaps sums up the issue many Liverpool fans had with Rodgers: at times he seems to have a slim grasp of reality; at least while talking to the press. While all managers talk up their team, and often have to avoid sounding defeatist, Leicester had two shots *all game*. A slight lapse from Adrián – if not a complete mistake, from a James Maddison strike after 80 minutes – meant Leicester scored with one of their two shots, and normally it would take five times as many attempts from similar positions to get the "value" of a single goal. It would have been a smash-and-grab on a par with the gang of diamond thieves who ram-raided the Millennium Dome in bright yellow industrial earth diggers. Thankfully, just as it had that day 19 years earlier – when the police closed in – justice was quickly served.

Sadio Mané had given the Reds a first half lead, but it required an injury-time penalty after Mané was kicked in the ankle by Marc Albrighton. Clearly his kick didn't *send* Mané to the floor, but with Evans covering, the contact would have illegally delayed the Senegalese by a split second – missing the ball and kicking someone in the foot or ankle is not allowed (whether they stay upright or not) – and taken away the clear chance to score. James Milner calmly slotted home, and Klopp's men won 2-1, to equal the best-ever start to a season by any club in the English top flight after eight games: equal with their own 1990/91 title defence, which, of course, later fell apart.

Leadership, Teamwork and What Makes Klopp So Special

After winning the Manager of the Month award in January 2019, Jürgen Klopp saluted, in a particularly succinct way that stands the test of time, the efforts of his backroom team, without whom, he insisted, such success would not be possible. "One hundred per cent teamwork. I know a few things about football but my best skill is to bring really good people together. I lead that group, that's true, and I have to make final decisions but I can only make good decisions if the information I get is brilliant. With the group I have here, if you can mix up the potential of the group with the best attitude you can get and you get quality."

It's abundantly clear to most observers that Jürgen Klopp has a personality as large as his physical presence. It's obvious that Liverpool have some elite coaches alongside him. It's also undeniable that the club's use of data, combining analytics with video scouting, has led to a run of recruitment that has been staggering in its success rate – not just in making successful purchases, but *game-changing* purchases.

But how does it all fit together? And how has Klopp somehow seemed to perfect all aspects of the art of management, so that he has created what is statistically one of the best teams the world has ever seen on a budget that is relatively humble?

We can look at testimonials from people within the game, but a look at how scholars, authors and academics define teamwork and leadership in other walks of life, as well as in other sports, can help unlock some of the secrets. Anyone could study these secrets of success, and learn them by rote, but it still takes someone with special skills – albeit skills that can genuinely be developed over a long period of time (as opposed to merely parroting the mantras) – to translate the ideas into exceptional levels of production. You could learn to play all the songs of the Beatles, but it wouldn't mean you would instantly get McCartney's knack for writing melody or Lennon's aura and acerbic wit. Leaders need to be *followed*, but you can make people follow you out of fear, using tactics of intimidation, but it will not foster loyalty; bullies can bully performances out of people, but those people are proven to become less engaged over time, and more fearful of making mistakes, and thus, playing it safe. You can try to be likeable, but will you be *authentic*? Will people see through the façade? Equally, being a 'nice guy' does not make you a loser, but it could entice people to take advantage; and thus you need to be firm, but fair. Will you be able to appeal to people from different backgrounds, and as you get older, will you still be able to mainline the minds of the young? (All of these points could relate to the ageing Jose Mourinho, and what has gone wrong for him. Though clearly an excellent manager in the 2000s, his youthful charisma disguised many flaws.)

Playwright and screenwriter Lucy Kirkwood is neither a football fan nor a Liverpool supporter. But she is an admirer of Jürgen Klopp. Writing in *The Observer* in early 2020 about "what's on her radar", she chose to include the Liverpool manager. "I'm not that interested in sport," she said, "and I've got no truck with people wishing plays were like football matches, but I'm so glad Jürgen Klopp is in the world and not only because my husband is a Liverpool fan. In the age of Donald Trump and Boris Johnson, he delights me as an example of what male leadership can look like: passionate, humorous, generous, kind, driven by humility and integrity and, above all, decency. My husband loads up clips from post-match interviews and match highlights for me to watch and without fail Klopp makes me laugh or my heart swell, whether he's complimenting the male translator on his erotic voice, or getting so excited at a victory over Norwich that he breaks his glasses. Also I have instant affection for anyone who's been a professional sportsperson and a smoker at the same time."

Klopp, whilst funny, likeable and humble, is clearly no shrinking violet. He can at times be 6'4" of Teutonic rage – an angry German barking orders has its own social and historical problems – and yet he seems universally loved, even by fans of rival teams who have every reason to loathe him. Perhaps it's because he shows *all* his emotions, rather than just anger (and his anger never lasts, or turns to bitterness. It's just an emotion, passing through him). He doesn't hide his flaws, and he doesn't seek to bullshit anyone. Being 'authentic' can be its own kind of bullshit in the modern age: everyone trying to *show* how real they are – "look at me, keeping it real!" – from social media accounts managed by PR firms. Klopp mixes intelligence with honesty, humour and decency.

New backup goalkeeper Adrián told the BBC in February 2020 that "Klopp usually tells us that we'll face many problems during the games, so we must be able to fix them. Any team can surprise you with a new system, for example. He's there to guide us. He visualises football very well from the sidelines and transmits this knowledge to the players in a masterful way … Jürgen is not only a top strategist, but also a great person. The best group management I've seen. [He's] next to the team through thick and thin."

Without wishing to sound like a hagiographer, Klopp has it all. Or rather, he has strengths in all areas, and a willingness to delegate to specialists in areas where he himself is merely very good rather than exceptional. And all this feeds into the way he creates a team; and the team around him multiply his effectiveness.

Team Building Exercise '99

Practice is obviously vital; almost all exceptional talents are proof of the well-known "10,000 hours" rule – it usually takes that much time, give or take a thousand hours or two, working at something to become considered elite. Then again, there is also the level of difficulty in practice undertaken, which can push the limits, just as exercising beyond comfort allows new muscle to build.

For teams, however, it's far more complex. These are always groups of disparate individuals, driven by different desires. What is the magic behind making a team exceed the sum of its parts?

Leading American organisational psychologist Adam Grant, writing for *The Huffington Post* in 2013, asked in the title of the piece, 'What's the Common Ingredient for Team Success in Surgery, Banking, Software, Airlines, and Basketball?'

Grant wrote: "What if work experience is overrated? In a brilliant study, researchers Robert Huckman and Gary Pisano tracked more than 200 cardiac surgeons at 43 hospitals. After analysing more than 38,000 procedures, it turned out that the surgeons didn't get better with practice. Their patient mortality rates were no better after 100 surgeries than after the first few.

"A closer look at the data revealed a fascinating pattern. The surgeons did get better as they gained more experience at a particular hospital. Each procedure performed at one hospital decreased patient mortality rates by an average of 1%. But the benefits of experience didn't carry over to other hospitals.

"The technologies weren't any different from one hospital to another; the *people* were. When the surgeons left their teams behind, it was as if they were starting over from scratch without any of the benefits of practice. Practice wasn't an individual act; it was a team process. As the surgeons worked with a core team of nurses and anaesthesiologists at one hospital, they developed effective routines that leveraged the unique talents of each member."

Of course, to become a surgeon requires thousands of hours of study and practice *before* becoming part of a team. But once they were fully qualified surgeons, the team around them became the most important factor in success. In football we idolise the individuals, yet few people think about why Mo Salah was not so good at Chelsea and yet has been so sensational at Liverpool; or why Philippe Coutinho became so exceptional at Liverpool and was not so good at Barcelona.

Myriad factors are in play: at the most basic level, they are not even the same players even from one game to next, given that their physical and mental states will never be 100% the same each time, no matter how close they get to that state through training and mental practices, and the players around them will be different from day to day (and the way the game unfolds will always be uniquely different). The opposition will be different; the same opposition can play well or play poorly, and you don't always know what version you'll get. The bigger the change, however, the greater the disruption. Moving to different clubs, and to different leagues, involves forming new relationships, facing new challenges and, to use a culinary metaphor relating to a mix of ingredients, if you represent the curry powder you will work well in a lamb korma and terribly in a lasagne (or so I have been told in relation to my strangely unpopular spaghetti carbonara vindaloo). Even the very same curry powder will work differently in an alternate Indian or Thai dish, depending on what the other ingredients are; some might enhance your flavour, others may overwhelm it. It's about the blend, the balance.

Of course, a footballer is a more complex entity than a mere mix of spices; a human has the capacity to work at altering their own qualities, even if it's not easy to change one's character or abilities overnight. But within a team, the individual is reliant on what's around him or her. And time spent together plays a role.

In the summer of 2019 I argued, in the face of the usual transfer-based hysteria that often makes those months unbearable (for some people, "winning" the transfer window seems more important than any actual football), that Liverpool were probably right to keep their powder dry in the transfer market, because the team was at a very good average age, and was increasing its interdependent skills. The previous summer, in 2018, both Spurs and Manchester City made virtually no additions to teams that were at good ages, and subsequently had their best seasons, by some of the biggest metrics, in their history (in City's case, three trophies was a club best; in Spurs' case, it was their first ever European Cup/Champions League final). Of course, a further year later, heading into 2019/20, they then had issues with some ageing players; and so they bought new players, and rather than improving, they regressed, to the point where they were miles adrift of the Reds. None of which is to say that buying new players was therefore a mistake; just that it can take time for a team to form, and grow, and sometimes it simply won't work out. If your players age-out, you need to replace them – you cannot keep a team together beyond its natural lifespan; but that change can often disrupt the shared wavelength – in the short term, at least – that everyone else has tuned in to. Indeed, this is why Klopp often chooses to let players adapt to Liverpool's football via months of training before they are exposed to the first team; which was also famously the way Liverpool used to do it during the halcyon days, perhaps as no coincidence. (Albeit back then, there was less fanfare about new arrivals, and players like Alan Hansen, Ian Rush, Ronnie Whelan and Steve Nicol were all fairly young when they arrived, but went straight into the reserves.)

In his piece, Grant continued: "In teams, it appears that shared experience matters more than individual experience. The best groups aren't necessarily the ones with the most stars, but rather the teams that have collaborated in the past. In a study of more than 1,000 security analysts led by Boris Groysberg, when star analysts moved to a new firm, it took them an average of at least five years to recover their star status – unless they moved with their teams. The star analysts who moved alone had 5% odds of receiving the highest ranking from investors, whereas those who transferred with their teams enjoyed a 10% chance of earning the top spot.

"Huckman and his colleagues found similar patterns in a study of more than 100 software development projects. The highest quality and on-time delivery rates were achieved not by the teams whose members had the most individual experience, but by the teams whose members had the most shared experience working together. Another study of product development teams showed that it typically took two to four years for members to gain sufficient experience working together to achieve their potential."

This last number is particularly interesting, as almost all of Liverpool's title-winning troops – certainly the key players – had been at the club (or in the first-team setup) for two to four years: Alisson, Trent Alexander-Arnold, Virgil van Dijk, Andy Robertson, Joël Matip, Gini Wijnaldum, Fabinho, Sadio Mané and Mo Salah; while Joe Gomez, Divock Origi, James Milner and Roberto Firmino were in their fifth season at the club, which doesn't fall too far outside the limit, and they were refreshed by the new talent around them. The only key first-XI player who was long-serving was Jordan Henderson, with a few of the squad players at the club for up to six or seven years, such as Adam Lallana and Dejan Lovren, who had gone from the first team to the fringes of the squad, albeit still making the occasional important contribution. The research suggests that if you have a team where half of them have been at a club ten years, and half of them are in their debut season, you could have the same average time spent at the club, but not the same levels of cohesion.

Selling an overvalued star to rebuild a squad is often a good move, but it's not without its dangers. The best example of it working to perfection is Ian Rush moving to Juventus in 1987, for a whopping £3.2m (at a time when the most an English club had ever paid was £1.5m). That £3.2m, agreed a year earlier, allowed Liverpool to reshape the entire attacking unit: John Aldridge, John Barnes, Peter Beardsley and Ray Houghton all arrived in 1987, to form what was, until the current team, arguably the best multi-pronged attack the club had ever possessed, as part of a team that rewrote the style book. But crucially, Aldridge arrived in January, and spent quite a lot of time on the bench as Rush played out the second half of his final season (before later returning in 1988, after his time in Italy proved a mistake). Houghton was the last to arrive, making his debut in late October 1987. In between came Barnes and Beardsley, both in the summer. But of course, that pair had been to the 1986 World Cup together as part of the England squad. So it was a gradual process, and the two key summer additions were already accustomed to one another's game. It perhaps also helped that the defence and central midfielders were already a well-established unit, providing their own platform of understanding within the side.

In the aforementioned article, Adam Grant stated that "Shared experience in teams is so important that Richard Hackman, one of the world's foremost experts on teams, went so far as to include it in the very definition of team effectiveness. In *Leading Teams*, he argues that in addition to assessing the quality and quantity of output, we should expand our measures of team effectiveness to include viability – whether the team retains its capability to work together in the future.

"The benefits of shared experience are visible outside knowledge work. Hackman referenced a NASA study showing that fatigued crews with experience flying together made significantly fewer errors than rested crews who had never flown together. He also pointed to an NTSB analysis of airline accidents revealing that 44% occurred on a crew's first flight together and 73% on a crew's first day. And an investigation of all NBA basketball games played from 1980 to 1994 showed that as teams gained more experience, they won more games. This was true even after accounting for player talent and age."

As ever, not everything fits neatly with the theory. "There are alternative explanations for some of these findings," Grant noted. "Many airline crews only do one flight or day together, meaning that there are more chances for accidents to occur on first flights and first days. Basketball executives and coaches work harder to keep successful teams together – and players are more motivated to stay with winning teams. Consistent with this idea, when NBA teams win more games in year one, they're more likely to stay together in year two. But the opposite also holds: NBA teams with more shared experience in year one win more games in year two.

"Interestingly, in the NBA and R&D, the gains from shared experience declined over time. The value of the first few years together was much greater than additional years accumulated. As teams stayed together longer, they had less to learn and faced a greater risk of becoming too rigid and predictable in their routines. At that point, rotating a member – or a coach – might be a critical step. But most teams never made it there. The vast majority of teams weren't together long enough to benefit from shared experience.

"Today, too many teams are temporary: people collaborate on a single project and never work together again. Teams need the opportunity to learn about each other's capabilities and develop productive routines. So once we get the right people on the bus, let's make sure they spend some time driving together."

This accurately describes Liverpool's process, and reinforces the idea that the squad, and the team, is perhaps ready for one more season together, as the Covid-19 crisis forces clubs to scale down their transfer plans ahead of 2020/21. The team is getting older, clearly, but no one in the best XI is within even two years of being *too old*.

Team of Teams
Retired US Army General Stanley McChrystal, former commander of Joint Special Operations Command (JSOC) in the mid-2000s, discusses the complexities of combining individuals into units in *Team of Teams: New Rules of Engagement for a Complex World*, released in 2020:

"A fighting force with good individual training, a solid handbook, and a sound strategy can execute a plan efficiently, and as long as the environment remains fairly static, odds of success are high. But a team fused by trust and purpose is much more potent. Such a group can improvise a coordinated response to dynamic, real-time developments. Groups like SEAL teams and flight crews operate in truly complex environments, where adaptive precision is key. Such situations outpace a single leader's ability to predict, monitor, and control. As a result, team members cannot simply depend on orders; teamwork is a process of reevaluation, negotiation, and adjustment; players are constantly sending messages to, and taking cues from, their teammates, and those players *must* be able to read one another's every move and intent. When a SEAL in a target house decides to enter a storeroom that was not on the floor plan they had studied, he has to know exactly how his teammates will respond if his action triggers a firefight, just as a soccer forward must be able to move to where his teammate will pass the ball. Harvard Business School teams expert Amy Edmondson explains, 'Great teams consist of individuals who have learned to trust each other. Over time, they have discovered each other's strengths and weaknesses, enabling them to play as a coordinated whole.' Without this trust, SEAL teams would just be a collection of fit soldiers."

Elsewhere in the book, McChrystal talks about the optimum size, in term of numbers (rather than height or girth), for 'teams'. Of course, in football, the team is always eleven players, so the *squad* size is the more pertinent issue here, and it's interesting to note how Jürgen Klopp has always wanted to keep the squad just below what many consider the optimum size; going with only 20-or-so senior players, with a series of talented youngsters available to fill in if required, rather than the 25 or more model. Versatility is another reason why Klopp can get away with a thinner squad: rather than have at least two specialists for every position, there are a series of multitaskers, who can adjust to different roles. So unless an injury crisis goes beyond six or seven players, the versatility of the squad should cover the shortfall.

McChrystal asks *How many cooks is too many?* in reference to the old proverb.

"In a small kitchen or office, four might be the ideal number. For a company with operations the size of Walmart, the break point is much higher. For some activities, like having an engaging conversation, diminishing marginal returns sets in after a few people. For other tasks, like producing a mechanical item via assembly line, you can add just as much value with the hundredth employee as with the first. For teams, this range is considerably narrower. Athletic teams, for instance, usually consist of fifteen to thirty people. Army Ranger platoons are composed of forty-two soldiers. SEAL squads contain between sixteen and twenty people. Beyond such numbers, teams begin to lose the 'oneness' that makes them adaptable. As the proverbial kitchen fills up, communication and trust break down, egos come into conflict, and the chemistry that fuelled innovation and agility becomes destructive. In many cases, this loss of adaptability dooms the enterprise."

Finally from McChrystal's book, there's a powerful paragraph on how the best teams operate:

"The team is better off with the cohesive ability to improvise as a unit, relying on both specialisation (goalies mostly stay in goal;

forwards mostly don't) and overlapping responsibilities (each can do some of the others' jobs in a pinch), as well as such familiarity with one another's habits and responses that they can anticipate instinctively one another's responses. The best teams […] know their coach (or commander or boss) trusts them to trust each other."

Again, all of this could be applied to Liverpool in 2019/20. There is the familiarity of habit to anticipate each other's actions, borne of years spent together and hard-drilled and challenging (but rewarding) training sessions. The players are trusted by the manager. There is specialisation – aside from Alisson and Andy Robertson, and one or two others (Dejan Lovren, Naby Keïta) – where they can do each other's jobs, with versatility an absolute hallmark of the Jürgen Klopp Liverpool side. Name almost any player and he can play in at least three positions; albeit my personal rule of thumb has always been to expect rounded players, unless utter specialists (like Alisson, obviously, or to go back 15 years, Peter Crouch), to be able to play one position 'removed' from their norm; i.e. one place infield/outfield, or one place upfield/downfield. Even Robertson, with whom Klopp sympathised in the autumn of 2017 when noting it is harder for those in the squad who only play one position to break into the team, can look comfortable in any area of the field, albeit he's yet to start in any position other than left-back.

Virgil van Dijk could be a central midfielder; as could Trent Alexander-Arnold. Fabinho can, and has, played right-back and centre-back. Roberto Firmino can play anywhere in the final third, or midfield. Gini Wijnaldum has played as a winger, attacking midfielder, holding midfielder, centre-back and second striker. James Milner has played every position in football bar goalkeeper. It's a kind of *totaalvoetbal*, where everyone knows his own role, and knows the roles of others, and none of it happens overnight. Teams that are more regimented, with more specialisation and less versatility, can more easily fall apart when the structures are broken, the team shape stretched.

Speaking in a 2020 interview sponsored by Standard Chartered, Klopp said: "My dream was always that we can play in any random shirt. But if you watch us playing, you say... 'ah, that's Liverpool'. Our identity is that clear. 'That's Liverpool'.

"… With new players, we have this agreement, we like you, that's why we signed you. But from now on, we expect much more. And if he agrees, he gets more attention, more education, better training. That's a clear agreement. If he's not happy with one of these parts, he can come and tell me. 'You told me this, and that, and it isn't happening'. The same applies, if I'm not happy with what he agreed I will go to him and tell him. This is a clear deal. A handshake deal, not official!"

"…We have clear rules on how we want to play. Where we want to defend. Where we want to pass it. How lively are you? How positive? How brave? Through all the ranks. All the teams."

Klopp is a cosmopolitan, a uniter of people – another strength of his leadership, in stark contrast to the preening self-regard and divisive policies of presidents and prime ministers seen during the pandemic; leaders full of strongman promises and populist rhetoric. Anyone can make bold statements when they want to be elected leader, or once they have seized power – it's much more difficult to lead by example, with empathy *and* strength, for more than a short period of time.

"I love football so much because it's a wonderful example of how different cultures can work together," Klopp said. "We are one group. That's my dream of the world, my dream of Europe. It is why I was not happy about Brexit, because I do not understand the world like this. In a football team, nobody cares where you are from. But it is still important to know about it, because we have to treat individuals differently. I can't treat Mané or Salah in the exact same way I treat Jordan Henderson who has grown up here. I try to understand why people are like they are. And the boys try to understand that as well. We want to function as a group and that means respecting the individual. A football dressing room is a wonderful example of how colourful the world can be. Use all the different cultures, all the different strengths, all the different educations to be the best team you can be.

"… Having eye contact in the massive moments, and you see their eyes widen, and you feel the same. That's everything for me. Same as a kid. I know football isn't that important, I just forget it constantly, especially around these moments and football games. I think that is allowed for these 95 minutes. We really can connect to each other, and create the best atmosphere ever. Seeing how much it means to other people, gives me a lot.

"Success doesn't change really. The time we spend together changes a little, because in the beginning I don't know them. I trust them because they are football players, and I think after 20 years in the job I understand how are they are. But the rules are still strict, and without discipline you cannot win in sports. It's just not possible. For the boys it's much easier to respect them because they are completely logical now, they know why we have these kind of rules."

It's About Philosophy, Not "Winning"

In his best-selling book, *Atomic Habits*, author James Clear – a once-promising baseball player until, aged 16, his face was staved in by an errant bat that left him in a coma – notes in bold capitals: "forget about goals, focus on systems instead".

In football, 'systems' could be read as 'philosophy': the methods, the style of play, the things worked on in training; and goals – which are not to be fixated over – are obviously *results*. So, don't focus on results, but on how the team plays. As such, a losing team could be improving, whilst a winning team may just be riding its luck and not actually progressing.

Progress is rarely linear – there are almost always setbacks and false steps – but the right ideas, if well practiced by good players, can become a winning formula. Look at Jürgen Klopp in October 2017, around the time of the 4-1 defeat by Spurs at Wembley: lots of people questioning why the team wasn't winning enough, and if he was as good as people made out. Indeed, the narrative was clear – with a 52% win rate, Klopp's record was identical to the win rate of Brendan Rodgers, *who was sacked* (even though he wasn't sacked *because of a 52% win rate*). My argument at the time was that, after the brilliant, barnstorming 2013/14, Rodgers' final 15 months saw a Hodgsonesque win percentage of around 40% (so results were getting worse over a far longer period of time than when Roy Hodgson himself was in charge), and the style of play was a mess. By contrast, in October 2017 there was a sense of Liverpool being an exciting team under Klopp, with a clear identity, but some skittish consistency, in part because the team (still largely the one he inherited) had players who made too many costly mistakes, and defenders and a goalkeeper who, whilst not bad players, were like punch-drunk boxers having taken too many beatings. It seemed ludicrous to me at the time to suggest that Liverpool were not better under Klopp than they had been under Rodgers, especially as the final year or two of a manager's reign are indicative of what he hands over to the new guy. Klopp did not inherit Luis Suarez, Steven Gerrard, Daniel Agger or Raheem Sterling, who all left between 2014 and 2015, and the Daniel Sturridge he found was physically broken.

Back then, Klopp was always talking about identity, ideas, philosophies; as indeed did Rodgers, as the argot became fashionable. But Klopp had already established an elite-identity team with an insanely young Borussia Dortmund side, that won back-to-back German titles (breaking the national points record in the process) and then reached a Champions League final that they were unlucky to lose (in part as Bayern Munich poached their best player on the eve of the game), all on a shoestring budget; the manager having taken over in 2008 when the club was on the brink of collapse. Rodgers had a clear identity with his Swansea side, of super-high possession, albeit often in deeper areas of the pitch (which worked wonders for a promoted club), and he talked a good game, but his Liverpool project was an utter chaos of altered approaches – some of which highlighted his adaptability (switching formations), but which overall ended up feeling like a dog's dinner. As results suffered, the philosophy went out the window in search of wins; understandable, perhaps, for a youngish manager in his first big job, trying to stave off the sack, but as he himself later accepted, making mistakes in the process. In 2020, Rodgers admitted that his role in transfers – which perhaps ultimately sank him at Liverpool – was badly handled (he now saw himself as more of a coach than an old-fashioned manager), and his war with the transfer committee meant the Reds were constantly compromising on new talent. The club was divided, the squad was a mishmash, and the side was not showing a clear playing style, nor was it winning very many games.

Enter Klopp.

And, two years into his reign, that turning point came in late 2017, when things started to really click – albeit mostly in Europe – and still without total consistency or defensive solidity. If the first two years represented anything – aside from two lost finals, and qualifying for the Champions League for only the second time in almost a decade – it was the implementation of an attitude, a philosophy and a *process*.

In *Atomic Habits*, James Clear notes: "If you're a coach, your goal might be to win a championship. Your system is the way you recruit players, manage your assistant coaches, and conduct practice. If you're an entrepreneur, your goal might be to build a million-dollar business. Your system is how you test product ideas, hire employees, and run marketing campaigns. If you're a musician, your goal might be to play a new piece. Your system is how often you practice, how you break down and tackle difficult measures, and your method for receiving feedback from your instructor.

"Now for the interesting question: If you completely ignored your goals and focused only on your system, would you still succeed? For example, if you were a basketball coach and you ignored your goal to win a championship and focused only on what your team does at practice each day, would you still get results? I think you would. The goal in any sport is to finish with the best score, but it would be ridiculous to spend the whole game staring at the scoreboard. The only way to actually win is to get better each day. In the words of three-time

Super Bowl winner Bill Walsh, 'The score takes care of itself.' The same is true for other areas of life. If you want better results, then forget about setting goals. Focus on your system instead."

When interviewed mere minutes after Liverpool were confirmed champions for the first time in 30 years, as he sat in a room at Formby Hall Golf Resort & Spa where the squad had watched the Chelsea versus Manchester City game, Jordan Henderson was asked by Joe Cole on BT Sport if there was a particular game where he thought the title was won. The captain explained, "I never ever wanted to think about the end goal. I never wanted to think about what would happen if we did win, or we didn't win a certain game. The focus was solely on the next game, and not what may or may not happen."

Sound familiar?

In the book, Clear lists four problems with focusing on goals rather than process. I'll share them here, albeit edited down to the opening statements for each:

"Problem #1: Winners and losers have the same goals. Goal setting suffers from a serious case of survivorship bias. We concentrate on the people who end up winning—the survivors—and mistakenly assume that ambitious goals led to their success while overlooking all of the people who had the same objective but didn't succeed. Every Olympian wants to win a gold medal.

"… Problem #2: Achieving a goal is only a momentary change. Imagine you have a messy room and you set a goal to clean it. If you summon the energy to tidy up, then you will have a clean room—for now. But if you maintain the same sloppy, pack-rat habits that led to a messy room in the first place, soon you'll be looking at a new pile of clutter and hoping for another burst of motivation. You're left chasing the same outcome because you never changed the system behind it."

"… Problem #3: Goals restrict your happiness. The implicit assumption behind any goal is this: "Once I reach my goal, then I'll be happy." The problem with a goals-first mentality is that you're continually putting happiness off until the next milestone. I've slipped into this trap so many times I've lost count. For years, happiness was always something for my future self to enjoy. I promised myself that once I gained twenty pounds of muscle or after my business was featured in the *New York Times*, then I could finally relax.

"… Problem #4: Goals are at odds with long-term progress. Finally, a goal-oriented mind-set can create a "yo-yo" effect. Many runners work hard for months, but as soon as they cross the finish line, they stop training. The race is no longer there to motivate them. When all of your hard work is focused on a particular goal, what is left to push you forward after you achieve it? This is why many people find themselves reverting to their old habits after accomplishing a goal. The purpose of setting goals is to win the game. The purpose of building systems is to continue playing the game."

Since day one at Liverpool, Klopp has focused on the process, not results. In an early game at Anfield in 2015 he took the team – looking sheepish – towards the Kop after the 2-2 draw salvaged against lowly West Brom, to much mocking from outsiders, and even some embarrassment from Liverpool fans; the goal had not been achieved – Liverpool failed to beat mediocre opposition. But a *process* was put in place. The team had tried, and the crowd had got behind them in a late search for the equaliser. *That* was the reason to celebrate. Winning or losing can be arbitrary at times, but unity provides strength. Liverpool could have won that game whilst playing poorly, and less might have been *achieved*. You can't completely control the outcome, but you can control the effort put in.

Heart

In December 2019, Pepijn Lijnders told Arthur Renard of *The Guardian*, "The heart of the team is the heart of the coach. So the character of the coach will become the character of the team in the long term. That's it. Because there is no stronger weapon than your own example. If I'm a disciplined coach, then I don't need to discipline the players. Our captains Hendo [Jordan Henderson] and Milly, together with Virgil [van Dijk], are so disciplined, which means the rest of the group doesn't need to be disciplined. There is a saying from [Theodore] Roosevelt which says: 'People don't care how much you know, until they know how much you care.'

"Jürgen does really care about the squad and his staff. Players will understand and absorb more of our philosophy when they feel how much we care about them."

Klopp is clearly a realistic optimist; a Stoic, in the ancient sense of the word – seeing solutions with every problem, rather than raising his hands in defeat and giving up. "He is able to give a completely different perception to a situation inside a few minutes," Lijnders explained, using the example of the away game in Barcelona in the semi-final of the Champions League in 2019. "We lost 3-0, but afterwards Jürgen said in the dressing room: 'The only team in the world who can overturn this defeat against Barcelona is us.' It gave the squad a boost, also because of the way we had played that night. When the players walked towards the coach there was already a different feeling."

Talking to James Pearce of *The Athletic* a month later, Lijnders said of his relationship with Klopp: "There's a super dynamic between us. It's much more than just assistant and manager. What I mean by that is that I believe you need 100 per cent trust in this job because we have to make so many decisions on a daily basis. I love working for him. He sees who I am, and respects that. We know what to expect from each other.

"Jürgen is a true leader. He's inspirational and motivational. He still surprises me every day with something he says. His brain works differently to a lot of other brains!

"He sees through situations and processes … And I think everyone who works with Jürgen has the feeling he really cares about you and your development. There is no ego, he purely searches for the right thing to do."

Lijnders explained how Klopp creates an apparently ego-free dressing room, which allows the team to become one. "He has this remarkable capacity to touch people with the words he selects. That's not easy, especially with this level of players. I find that intriguing, how it's possible, the convincing way he has and that ability to touch people. You are dealing with a lot of egos in football but in our club it looks like there are no egos.

"Jürgen has created an environment where everyone has bought into it. He solves problems before they arise. He has this capacity of making sure that certain things won't happen because he speaks about them. The level of respect the players have for him is huge.

"No written word, no spoken plea, can teach our team what they should be, nor all the books on the shelves, it's what the coach is himself. Do you know what I mean? The character of the coach becomes the character of the team. You can see it throughout the club. That's the power of Jürgen's personality."

Raphael Honigstein, whose book on Klopp, *Bring The Noise*, provides an excellent insight into the processes the manager and his staff developed back in Germany, wrote in *The Athletic* after the Reds clinched the title that, "This season's achievement has put Klopp into a managerial category all of his own, at least until the Champions League resumes in August: he's the one manager working at a top-level club who has achieved all the goals for which he was hired."

Indeed, in just three jobs over a 19-year period, Klopp has massively exceeded expectations at each club he's managed. Within a few years, Mainz were taken from the poorest club in the second tier up into the top tier for the first time in their history. Dortmund, also financially parlous, became the best team in the *Bundesliga*, and were close to repeating the feat in Europe.

Martin Quast, a German football reporter and one of Klopp's oldest friends (they met when Klopp was a young player, back in 1990), told Honigstein: "Kloppo doesn't know the meaning of the word 'satisfaction'. He will be deeply happy, of course, but there's no sense of 'this is it' nor of 'I've finally done it'. It's never about him for him, and it's also never about proving a point for him. He doesn't draw motivation from negativity, whether that's other people's attitudes or a personal fear of failure. Kloppo does what he does because he loves football, he loves life, and especially what winning feels like. More importantly, he loves sharing these wonderful moments with those who feel the same.

"… He's not one to fret about things he has no control over," Quast said about the fact that Liverpool were not able to have a trophy parade. "In fact, his ability to take setbacks big and small in his stride is one of his most remarkable features. He always finds a way to turn a negative into a positive. It's a little bit weird right now but he knows that people won't value the trophy any less. And they will party eventually, I'm sure.

"…He doesn't want to be at the centre of it all, and he would never agree to have a statue of himself put up. When someone suggested that idea at Mainz, Kloppo said statues were only good for collecting bird droppings at the top and for dogs peeing on them at the bottom."

Clashes of the Titans

When Liverpool could only manage a draw at Old Trafford on October 20th, with United languishing in the bottom half of the table, few thought the Reds would resume a winning league run that would take them well into 2020.

It's fair to say that Liverpool did not have a lot of luck, with the referee, and VAR, making life much harder for Jürgen Klopp's men, and helping out Ole Gunnar Solskjær's team to an opening goal, and denying Liverpool an equaliser. The game seemed to be getting away from the Reds as the clock ran down. Klopp made changes in the second half, with Naby Keïta and Adam Lallana coming on for the closing stages. In the 84th minute United replaced their goalscorer

Marcus Rashford with Anthony Martial, and not a single home player touched the ball from that point until, a minute later, it was in the back of their net. Liverpool began moving the ball from side to side at the back, trying to find a forward pass, before turning and trying down the other side. The first truly cutting pass was from Trent Alexander-Arnold, infield towards the edge of the area, to Roberto Firmino, who had three players around him. The ball bounced up a bit as he controlled it, but then he used the outside of his boot – up by his heel – to flick it away from Harry Maguire, yet that allowed two United midfielders to try and win the ball from the other side of the striker. As both Fred and Scott McTominay stuck out legs to stretch and get a touch, Firmino dinked the ball in between the pair of them, to his compatriot Fabinho. For the first time United were now slightly out of shape: too many men had gone to Firmino, and now their right flank was slightly exposed. At the moment Fabinho – dead-centre of the pitch – laid the ball to Keïta there were four Liverpool players in white to the left of the no.3, and only three for United; with six home players temporarily out of the game on their own left side of that axis, albeit not exactly stranded. Keïta looked to play the ball infield, but by then United had shuttled back into shape to close that avenue; albeit there was still one player in oceans of space, where United could not move quickly enough to shut down. Keïta laid the ball out wide to that man – Andy Robertson – and, with the help of a Firmino dummy, his low cross across the face of the six-yard box evaded everyone bar the late-arriving Lallana, who prodded home from four yards with just five minutes remaining. It was Lallana's first goal in 29 Premier League appearances, having last scored against Middlesbrough in May 2017. (With an open goal beckoning, the only surprise was that Lallana did not try to Cruyff-turn the ball home.)

Before the full-time whistle it looked like Alex Oxlade-Chamberlain had fired the Reds to victory, but his arrowing low drive whistled an inch past the post. Despite not being at their best, Liverpool had 68% of the possession, 10 shots to seven, and four to two on target, but could not snatch the victory; with the averages across all the main xG models having Liverpool edge the game, but only by one-third of a goal. (Of course, United's one big chance – their goal – should have been a free-kick to Liverpool instead.) United registered their second lowest possession figure (32.1%) in a Premier League home match since 2003/04, second only to 32.06% – also against Liverpool – in March 2018. Quite what Sir Alex Ferguson must have been thinking, having recently survived a near-death experience with a brain haemorrhage, only to be served up a tepid and tentative United team hanging on against a Liverpool team running away with the title, is anyone's guess. Almost three decades after celebrating knocking Liverpool off their perch, Ferguson was thankfully now well enough to see the reversal of fortunes; the cycle almost complete.

As such, the Reds' run of 17 consecutive league wins fell one short of Manchester City's record of 18 from two seasons earlier – but Klopp's men immediately started on a new run to have a second bite at that particular cherry.

The dropped points could have felt costly – although winning at Old Trafford has always been rare (and now it was even rare for *Manchester United,* too). Despite Manchester City winning away at Crystal Palace on the same weekend, Pep Guardiola's men had lost 2-0 at home to Wolves in the previous round of games. The Reds' lead now stood at six points, with another Big Six game out of the way – their third in the league in just nine matches. A week later they would play their fourth.

"Spursy"

Next up were Spurs at Anfield, seeking atonement for their defeat in Madrid when they conceded a second-minute penalty in the biggest game in their history (you wait all that time for a Champions League final and then almost literally *hand* it over in the opening exchange). And it was indeed their turn to take a ludicrously early lead, going 1-0 up in less than 60 seconds, as Son Heung-min's shot rebounded off the post – via a deflection off the head of Dejan Lovren – for Harry Kane to stoop and head past the helpless Alisson as the ball rolled fortuitously across the six-yard box.

Liverpool then spurned a whole host of first-half chances, missing the target from close range, and when their aim was true, finding Paulo Gazzaniga in top form. The second half continued in the same vein, as Spurs' keeper blocked a close-range Roberto Firmino header, before the visitors broke and Son hit the bar.

Liverpool got back into the game seven minutes into the second half when Son ran the ball out of play for a Liverpool throw. There was no great magic here; no throw-in coach required: it was simple, and unpressurised, with the ball played between the Liverpool centre-backs and Fabinho, with Spurs sitting off. The move progressed, and for a third time Fabinho tried something ambitious out to the right; this time to devastating effect, with a scooped cross into the right-side of the box. Roberto Firmino appeared to be pushed over in the area as the ball sailed through to the inrushing Henderson, who squeezed a left-footed half-volley – hit into the ground – into the far corner. It was his first league goal at Anfield in 1,414 days. (Thankfully he wouldn't have to wait as long for his next one.)

With fifteen minutes to go Spurs were still trying to find the winner on the break; a ball over the top to Son was brilliantly cut out by Alexander-Arnold with a last-man header on the stretch. As Christian Eriksen tried to find the time to make another pass, Gini Wijnaldum robbed him and Alexander-Arnold nipped in to instinctively launch a high ball into the inside-left channel; half clearance, half preplanned tactic to put Sadio Mané away whenever possible. Mané, surrounded by two Spurs' defenders with a third on the cover, drove into the box but Serge Aurier managed to slide in – albeit awkwardly – and win the ball. However, by going to ground the Frenchman was unable to beat Mané to the loose ball as it bounced on the edge of the six-yard box. Mané got his body in the way at the exact moment Aurier went to boot the ball out for a throw, succeeding in only booting Mané on the back of the calf. Anthony Taylor had no hesitation in pointing to the spot, and VAR had no objections either as Gary Neville, on Sky, said "there's absolutely no chance that will be overturned", such was its stonewall nature.

It was only Liverpool's second Kop-end penalty in the league in almost two and a half years, and it needed to be a near-assault to be given; but given it was. Mo Salah, with his new technique of skipping sideways to his right in an arc when approaching the ball, before straightening up as he drew closer, lashed a low left-footed drive past the helpless Gazzaniga. Having conceded two penalties to Spurs at the Kop end in 2017/18, Liverpool were now getting some revenge from the spot – with this goal turning a draw into a win, whilst in Madrid, the 2nd-minute penalty essentially won the Reds the Champions League.

As at Old Trafford, Liverpool had 68% possession, and this time it was backed up by a *ton* of shots; over 20. Gazzaniga made 12 saves, the most by a goalkeeper in the Premier League since David de Gea against Arsenal in December 2017 (14). When Mauricio Pochettino – who would soon lose his job – said his side "deserved more", one can only assume he meant more of a battering. It was one from Brendan Rodgers' school of reality denial.

Daniel Rhodes, writing for TTT in his post-match analysis, noted that Liverpool had "Nearly twice the amount of shots (21 – 11), and four times the amount of shots on target (13 – 4). During Klopp's three full seasons, this is the third highest amount Liverpool have ever had in a game: 17 vs Watford (6-1); 15 vs Sunderland (1-0) and 13 vs Palace

(1-0) were the other occasions when the Reds tested the opposition keeper so frequently."

Klopp was naturally effusive about his team. "I really liked the way we played against really tough opponents. It was a wonderful game of football, it's how you wish games should be. The boys delivered. We had chance after chance and the keeper had sensational save after sensational save.

"At half-time I said this game had only one problem – the scoreline. When Tottenham had the ball their counter-attacks were incredible. We won the game and deserved it."

Thrilling! Late Late Resurrection At Villa
When, in early November, Manchester City turned around a 1-0 deficit at home to Southampton with two late goals, to take the lead with just four minutes left, Liverpool – on a rare occasion when the two title-chasing titans both played Saturday 3pm kick-offs – still trailed 1-0 at Aston Villa, to a goal from a free-kick that was only marginally onside according to several minutes of VAR-based analysis. The Reds, on 28 points after ten games, looked set to remain on 28 points after 11; while City would be up to 25.

It looked like City would be coming to Merseyside a week later knowing that a win at Anfield would take them top on goal difference, in which metric their superiority was almost at double-figures. What's more, their 86th-minute winner was from an unlikely source: full-back Kyle Walker (which always seems like an unexpected bonus, as if fated). It was the moment the title race tilted back in City's favour.

Or was it?

Days after Halloween, Liverpool looked so dead and buried at Villa Park that only a reenactment of the *Thriller* video would suffice. Step forward Liverpool's own full-back hero, Andy Robertson. The funk of forty-thousand years and the grisly ghouls from every tomb had nothing on the Scottish left-back, who bullet-headed in an improbable equaliser from a beautiful deep Sadio Mané cross, just when the phrase "at the death" was about to kick in.

And when Trent Alexander-Arnold's delicious injury-time free-kick – heading into the top corner, with under 60 seconds of added time left to play – deflected narrowly over, it looked like the chance was gone; a draw against an incredibly spirited and organised Villa side was looking like a decent result, but possibly not enough with City starting to find their groove. There was barely even time to take the resultant corner. However, three days after the Reds' 5-5 comeback in the League Cup against Arsenal (which the young XI won on penalties), this

Liverpool team – no matter who was wearing the shirt – was as devastating in the 95th minute as probably any team in history, rescuing results with the last kicks of games – or in this case, the last header, with Sadio Mané flicking in at the near post from the corner just as a high boot conked him in the face.

At a quarter-to-five, Man City were within three points of Liverpool. By ten-to-five, Liverpool were six points clear once again.

Man City At Anfield: Title Decider In November?
Arriving at Anfield with a chance to narrow the gap to three points, Man City were starting their first league game of the season without the injured Ederson in goal. By contrast, Liverpool had won all of the league games that Alisson Becker had missed – Adrián deputising superbly well for the most part – so how would City cope with their number two, Claudio Bravo?

With the Reds going into the game on 31 points, the gap at the top stood at five after eleven games – although the lead was now over *Leicester and Chelsea*, City being 4th with 25 points – and this was a chance for some serious daylight to be put between the champions-elect and the reigning title-holders.

City started much the brighter of the two sides: the first few minutes spent with Pep Guardiola's team attacking the Kop end, and winning a couple of corners. But the game changed on a hugely pivotal and controversial moment. A Liverpool attack broke down, and as Kevin de Bruyne challenged Virgil van Dijk over a dropping ball in the Reds' half, the bounce fell infield to the advancing Bernardo Silva. As Lovren produced a block-tackle, the ball flew against Silva's hand and then ricocheted onto Trent Alexander-Arnold's arm three yards away, in the centre of a crowded box. Michael Oliver waved play-on, as Sergio Agüero and de Bruyne stopped to ask for a penalty. Liverpool had no fewer than five players around the ball, and Jordan Henderson and Fabinho were both about to enter the area as cover, as van Dijk calmly played a pass from the penalty spot out to Andy Robertson.

Robertson fed a ball down the line to Mané, and when he picked the ball up 20 yards inside his own half the Reds had already bypassed *seven* City players. As Mané advanced down the pitch he slowed, awaiting support, allowing Roberto Firmino to make a run into the space behind the City backline. By this stage the speed of the attack had faltered, and Rodri had got back to bolster City's rearguard, so it was three Liverpool attackers versus four defenders in blue. No angles for passes opened up, so Mané went for the line, but – given the speed at which football moves – City now had six players back. Mané's cross was low and found only a blue shirt, as Angelino intercepted and İlkay Gündoğan played a slightly strange, powerless clearance straight to Fabinho, who showed him in return what a *fast-moving* ball looks like. From 25 yards the Brazilian fizzed in a rocket, and Bravo stood no chance. *Goooooooooal!* as they more-or-less say in Fabinho's homeland.

The goal led to a heated debate between the City players and the officials, as VAR double-checked the details over what was a hitherto unique situation in English football. While the ball had clearly struck Alexander-Arnold's arm, it was from fairly close range, and the referees themselves had said at the start of the season that handballs following ricochets would be less likely to be given as penalties. However, this was doubly complicated, thanks to the new rules, as the ball had also ricocheted off *Silva's* hand, and in contrast to defending, *attacking* handballs would now be automatically penalised – even if utterly unintentional – if they led to a goalscoring opportunity for their team. So, Silva's handball would have "created" a penalty for City that would then have been overruled (so City's claim for a penalty was fairly denied), with Liverpool instead given a free-kick for the unintentional infringement by the City winger. But to disallow Liverpool's goal in order to bring the ball back 80 yards for a free-kick to Liverpool in their own box would have been ludicrous. The debate then moved on to whether Alexander-Arnold's handball in the buildup to *Liverpool's* goal, in starting the swift counterattack, meant Fabinho's goal should have been ruled out. This was complicated by the fact that the accidental handball occurred about 80 yards from the opposition goal, and City also cleared the ball from their own box – and so the game arguably entered a different phase of play. The net sum was that City did not get their penalty and Liverpool did not have their goal ruled out in order to be given a free-kick inside their own box. Which, overall, felt entirely fair, and presented another reason why Michael Oliver is regarded (Manchester aside) as the best ref in England – *and by a country mile.* Once the VAR check was complete the Liverpool fans had a second reason to celebrate the goal, and did so with great gusto.

It was only Fabinho's second goal for Liverpool, and it was scored from about 24 yards further out than his previous effort, a header against Newcastle when almost on the goal-line. It also highlighted how – since the departure of Philippe Coutinho and more recently, Daniel Sturridge – Liverpool had become more expert at closer-range goals, with the long-range pile-driver an almost literal blast from the past.

Despite reducing in quantity, these types of long-range shots remain important, not least because they keep opposition teams guessing (you don't have to rush out to block a shot if you know *there will never be a shot*) – and Oxlade-Chamberlain remains a key contributor of the thunderbolt – but in the age of expected goals, teams realise that these are lower value, speculative attempts that, overall, are not to be resorted to too often. Season on season, Liverpool take fewer and fewer shots from distance, as discussed in more detail in *Mentality Monsters*. Feinting to shoot can often create *better* opportunities, but defenders have to believe that a shot is coming in order to fully commit themselves and buy the dummy. Plus, sometimes such shots will fly into the top corner, as Fabinho's did here.

The key thing to remember is that it may take some players over 50 shots to get a goal from outside the box, and as such, what is the incalculable value of all those "wasted" attacks? Equally, did those shots make defenders think twice and enable a long-shot addict like Coutinho to then disguise a dinked through-ball, or did they lead to goalkeeper spillages and corners that could be profited from? What the data does show is that constant strikes from distance are usually a desperate act, and often destroy the momentum a team may be building up, especially if the goalkeeper takes 90 seconds to place the ball for a goalkick. Choosing better positions to shoot from is not the same as trying to walk the ball into the net; simply, only shooting when the odds are good enough, and mainly when the space to shoot – as it did for Fabinho – opens up to the point where to refuse the shot almost seems rude.

With City still dazed by this blindsiding blow, the Reds turned the screw, with a goal that was utterly remarkable in its own way. Guardiola's men lost possession in the Liverpool half by gifting the ball to Fabinho, a player City had once scouted as a replacement for Fernandinho. Fabinho found Alexander-Arnold with a square pass level with the base of the centre-circle. The key to the beauty of the goal was when the young right-back turned back onto his left foot, which opened up the obvious pass back to Alisson; the kind of moment when high-pressing teams trigger a movement to win the ball. Right on cue, both de Bruyne and Agüero made runs to intercept the back-pass, and, just crossing the halfway line, Bernardo started to sprint forward, to join the press on Liverpool's defensive unit. At that precise moment it looked like the Reds could be in trouble; but one shimmy – one single shimmy – and it was City on the rack. Bernardo began to press forward just in time to leave a gaping chasm into which Andy Robertson strode; the art of the transition perfectly highlighted when Alexander-Arnold turned and found the space with a sublime pass from his weaker foot. By the time City's younger Silva got back to the base of the centre-circle in his own half, Robertson was ten yards ahead, delineated perfectly by the cut of the Anfield grass. Such was the quality of the pass he received, and such was the sureness of his first touch, that his second touch, now just 20 yards outside the City box, was to swing in an undefendable cross that bounced beautifully on the penalty spot and onto the head of the onrushing Mo Salah. In four passes the Reds zigzagged from flank to flank, back to front, and from the back-foot to scoring a goal. The game was not even a quarter of an hour old, and already City's hopes of getting a much-needed win were dead. This was classic blitzkrieging Liverpool, as seen more frequently in Klopp's early seasons – before his teams increased their share of possession, to the point where they dominated most teams (and even, at times, Manchester City).

Liverpool almost went 3-0 up with another terrifyingly quick but skilful move from one end to the other; Alisson controlling the ball on the edge of his own six-yard box before pinging a beauty of a pass to Alexander-Arnold. The young Scouser still had a lot to do, taking the ball on the touchline ten yards inside his own half with a nonchalance that belied three things: the speed of the pass he was receiving, his proximity to being out of play (so any miscontrol and the ball was out) and the fact that the ball was about four feet off the ground when he stopped it dead. He then sprinted infield like a winger, going between two City midfielders, before laying the ball to Roberto Firmino, whose sharp turn and shot was too close to Bravo.

City then had a half-chance when Agüero dragged a shot wide from an acute angle, but Liverpool themselves had another half-chance when Salah curled a shot from 25 yards, but like Firmino's effort it was too close to a goalkeeper who otherwise struggles to extend his reach.

Early in the second half, the game was essentially over as a contest when Liverpool won a throw-in 40 yards from the City goal. Firmino was in the traditional centre-forward position, give or take a few yards, but he made a sudden dart towards the flank (almost as if the Reds work on these types of things with a specialist). Rodri looked confused, and passed him over to Gündoğan, who was a little late in reacting; by the time he tried to intercept, Firmino had flicked the ball back to Alexander-Arnold and the Liverpool striker quickly moved into the space Gündoğan had vacated. When Alexander-Arnold played the ball down the line to Jordan Henderson, Firmino was unmarked in the 'hole', Mo Salah was being man-marked tightly by Fernandinho in the centre-forward position, and, on the opposite flank, Mané was holding a very wide position, rather than moving inside early as many goal-hungry wide players – himself included – normally would.

Henderson, playing on the right of midfield, decided to take the unlikely path of going outside not one but two City players in a bid to reach the byline; but even as he got close to the line, Mané was still not in the box. Somehow Henderson managed to achieve his aim, and, almost from the corner flag, hit a powerful deep cross whose shape was itself a work of art: just high enough to bypass four City defenders and the diminutive Bravo, but with the power to stay in the air for 50 yards; and just low enough to come down perfectly for Mané – arriving at full-speed – at the far post. Any notion that Henderson's cross was just hit to a lucky area seems at odds with the positioning of Mané.

Mané's header – that, from a position wide of the goal, had to go back across keeper to be on target – was straight at the scrambling Bravo, but from such a close range, and with such power, there was nothing the Chilean keeper could do except frantically flap as the ball bounced off his body and span into the inside of the side-netting. Half the Liverpool team ran to Mané, but those on the other side of the pitch jumped on Henderson. The second half had barely begun but the match was already as good as won.

City rallied, as you would expect from a team with their quality (and nothing left to lose), and Liverpool looked to try and keep things tight, playing more on the break. As such, the visitors had chances – clearly dependent on game-state – but Bernardo Silva's goal, after 78 minutes, left little time to build up a really strong head of steam. The most cutting thing they could achieve on the pitch was when Guardiola sarcastically thanked Michael Oliver – not once, but twice, just to make it clear – after the final whistle. Guardiola had also earlier performed a manic touchline appeal for a second penalty, but the ball was struck right at Alexander-Arnold's hand from close range, and his arm was in a natural position by his side. The City manager was clutching at straws, knowing that his side's hopes of a third successive league title had just taken a serious blow.

It Gets Easier
Games against Crystal Palace and Brighton – those strange "local" rivals – followed. The game at Palace was dominated by another VAR controversy (a disallowed goal for the hosts when Jordan Ayew pushed Dejan Lovren over in the box, as a corner flew over their heads), although in this case it was hard to see what the fuss was all about; whilst the Reds' game against Brighton saw Liverpool suffer a clear refereeing mistake that no one seemed to notice at the time.

The Reds went 1-0 up at Palace, through a scuffed Mané half-volley, but Wilfried Zaha equalised with eight minutes left, and time was running out. However, with five minutes remaining the Reds forced an almighty scramble from a corner, and Roberto Firmino calmly swept home the winner.

With a corner routine rescuing the Reds at Palace, Jürgen Klopp's men were in full "dig out wins" mode. Days later, Dejan Lovren headed a set-piece equaliser against Napoli, to more-or-less secure passage into the knockout stages of the Champions League. Another few days on, and Brighton were put to the sword by two more simple-looking set-pieces, as Liverpool's entire game was reduced, in some circles, to something perfunctory; as if this was *all they ever did.*

Brighton got a late goal back, after Alisson was correctly sent off for handling outside the box, as Lewis Dunk scored from the resultant free-kick. However, Martin Atkinson was again costing Liverpool goals; allowing the free-kick to be taken in a way that the new rules said was illegal. It took Keith Hackett, one of the most experienced referees England has ever seen, and a former leader of the country's refereeing body (the PGMOL) to come out and point out the error: "The Brighton goal should have been disallowed. The Liverpool wall was formed with three or more players. Brighton's attackers were in the wall not one yard away." It was a small technical point, but a correct one; and Adrián was unsighted by the player, as – only just on the field as an emergency sub – Atkinson let Brighton take the free-kick quickly.

Jürgen Klopp was simply relieved to get the three points, with his side looking tired after yet another big Champions League game three days earlier. "It was difficult this game because Brighton are a good football side. They had a lot of possession and we had to work really hard. I loved that the boys were prepared to do that after a busy week."

Killing xG – How The Reds Destroyed Solid Statistical Models

As Liverpool continued to streak ahead in the title race, more and more observers seemed to note that it was either in some way lucky (excluding the ludicrous tinfoil helmet brigade that said VAR was a conspiracy implemented to help the Reds win the title), or that the underlying numbers did not back up such hitherto unseen supremacy.

Obviously *some* luck is needed along the way, when on such an unprecedented run (after all, *any* team will need its share of good fortune at the right times, just as any boxer can be on the end of a knockout blow if it catches him right), but Jürgen Klopp's team seemed to be doing things in a way that the statistical models like expected goals (xG) could not adequately explain. As the saying goes, "All models are wrong, but some models are useful".

At a time when Liverpool were 25 points clear, xG models said that Manchester City should instead have been ahead in the table, and yet witnessing City *actually play*, there was a nervousness (at times) and a flakiness (at times) that meant they often shot themselves in the foot. Indeed, they had no real defensive solidity, and little individual defensive brilliance, which meant that their freewheeling all-out attacking style was like a boxer – to continue the pugilistic analogy – windmilling the haymakers only to be shown to have a glass jaw at the first firm jab. Overall, xG is a brilliant tool, but it doesn't explain *everything* in football. It is better than the other commonly used metrics – possession, shots at goal, corners won – in explaining results, but it doesn't allow for the model-breaking excellence of dead-eye finishing, supreme defending and world-class goalkeeping. (And of course, Liverpool have all of those.)

After all, xG is based on the *average*, and at either end of the pitch the Reds were far from that. Indeed, the story of Liverpool's season was, in part, their *utter brilliance* at both ends of the pitch. The midfield also did an often unheralded job – protecting the defence, keeping the ball, pressing like dervishes, and weighing in with a few goals and killer assists (before belatedly someone like Jordan Henderson started being taken very seriously) – but their main role was to provide a solid base; to *control the game*, essentially, rather than to win it as individuals. But it was the men ahead of and behind them who essentially killed the xG model.

Indeed, Liverpool do so many unique things in the way they play, such as mixing the aerial ability and set-piece prowess of a lower-budget team (with world-beating, goal-creating throw-ins) with the passing and skill of the elite aesthetes, allied to the intense pressing made famous by Klopp at Dortmund, to provide an all-round game that is arguably as close to perfect as has been seen. Liverpool topped various metrics for the 2019/20 season – just not xG.

In essence, xG is a database of all the shots ever taken – since stats companies started recording them – from any position on the pitch, which distils them into a figure that shows the probability of scoring from such a chance, with the more complex models working in other variables, such as the position of the defenders and the goalkeeper, and what kind of finish was required, such as a header or a volley.

However, it doesn't allow for *unique* talents. Even then, many of the best players will be merely human a lot of the time, with plenty of mortal moments that contribute to the overall average. But the very best players obviously tend to do something special *more often*, lest they just be another regular player. Lionel Messi regularly outperforms the xG model, because he can score more regularly from all manner of shooting positions that prove difficult for less sublime talents. Equally, some specialist players are better than average when shooting from 30 yards, even though a goal is, on the whole, a low-probability outcome from such distances – perhaps one-in-fifty.

At the other end of the pitch to Messi, Alisson Becker outperformed xG by a world-class level that, frankly, put him in a league of his own. Opta noted that he was preventing 0.74 goals per game with his saves well into 2019/20, more than three times as much as Ederson of Manchester City, and David de Gea of Manchester United, who ranked 2nd and 3rd, with 0.23 and 0.17 respectively. Dan Kennett of *Anfield Index Under Pressure* and alumnus of *The Tomkins Times* stated a little while before the Watford match (when the keeper's 'luck' ran out) that "Alisson Becker has saved 50 of the last 54 shots on target he has faced in all competitions (93%)."

For all the benefits of xG, there are things that are harder to quantify with simple numbers in isolation, like resilience, or the flow of a match and how much pressure a team puts on the opposition, dependent on game state. You can track data for the ebb and flow of any given match, but it won't be clearly represented by the mere sum of a team's xG on any given day. Like the scoreline, it doesn't tell the story of *when* and *how* the goals were scored (or chances created); although some analysts create graphs that show how the xG is accumulated during a game, spread across the 90 minutes, which can be more revealing. A great example is the 2018/19 Champions League final, in which Spurs took several late shots – few were actual "chances" – on account of Liverpool sitting back to defend the 1-0 lead; and while the Reds wouldn't have been looking to see Alisson forced into making a series of saves, Spurs' domination of the end of the match was clearly driven by game state, as they threw caution to the wind – and with Jürgen Klopp's men very wary of the clear threat the Londoners posed on the break.

And in 2019/20, Liverpool's brilliance seemed to be in picking and choosing *when to strike*, in terms of the state of the game, in stark contrast to the early Klopp years, when the team seemed to go all-out for 70 minutes and then collapse. As the team naturally progressed from a young side to its recent average age of 26.5 – a prime title-winning stage (not too young, not too old) – it seemed to have developed real *nous*; which was supplemented by the fact that the team, *as a whole,* had more-or-less been together for two to three years, and in that time it had reached two Champions League finals and contested the league title with the third-highest ever points tally seen in English football.

Indeed, rather than mirror the spirited tyros of his Dortmund team, with an average age of just 23, Klopp's side seemed to gradually acquire the wily game-control management skills associated with the Real Madrid and Bayern Munich teams of recent times, when they racked up Champions League successes almost by force of habit, as well as force of will. What perhaps marked Liverpool out as unique compared to a lot of those great "older heads" sides of the past decade, where success was built on a ton of experience, was that Liverpool still had the pace and vigour of youth. (And of course, it was also not a cynical team, in stark contrast to the sickening shithousery of Sergio Ramos at Madrid.)

Going into 2019/20, Liverpool had the experience of various European campaigns, a near-miss on the league title, but not one single first-XI player was old and slow, and in need of compensatory attributes from someone younger to balance out his effectiveness. Every single Liverpool player, bar the evergreen squad man James Milner (and the lesser-seen Adam Lallana), was absolutely in their prime, or approaching it. Joe Gomez was not covering for an ageing, slowing partner; while both Sadio Mané and Mo Salah weren't attacking ahead of slower full-backs who tentatively backed up play, but instead, were often cutting inside to let those bundles of energy overlap. There was no slow, goal-hanging centre-forward, offering nothing outside the box, letting the young guns do his running. And while Jordan Henderson and Gini Wijnaldum were approaching their 30s, they still retained the athleticism for which they were famous.

After 25 games – two-thirds of the season – as the league enjoyed the country's first official midwinter break (and before it "enjoyed" what felt like a *post-apocalyptic* break), it was almost two years since Klopp's men had been two goals behind in a league game; going back to the trip to Old Trafford in March 2018 – a massive 71 games, when no other Premier League club could boast better than a run of nine. In the same period, Manchester City had been two or more goals behind in no fewer than *seven* league matches, including a three-goal deficit at Anfield earlier in the season, which ended 3-1. City had also been two goals behind against Crystal Palace, Norwich City and Wolves, as well as Chelsea, Manchester United and Spurs.

(Of course, following the midwinter break, and before the global Covid-19 lockdown, that Reds' record would be shattered at Watford. This in and of itself should have been taken as a portent of impending doom, as the world went *weird*.)

Between the Reds' 2-1 defeat at Old Trafford on March 10th 2018 and mid-February 2020, the Reds only conceded two goals in a league game on six occasions: the 2-2 draw at West Brom at the time of the Champions League semi-finals in 2018 (with several stars rested and players like Alberto Moreno, Ragnar Klavan and Danny Ings in the XI), then the unlucky 2-1 defeat at the Etihad at the start of 2019, followed by the crazy 4-3 win over Crystal Palace the same month, the 4-2 win over Burnley in March 2019, the 3-2 win at Newcastle right at the end of 2018/19, and just once in 2019/20, in the 5-2 win over Everton, when Klopp rested half his team.

Long Shots

The other issue with using xG totals to assess which team has been the best is that – like all averages – it can obscure strengths or weaknesses in a particular area. In 2019/20, this was true when it came to the two main title-challenging teams, and their ability to deal with opposition shots from distance.

The website *Understat* breaks down expected goal figures in all kinds of different ways. By formation, game state, attack speed; you name it. The figures they have for shot zones made for interesting reading for Liverpool and Manchester City, at the time of the Covid-19-enforced break.

Jürgen Klopp's team had conceded two goals from outside the box, from chances collectively worth 3.8 expected goals, and on both occasions Adrián was between the sticks. Alisson Becker is extremely strong in this regard, as the only Premier League goal he has let in from beyond the edge of his penalty area occurred in strange circumstances. Everyone in Anfield, aside from referee Andre Marriner, could see the Brazilian was being impeded by James Tarkowski early in a match against Burnley – two players pushed down on him – which allowed Ashley Westwood to score directly from a corner. That aside, Becker's record from long shots has been flawless; beaten just once from outside the box in his Liverpool career (by a *shot*, not a corner), when Lionel Messi hit a free-kick so sublime that no keeper could have stopped it.

The same can't be said for Ederson or Claudio Bravo, and it has proved costly to the defending champions. By the time the league was mothballed in March, City had already conceded *seven* goals from outside the box, despite the chances being valued at just 2.8 xG by *Understat*.

And while correlation is not causation, there's certainly a theme. In six of the 10 league games which Pep Guardiola's side failed to win prior to the lockdown, they conceded a goal from further than 18 yards out. Some of them – Adama Traoré's effort at the Etihad or Scott McTominay's in the derby – simply turned a one-goal deficit into a 2-0 defeat very late on (albeit ruling out the chance of a last-gasp City equaliser). But some had a far more serious impact upon the result, and were very low quality opportunities.

City had conceded four goals valued at just 0.02 xG; one-in-fifty chances, in other words. Érik Lamela scored in the first half of a 2-2 draw in Manchester, while former Red Jonjo Shelvey scored an 87th-minute equaliser for Newcastle in November. Wolves' fightback from 2-0 down to beat City at Molineux began with another long range Traoré strike, and the most memorable of these goals for Liverpool fans was Fabinho's pile-driver, which set the Reds on their way to a 3-1 win in November. The result put Klopp's men nine points clear of City, and the gap only widened afterwards.

Game State

A secret of their success was that Liverpool didn't *waste* goals. In his column for the *Liverpool Echo* in early February 2020, Andrew Beasley noted:

"The chances they [Man City] have had when at least two goals ahead this season work out at 3.1 expected goals per 90 minutes, compared to Liverpool's average of 2.2. That's all well and good, and can lead to entertaining 8-0 wins for your fans to enjoy, but it doesn't earn you any more points.

"As Jürgen Klopp noted, 'Eight times 1-0 is better than one time 8-0'. Liverpool have 11 one-goal wins so far this season, while City have just four."

After the publication of that article, Liverpool's next three league victories – prior to the coronavirus shutdown – were 1-0, 3-2 and 2-1, to take it to 14 single-goal victories. (City themselves won one of their subsequent games by a one-goal margin – away to Leicester – but in playing catch-up after cancelled fixtures, they beat West Ham 2-0, then lost 2-0 at Manchester United.)

Andrew continued: "Arguably the Reds' greatest strength this season has been the consistency of their underlying performance, regardless of the scoreline. Whether they have been ahead, level or behind, Liverpool's expected goal difference per 90 minutes has always ranged between 1.1 and 1.6.

"But City's performances have fluctuated by a far wider margin. When they have been at least two goals ahead they have been 1.9 expected goals per 90 minutes better than their opponents, but when trailing by a goal that figure drops to just 0.5. Their best work has been wasted when they don't really need it, and often absent when they absolutely do.

"And it has been reflected in the results. Both Liverpool and City have won three and drawn one of the matches in which they have trailed in 2019/20. The difference is, Klopp's team have only been behind in four matches while Guardiola's have been losing in 10.

"Another great asset for Liverpool this season is they have yet to go two goals behind, where City have been in five of their six losses. The quality of chances given up by the two teams explains why too."

In the month of football that followed Andrew writing this article, Liverpool not only finally went 2-0 behind, but that game ended with a 3-0 defeat at Watford. However, City also added another 2-0 reversal, against their city rivals. Not only that, but 2-0 was actually a fair reflection of the game, according to the xG figures. For once, City didn't boss the game.

Andrew continued: "The average expected goal value of a shot in the Premier League this season has been 0.11. Liverpool and Manchester City have been the top two teams for xG per shot in attack, with an average of 0.14, but are ranked 3rd (0.10, Liverpool) and 19th (0.14, City) respectively in defence.

"Where a shot conceded by a losing Liverpool team has been worth 0.08 expected goals in 2019/20, for City that figure is 0.14. Even worse, it has been 0.20 when one goal down, showing why they've often gone further behind."

In essence, when City were behind they ended up gifting high quality chances to the opposition, but Liverpool, when behind, remained defensively solid.

Mark Cohen looked further into game state later that same week for an article on TTT:

"The issues only come into focus when we look closer. City are spending 17% of their minutes behind in games, and when you see their goal difference of +13 at state '0', understand that they've scored 23, but conceded 10. That's a lot of goals to concede when level. Remember how teams feel anything is possible when the game is level? You don't want to see teams able to take it to you with such alacrity. At some points last season, I remember thinking that nobody could even lay a glove on City in the run in, let alone knock them down, but that is clearly no longer the case.

"… Also, they appear mentally fragile. At the 'goal difference -1' state, they are just 0.53 xG better than their opponents. This stands in stark contrast to the other game states where they are all at nearly 1.5 or higher. It means they get mentally stung by conceding, and struggle to revive themselves. Indeed, so shocking are City once behind, that they actually have a negative *proper* goal difference, at -2.

"They are also spending 10% longer with the scores level this season than in 2018/19. Worse still, they spent just 4% of their entire season behind last year, seeing a 400% increase so far this term at 17%."

Mark noted that City "have been quite unlucky too, with both the Spurs fixtures good examples – City should have won each by three or four goals, but took just a point across the matches." However, it was a case that when they were bad, they were much worse than in the past.

After Mark's piece, City subsequently spent sixty minutes trailing against Manchester United at Old Trafford, which amounted to 22% of the playing time that City undertook in the weeks following the calculation of the aforementioned stats and the moment of the coronavirus shutdown; anything City did after lockdown was likely to be too little, too late.

Mark provided some stark contrast, backed by statistical evidence, of the way Liverpool were much more machine-like and efficient, with what appeared to be greater *resilience* – a vital trait in sport.

"Under Jürgen Klopp, Liverpool have morphed from an exciting attacking, but erratic, team, into one that can easily shift through the gears, both up or down, depending on the game state. Yes the goals flow, but the first standout figure is the Reds' performance when more than one goal to the good is only roughly half as good as City's. Liverpool have an xG of 1.08 at this state, City 1.81. They've scored 14 times, Liverpool only four.

"But this might be the single clearest difference in the two teams' mentality. City have an ability to drill teams into the ground, once the team is already beaten. Liverpool on the other hand, possess a much greater ability to make sure the team is beaten, but to then conserve energy that is not required.

"Look at game state Goal difference >+1, and it shows how capable Klopp's team are at switching gears from all out aggressive pressing and dominance to energy conservation."

In other words, once they went more than one goal clear in a game, Liverpool stopped scoring goals, and their *expected goals* tally fell by almost a third.

When the game state was equal, "Liverpool are so dominant at the ends that it's practically game over. Whilst City create a higher xG, 1.81 to 1.35, a sizeable difference, we need to understand that in terms of the *actual* goals scored and conceded, City are at 23-10 for this period, whereas Liverpool are at 27-4, nearly double them.

"It would be easy to put this down to luck, but it would be much better placed to understand that the Reds don't begin too many games at full tilt.

"Again this is quite at odds with City, this time from Gary Fulcher's ever-excellent pre-match previews on TTT:

"Liverpool, from the 31st to 45th minute, have scored 16 times, conceding just two. City in that same period have scored 10 and conceded three, still excellent but again, half the goal difference. Liverpool have won many matches during this period. For further comparison, Leicester in third, are +7 too, but are at zero GD for the rest of the first half, whereas the Reds are at +11 for the other periods."

Quirky Corners
One of the strangest statistical quirks of the season related to corners (albeit not necessarily, in 2019/20, "corner taken quickly!"). While corners do not offer a clear correlation with success – unless you are looking for a decisive late goal against some somnambulist Catalans – they are still a metric that indicates some type of pressure. Gérard Houllier once famously stated that his Reds team had deserved a win because they had more corners, and his argument has not aged well.

Two-thirds of the way through the 2019/20 season, the Reds ranked way down in 7th – surprisingly low – for fewest corners conceded, at 118. To put this into context, Manchester City had conceded just 69, and Chelsea 80. Everton actually ranked 3rd, on 107, then came Wolves, Leicester and Manchester United, all before the Reds appear on 118 – just ahead of Brighton on 125.

Why were Liverpool conceding so many corners? It seems outlandish – and I originally mooted it as a joke – but could some have been conceded *on purpose?* If that seems ludicrous, consider that, shortly before the lockdown (just before West Ham had some joy with one, and soon after Atlético Madrid had similar fortune in the Champions League game in Spain), the Reds had conceded just *one* league goal from a corner, to rank as the most effective Premier League team at defending them (0.85% of those faced led to goals), whereas Chelsea and Manchester United were conceding from over 7% of the corners they faced. But more tellingly, up to February, Liverpool were actually far more potent at scoring from *opposition* corners than they were harmed by them.

A corner is one way to make sure that the opposition shifts at least five or six – if not more – of its players upfield, which can be hard to get them to do in open play; and even if you defend that corner with everyone back, if you can break at pace in synchronised patterns, you can turn the situation to your advantage – as you charge forward, and they backpedal, facing their own goal and the formation all out of shape.

It seems almost too risky to be true – an opposition corner is something to fear – and yet the data suggests that if Liverpool weren't doing it deliberately, *maybe they should have been.* Alex Oxlade-

Chamberlain's goal at the London Stadium against West Ham at the end of January 2020 was the third the Reds had scored in the league straight from an opposition corner (compared to just one conceded), whilst numerous other Liverpool goals came from turning deep defence into attack – including a wide free-kick not too dissimilar to a corner in the penultimate game against Chelsea, which also led to Oxlade-Chamberlain scoring.

Even more strangely, Liverpool were not winning an especially high number of corners themselves – just 154 after 25 games, compared to Manchester City's 208. Corners won and corners conceded was one of the few metrics where Liverpool looked nothing like title contenders, and not even *top-four* contenders; but corners *scored* from, and *corner-goals against*, showed the ruthless efficiency of Klopp's team: a clear case of quality over quantity.

Possession
While outright possession is generally less fetishised than in the past, the top team in this metric (after 25 games) were the usual pass-masters Manchester City, at 61%, while Liverpool were 2nd, at 58%. On the whole, the big clubs ranked higher, but Brighton were 5th and Norwich 9th – to show that you can have an above-average amount of possession and still be in a relegation battle (while Sheffield United were battling for the top six with an average of just 44% of the ball, ranking 18th). As with shots or corners, simply having a lot of something is one thing – it's what you *do with it* all that counts. Liverpool being *close* to 60% for possession is key as, for all the talk of the long passes that somehow morphed into Liverpool being a "long-ball team", to post such large overall possession stats shows that games could be controlled with the ball – either to build attacks, or to take the sting out of the situation with sterile ball retention; all the time possessing the option of the fast counterattack or the long-diagonal pass into space on the flanks.

Pressing Concerns (Or Lack Thereof)
Andrew Beasley also looked at the Reds' pressing figures for an article on *The Tomkins Times,* as we sought to assess the Reds' DNA in becoming the best team in the world.

"Until recently, pressing was not something that was measured far and wide, with data not widely available. Thanks to *Statsbomb*'s data on *FBref.com*, which covers the last three seasons, that has changed.

"By using a different data source to the previous work mentioned, the findings will inevitably be different. However, they provide an interesting insight into how Liverpool stand above other teams, and also how the Reds' illustrious front three press in different ways and with changing volumes over the years.

"Before we continue, a quick definition of pressures. These are the 'number of times applying pressure to an opposing player who is receiving, carrying or releasing the ball', and being successful at doing this is the 'number of times the squad gained possession within five seconds of applying pressure'."

Across a whole campaign, the Premier League now presses more than most other elite European leagues, averaging over 170 per match in each of the past two seasons, which is higher than any single season in the *Bundesliga, Serie A, La Liga* or *Ligue Une* when looking back to the start of 2017/18. (Weirdly, that season, 2017/18, the Premier League posted the fewest average pressures per match from the sample of 15 – three campaigns apiece, spread across the five major leagues – at just 137; after which, the English game became turbocharged – moving into the 170s – perhaps due to the arrival of new managers with high-pressing styles, such as Southampton's Ralf Hasenhüttl, Graham Potter at Brighton, Daniel Farke at Norwich and before them, David Wagner at Huddersfield. The Germanic influence is clear.)

Andrew noted: "Liverpool have consistently been above the Premier League average for the effectiveness of their pressing. However, the data here suggests that where English football as a whole often leads the way in volume, it can't match up to Germany in *efficiency*."

(Sometimes a stereotype exists for a reason.)

In true Teutonic style, Liverpool do not actually press in extreme *quantity*, but do so with incredible efficacy. This is one more metric where the exceptional nature of Klopp's team can be found in certain underlying numbers, even if others will continue to note that they didn't create the best xG. The Reds rank below halfway in each of the past three seasons for *quantity* of pressing actions, although this is partly due to an increase in possession (only Manchester City have more of the ball); indeed, Klopp's side have progressed from hard and rabid pressers to ball-retainers. But when they lose the ball they are ruthless and more organised in getting it back, as befits a team that has largely spent 2-4 years together, evolving and developing.

Indeed, Klopp's side, in terms of percentage, have made the most *successful* pressures since the beginning of 2017/18, which makes them the most effective team in the Premier League. In the past two seasons alone (up to the Covid-19 hiatus), Liverpool were averaging a 32% success rate with presses, a figure that only Manchester City and Spurs from 2017/18 could better in 60 team seasons (20 teams, 2017-2020). The Premier League's average success rate for pressures in that period was 28%, and while 32% may not seem like that much more, it is a 14% increase on the league's baseline; and anything you do better than everyone else – even by a couple of percent – goes into the 'marginal gains' category. And while their success rate was not 14% greater than Manchester City's, given City's own above-average pressurising, the increase was still 7% on Pep Guardiola's men.

Then there is the metric of how many opposition passes are made for each pressure put upon them.

"To gauge who is best for pressure success rate," Andrew stated, "we have to account for how much of the ball each team has. We can divide the number of touches each team's opponents have had – and discount dead ball situations like corners, free-kicks, goal kicks and so on – by the number of pressures to see which team has closed down opposition sides most frequently."

Over the three seasons, the Reds allowed an average of 3.09 touches per pressure, which is lower (and therefore better) than Manchester City's 3.17. As Andrew continues:

"Liverpool haven't posted the best individual season, but have been the strongest over a longer period. It's worth noting that the Reds' figure was 3.29 in 2017/18, then improved to 2.99 in 2018/19 and has held at the same level in 2019/20."

As such, this is another area that backs up the improvement in results seen across the past two seasons.

"The only better examples [from the 60 "team seasons"] are Manchester City (2.93) and Chelsea (2.96) in 2018/19, but they have since dropped off slightly (to 3.21 and 3.00 respectively) while Liverpool have maintained their form."

And again, this is more forensic evidence of why City have fallen behind Liverpool in the past 12 months.

So how have Liverpool become so proficient at pressing? An article on *The Athletic* gave a small but priceless insight into the answer. An unnamed Liverpool source was quoted as saying the following regarding the work conducted by the club's Director of Research, Ian Graham:

"He and his team process these algorithms to identify trends and find players to fit into the system. This is presented to senior scouts, and Klopp has the final say. These guys are phenomenal. I wouldn't like to play chess against them.

"One of the impressive things: they can work out the speed at which the opponent moves and controls the ball. From there, we can identify pressing 'victims' and tell our players to apply pressure to specific opponents."

Sensing which opposition player to press – the weak link in their passing chain – has always been part of the best pressing philosophies, but now there's the analytical team with their databases, to precisely pinpoint who and where to pressure.

Andrew went on to write: "The line regarding recruitment from *The Athletic* article makes it worthwhile to check the player statistics from 2019/20 too [...] Ex-Red Dominic Solanke has made the most pressures per 90 minutes in Europe's big five leagues this season, if we look to men who've played at least 1,170 minutes. And Danny Ings ranks 13th. The fact these south coast sides don't have too much possession is clearly relevant; Liverpool only have one player in the continent's top 150 players, with the skipper, Jordan Henderson, scraping in at number 149.

"However, the Premier League alone contains six teams who've averaged less possession than Bournemouth (and nine below Southampton) and the majority of their players aren't pressing this many times per match. Whether this is why Solanke and Ings were signed, or whether Klopp's influence has made them this way is up for debate, but they are posting impressive figures."

"If we focus on Europe's most frequent pressers in the final third, Solanke – who, per 90 minutes, still remains Liverpool's most frequent final third presser over the last three seasons (albeit from a small sample from his brief time at the club) – and Ings are still both in the top 13. This time they are joined in the top 25 by Mohamed Salah (17th) and Roberto Firmino (22nd), while Sadio Mané is 93rd.

"Those three Liverpool forwards alone have made 750 pressures in the opposition's defensive third this season, just 82 fewer than the entire Newcastle squad have managed. The front three's efforts, combined with able support from Gini Wijnaldum, Andy Robertson, Alex Oxlade-Chamberlain and Jordan Henderson – all of whom have added between 85 and 95 – has seen Liverpool make more final third pressures this season with nine games to play than they did in 2017/18 in total."

So while Liverpool don't press like dervishes all over the pitch, the press by the forwards – and the midfielders who burst forward – is another area where Klopp's team excels in the data. (Naby Keïta is often the best midfield presser – frequently posting insanely good figures – but hadn't played enough football in 2019/20.)

"The Reds' tally of 1,424," Andrew noted, regarding final-third presses, "is currently the most in any of Europe's top leagues, and their average of 49 per match is more than any Premier League team has recorded in any of the last three campaigns. In the last three seasons, the proportion of Liverpool's total pressures which have been in the final third has grown each year."

In his in-depth study for the site, Andrew also noted that it wasn't just the *area* of the pitch where the pressing was changing, as the Reds hemmed teams back into their own third, and/or those teams chose to try and shell it out with ten men back. There were also stark changes amongst *who* pressed. While Mo Salah may not be scoring goals as freely as he did in his sparkling debut campaign, his other work perhaps goes unnoticed. For example, in 2018/19 he ranked 2nd in the entire Premier League for sprints made, at over 600. But a further season on, and his pressing numbers in the final third had skyrocketed, from an average of around six per game in 2017/18 to 12 per game in 2019/20, neatly seeing a double from his first to third seasons, with a halfway-step (nine per game) sitting neatly in between in 2018/19. While he can at times be too greedy and not pass to teammates in better positions, his overall work for the team cannot be overlooked.

Indeed, in the process he overtook the press-mungous Roberto Firmino, who has averaged between 10 and 11 presses (in the final third) per game in each of the past three seasons. The third and final member of the fabulous front three, Sadio Mané, presses the least in the final third, but even so, is up from six per game in 2017/18 to an average of eight in each of the past two campaigns. But with Mané it's not a question of inferior work-rate: he has made 310 pressures in Liverpool's *defensive* third over the last three seasons, whereas Firmino (167) and Salah (141) have only 308 between them. As such, Mané is the one who drops deeper in open play, while Salah is stationed further upfield, and Firmino flits between the two.

Andrew highlighted one game in particular that showcased the differences between the Reds' no.10 and their no.9 and no.11.

"Mané's efforts in the vital 3-1 win over Manchester City this season are worth highlighting. Liverpool's front three have collectively made 291 league appearances over the last three years, and in that City match the Senegalese made the most defensive-third pressures seen by any of them in any of those matches (17), and the joint-eighth most in the middle third too (again 17). With a further nine in the final third, his total of 43 gave him the fifth most by one of the established front three in the last 105 league games, and he scored a goal too."

It is statistics like this that show what many people might not see or appreciate when viewing a game: the individual off-the-ball contributions that don't show up in goals or assist tallies, *but which win games*.

The podcast *Anfield Index Under Pressure*, which involves some fine *Tomkins Times* alumni, do some of the best pressing analysis you can find anywhere on the internet (or indeed, anywhere *full stop*). They recently ran a comparison of how the Reds' pressing has changed in relation to areas of the pitch and to game state.

"The first two full years are all over the pitch and no real differences based on game state."

Then, looking at 2018/19, they note, there was "real discipline in the zones Liverpool are pressing for the first time, and there is a small shift when leading. This year [2019/20] … when level, the press is right across the attacking half with very little in Liverpool's half. And there is a clear contrast with when Liverpool are winning."

Liverpool, the *Under Pressure* guys asserted, "are pressing 40% less (FORTY) when leading by one goal compared to the previous two seasons".

This level of energy conservation may explain why, instead of trying to win 8-0, the Reds often 'got out' (though some will say 'got away') with a narrow victory, and had fresher legs a few days later, when the next fixture rolled around – in order to win again.

Pass Rather Than Dribble

Another part of Liverpool's DNA under Klopp, as ferreted from the data by Andrew Beasley from the *Statsbomb* databank in June 2020, is a clear change that took place at the start of 2018/19, at the time Liverpool became the best team in England over a two-year period, and champions of Europe and the world.

Clearly Liverpool have a lot of the ball. They make a lot of passes (ranking as the 6th highest amount in Europe's top five top divisions), and they make a lot of dribbles, or ball-carries (ranking 8th in total from that sample of 98 teams in England, Spain, Germany, France and Italy), with the distance gained from ball-carries ranking 10th.

"However," Andrew noted, "when you divide distance by carries, you find that Jürgen Klopp's side move the ball by dribbling the shortest amount on average of any club from the big leagues. You can see why this proved eye-catching.

"What's more, when I added the data from 2018/19 to the spreadsheet, that season's Reds' average was even shorter, and the lowest figure from the last 196 team seasons in a top league [2018-2020]."

However, in 2017/18, when Liverpool amassed far fewer league points, the pattern was not the same. It was only in 2018/19 that the style moved to one of lots of passing and *short* bursts of dribbling, rather than players carrying the ball great distances on their own. Perhaps this general lack of long-distance individual dribbling is one of those factors that made people think that Liverpool were not as "exciting" as their success suggested they should be; but the pass-and-move goals described throughout this book should dispel that notion. When you have Trent Alexander-Arnold and Virgil van Dijk (and even Alisson and Andy Robertson, as well as Fabinho and Jordan Henderson dropping into the quarterback role), then you can advance the ball 50 yards within a heartbeat, and an accurate ball flying over the heads of the opposition towards the wing cannot be tackled.

A misplaced pass in such an era can still prove costly (mainly if it is hit low and is intercepted), but a dribble is generally riskier, and slower. (And as noted in the chapter on throw-ins, longer passes out wide that opposition full-backs head for throws lead only to another angle of attack, as part of the constant pushing and pulling at an opposition's shape.)

As the club's data analysts may have pointed out with their computer modelling, the shortest route from point A to point B is a straight line, and even a slow pass can travel at twice the speed of a fast dribble. (Even Usain Bolt at his fastest, without having to dribble a football that would slow him considerably, couldn't reach even 30mph; but a longer pass can easily be at 40 or 50mph, with a bit of fizz.) If you want to catch the opposition out of position, a laser-guided pass to the opposite flank will do far more damage, far more quickly, than someone running with the ball – which may *look* quick, and impressive, but is logically a slower way to progress the ball.

As with so many other things about Liverpool in recent times, it's *almost* as if all this is carefully planned, to the nth degree.

The Dirty Dozen Goals: Liverpool Move From Set-Piece Brilliance To Open Play Effervescence

A lot was made of Liverpool's set-piece plays at the end of November, but there was a moment in the Brighton game that highlighted how dangerous the Reds could be. While much was made of the set-pieces that led to the two goals, I was fixated on one particular move, that didn't even make it onto that evening's *Match of the Day*.

Andy Robertson and Gini Wijnaldum neatly exchanged passes on the edge of their own area under some pressure from the Brighton pressers, before Robertson played a ball down the line to Mané, who, with great skill and acceleration, span past his marker just before the halfway line.

Davy Pröpper, the Brighton midfielder, pulled him, but Mané kept going. Pröpper then *tripped* Mané with a cynical leg across his thighs, but Mané kept running whilst trying to maintain his balance, which he successfully regained a few yards later after looking like he might stumble flat on his face; proof that players can often stay upright if they *want* to, but of course, had Pröpper been quicker, Mané would have lost the advantage by trying to keep playing (which is why players go down in the box when fouled, as refs ignore any split-second advantage that is lost, and a split-second is usually all it takes for a block to come in). Mané then faced up the right-back, but cut the ball inside to Roberto Firmino. At this stage it was a three on five, nearing the Brighton box, with Firmino passing the ball to the only other Liverpool player on the break, Mo Salah.

But bombing forward from midfield was Alex Oxlade-Chamberlain, and Salah laid off the deftest first-touch pass into his path. Oxlade-Chamberlain shot first-time towards the top corner but didn't quite get the power he wanted, and the keeper, reading the intent, pulled off a smart save. From defending to almost scoring in a handful of beautiful movements across almost 80 yards of pitch.

"Well, it was a stunning move" said the commentator on the Sky live feed that later ran as their *Game of the Day*. "The buildup is fabulous" said co-commentator Davie Provan, who adds after the replay has concluded, "A lovely bit of football!".

The half-time whistle went shortly after what would have arguably been Liverpool's goal of the season; certainly a contender. Yet this wonderful passage of play didn't even make the highlights on BBC's *Match of the Day* – even though it was outstanding, but also – presumably – incredibly easy to edit, as it was, after all, at the very end of the half. But no, it was lost on the cutting room floor, not to even be dragged up in the post-match analysis as sometimes happens to other strangely ignored bits of play in the highlights. However, they did show Salah running onto a difficult through-ball in the second half – played too far ahead of the Egyptian – which Lewis Dunk, well outside his box, cleared, complete with not one but *two* replays. It was largely a non-event; utterly baffling – going nowhere, doing nothing – until you realised the *narrative*.

The narrative was all about how well Dunk played (and he did indeed play well) and not about an honest appraisal of the *game*, its balance, nor its best moment by far. As the match was not shown live, then mostly only Liverpool fans would have seen it. Was it any wonder that the Reds weren't getting the full credit they deserved from neutrals at this point, and there was constant talk about "unconvincing" Liverpool? Or that the two set-piece goals the Reds scored in order to beat Brighton were some kind of "typical" Liverpool goal? It would be more acceptable had they not shown a merely decent bit of defending in an attack that was not worthy of airtime; then showed a replay.

Not only did *Match of the Day* omit the Reds' best move of the match, but they also failed to spot the illegality of the goal that Brighton scored. It may seem petty worrying about such things, but in addition to the noisy neutrals, a lot of football journalists will watch only the highlights of such games (after all, who can watch all 90 minutes of every match?), and fail to grasp some of the subtleties that were at play. If those writers were not impressed by Liverpool, that's one thing; but if they're not getting some of the most important pieces of information there can never be fair and balanced opinion pieces.

(None of which is to say that BBC Sport, which is based in Manchester, has an agenda.)

Let The Floodgates Open
If the two routine headed goals from corners were enough to undo Brighton and set in motion a narrative that Liverpool didn't play attractive football (given that recency bias meant all previous goals were thus ignored, and confirmation bias meant only set-piece goals rang the bells of those Pavlovian dogs seeking to see just what they wanted), that narrow-minded narrative should have been well and truly blown apart in the remaining December fixtures. Liverpool went into hyperdrive, warp-speeding their way to win after win.

Indeed, the next *two dozen* goals were virtually all works of art, none of which was due to a set piece.

And straight after Brighton, the following dozen goals only involved one single headed moment *anywhere in the move* (except in the Reds' own box when making a defensive clearance), and not a single set-piece; and relied instead on skill, speed, movement, pinpoint assists, cross-field passing and sublime finishing. Almost all started in the Reds' own half, as they cut through teams like a hot knife through extra-spreadable butter left out in the sun.

One game, in particular, is worthy of an in-depth look.

Merry Christmas, Everton
Liverpool started the run with five of the best goals you'll ever see in one single game, with a mix of just about every type of skill necessary – bar, weirdly, the use of a head. It just happened to be against Everton, whose boss, Marco Silva, was duly sacked the next day.

These were almost like *golf* goals, with stunning long-range drives hit with fizz and backspin, followed by accurate putts into the back of the net.

Silva's men lined up 5-4-1 in the midweek Anfield fixture, apparently including a defender for every goal they planned to concede. Adrián replaced the suspended Alisson, and, just days after the tired performance against Brighton, which itself came just days after the hard-fought draw against Napoli, Jürgen Klopp – to widespread surprise – rotated no less than *half* his team, leaving out Mo Salah and Roberto Firmino, amongst other usual regulars, and starting Xherdan Shaqiri, Divock Origi and Adam Lallana. To some it seemed an almost reckless move, in this most heightened of atmospheres, and yet the

Reds' "reserves" dismantled the Toffees. (Later in the season Klopp would see how his third XI – the kids – would fare against Everton, and again he had success. At that point he must have been tempted to field the U12s, just for laughs.)

The Dirty Dozen began with a bit of a scramble in Liverpool's own six-yard box, as James Milner's clearance careered off Gini Wijnaldum and flew in the air towards his own goal. But that was as messy as it would get. Andy Robertson headed clear from the edge of his own six-yard box to Adam Lallana, who scampered away with the ball, releasing Sadio Mané in the middle of the Reds' own half. Lallana found himself in acres of space – in the middle of his own private 25-yard exclusion zone, between Everton's defenders and their bypassed midfield – and screaming for the ball with arms outstretched; but Mané had other ideas.

The Senegalese advanced to just inside the Everton half and played one of the most perfect slide-rule passes you will ever see, curled across the tight-cut grass with the precision and weight of a crown-green bowler trying to nestle the bowl against the jack. Divock Origi, running with two Everton defenders (having been wrestled earlier in the move by Yerry Mina in an attempt to stop the breakaway), almost glided past the two in blue as the ball curved in behind them; Origi taking one touch – with an expert lengthening of a single stride – to take the advancing Jordan Pickford completely out of the game, and slot home into the empty net. The Belgian's first touch was essentially both getting the ball under control whilst simultaneously taking it past Pickford, and his second touch was a tap-in. Such moments are rare in football; killing two birds with one stone, in a split-second, with the outcome a gaping goal.

The second goal began with a Liverpool throw by Robertson, boxed in by his own corner flag. He received the ball back and punted it high and across the pitch: the tactic of trying to exploit the way the opposition all head towards the thrower, and leave big spaces on the opposite flank (who could have thought of such a dastardly idea?). The problem was that it was Xherdan Shaqiri trying to win a header against someone about three feet taller, and so, despite Lallana being free infield – and Alexander-Arnold free had he headed it out to the right – the little Swiss got nowhere near making contact. But Dejan Lovren, on the edge of his own box, prodded it to Alexander-Arnold (still in space) which, in itself, is almost like creating a chance these days. Once Alexander-Arnold took possession, the Everton players – still clustered towards the Reds' left-back position, began to sprint back, and chase infield. The young Scouser let the ball run across his body and, after a single touch and from the midway point of his own half, fizzed an arrowing pass right onto the thigh of Mané some 50 yards away in the inside-left channel – switching the play again, just as Everton were trying to *unswitch* from the previous cross-field pass. (As with the second goal against Manchester City, it was the old double-switcheroo.)

This time Mané cut inside and played a reverse right-foot pass into the tiny area of space into which the tiny Shaqiri was bursting and, with the tiniest of touches, the Swiss sent the ball past the tiny-armed Pickford and into the back of the net with the most satisfying velocity possible: indeed, a *tiny* touch – feathered, just enough to make defenders look extra flummoxed, as they watched it trickle into the net.

The third continued the run of own-half moves, after Richarlison left his studs on Shaqiri's ankle, one of several bad tackles from both sides. Four back-four passes on from the free-kick, Lovren, under no pressure, had time to pick a lofted pass from the middle of his own half that, before it could land just on the edge of the visitors' area, Origi plucked down with a sublime first touch, and, despite the ball then bouncing awkwardly on the Belgian – too close to his body – he readjusted and lobbed a difficult half-volley over the hapless and stranded Pickford, whose arms were *never* going to be long enough, even if he was standing on a stepladder.

The fourth yet again saw Mané as the instigator down the left flank. It started with no fewer than ten players on the edge of Liverpool's six-yard box: half in red, half in blue, as Jürgen Klopp's men defended the second-phase of a corner. Virgil van Dijk, out-muscling Dominic Calvert-Lewin, headed a deep cross out to Alexander-Arnold, who, still in his own box but on the left side, seemed to already be thinking about scoring a goal. He laid the ball off to Mané, and carried on motoring. Mané evaded a rugby tackle from the suitably bulky Alex Iwobi, and fed the ball back out wide to Alexander-Arnold who was still bursting forward. At that point it was two in red versus a lone Everton defender: the only three players in the Everton half, bar the keeper. The Liverpool right-back simply kept running with the ball. Shaqiri – on the far side – looked like the obvious pass, with the Swiss initially the only other Red entering the picture. But, as Liverpool's no.66 reached the edge of the area he tucked the ball inside to Mané, who had sprinted 60 yards to be in position to side-foot a left-footed finish into the corner, past the despairing dive of Pickford, who ended up picking the ball out of an Anfield net for the fifth time in less than 45 minutes of football (having famously gifted Origi a winner in the final minute of injury time a year earlier, from which memes about him being a Tyrannosaurus rex in disguise sprung up).

Anatomy of a Goal
This particular goal is especially interesting as, during the BBC's 2019 *Royal Institution Christmas Lectures*, mathematician Hannah Fry spoke on air to Tim Waskett, an astrophysicist who has been a member of Liverpool's backroom analytics team since 2012. The lectures are primarily aimed at children and teenagers, and the discussion was brief, but after a fairly bog-standard explanation of expected goals, Waskett detailed the probability model that calculates and recalculates the likelihood of a goal being scored from any position on the pitch, at a rate of 25 calculations per second – with over a million therefore generated each and every game.

"For roughly 200 games per weekend we get data involving every single ball touch in the game," Waskett explained. "The way the data is collected, every time that a player passes the ball, they'll mark it on the pitch and they'll say, this is the position on the pitch and the player who made that pass."

Waskett and Fry used the example of two youth players in the studio being filmed from overhead cameras, with the studio floor marked out like the game Battleships, or the algebraic notation used for chess: two axes, which, when triangulated, detail a position on the board, or in this case, the football pitch.

"For every game," Waskett explained, "we get approximately 2,000 ball-touch events. And that tells us the position of the player who makes the pass. For the Premier League games, we get what we call 'tracking data'. And this is from cameras all around the stadium, monitoring the position of all of the players. And so 22 players plus the position of the ball, and it does that for 25 frames a second. For the full 90 minutes, so you end up with approximately 1.5 million data points.

"This data can give us a goal value for every position and for every player on the pitch. We've got a little animation."

The animation starts with a team in red (Liverpool), represented as eleven small circles dotted around the pitch, with numbers correlating to shirt numbers, plus a team of eleven blue circles, with the ball – a yellow circle – in Liverpool's own area. Around the players are morphing seas of colour, that grow and shrink, intensify and desaturate, depending on how the move unfolds. The positioning of the Reds' players at the start of the move, and the numbers on the back of the two blue circles nearest the keeper (seven and nine), instantly suggested the Mané goal against Everton, even though the opposition was never named.

"This is what we call pitch control," Waskett said. "You can see the players are in the circles there, and the arrows represent the direction and speed that they can travel in. And you've got a blue team and a red team. The red team here is actually Liverpool, and the areas in red are places that the Liverpool players can get to sooner than the players who are in blue, based on how quickly people run and based on where the ball is. For example, the ball in this particular example is that yellow dot there. And if this player who is currently in possession of the ball is number 10, Sadio Mané, his best option at this stage is to probably pass to one of these red areas. And in fact, he ends up passing the ball up into this red zone here to be picked up by player 66, which is Trent Alexander-Arnold."

The animation reads almost like a weather map, detailing the time-elapsing changes in high and low-pressure areas, isobars spreading and contracting 25 times a second; weather fronts colliding, frontal zones converging. (Incidentally, shortly after writing this paragraph I learned that Waskett used to design weather prediction systems in his spare time before joining Liverpool FC, which may explain a lot.) In this case, it looks like there's a hurricane brewing. Instead, it's Alexander-Arnold and Mané marauding up the pitch.

At this stage the likelihood of a goal being scored within the next 15 seconds is displayed as just 1.5%. The image – with the sprawling colours and densities of a heatmap – highlights the best areas for the right-back to pass or dribble into, and the deeper the shade of red the more likely the radical increase in the chances of a goal being scored. Of course, Alexander-Arnold himself cannot see these images, which at the time of the game exist as nothing but a series of data points on computers that, as far as we know, have yet to be WIFId directly into the young Scouser's brain (although his vision *is* uncanny, and perhaps Uefa should investigate him for being part of *The Matrix*). The model shows that the very best options are to pass to Sadio Mané, ahead of him on the flank, or to take the ball into that area himself; either way, that's the best route to a goal. But as he approaches the halfway line there's another high-probability area of the pitch whose redness intensifies: approximately one-third of the attacking half, ahead of Xherdan Shaqiri, as the Swiss winger runs past Everton players and crosses the halfway line; moving towards a prime position.

With the animation paused as the Reds bear down on goal – at the point before Alexander-Arnold lays off the pass to Mané on the edge of the Everton area – Fry interjects to ask Waskett, "Are you using this information to look at what did happen and work out what should have happened?"

Waskett: "So we use this in a number of ways. The main way we use this is to evaluate player performance after the game. What was the result of this sequence? So if you pause it right about now, you can see Trent Alexander-Arnold now has the ball very close to the goal. He's in a good position, but his best option now is to pass into this red area here where it can either be received by Mané or Shaqiri, who was number 23 down here; one of these two players is most likely to get to this red zone. And in actual fact, what happens in this particular situation is that Mané receives the ball, around about here, and he scores a goal."

What's interesting is that, even here, Shaqiri was deemed the better option; or rather, the glowing red space just ahead of Shaqiri, in the box, for him to run into, was the prime area to attack. This indeed looked to be the *obvious* choice for the pass – at the match for those at a high enough vantage point to see the spatial relationships, on the television, and from the data animation – although with an Everton defender in the way, it would have to be curled or lofted, which would make it a more tricky endeavour (albeit not beyond the talents of Alexander-Arnold). And even when Alexander-Arnold has the ball as he approached the Everton box, the likelihood of a goal still only rises to 7.2%. Mané is outside the box, so it would not be classified as a 'big chance', and it required a first-time shot with no time to steady himself with a touch – but he swept the ball home with consummate ease.

Back To Reality
Before Mané's goal, Everton had scored a scrappy close-range effort from Michael Keane to make it 2-1 – at the point in the first-half when Liverpool looked like running up a cricket score – and then again – with a Richarlison header – to make it 4-2 just before the half ended; but there was to be one more goal in the game as, yet again, Pickford fished the ball out of the Kop-end net right at the end of another defeat. It came after the Reds missed some glorious chances fashioned by yet more fast flowing – and at times *direct* – football, including two ultra-incisive passes by Jordan Henderson to Mané, who spurned both one-on-ones (albeit in the second he was nudged by Pickford in what should have been a penalty, seeing as the keeper didn't touch the ball and put the striker off balance *just enough* to force him wide and allow a defender to get back and cover).

The final goal was the only one not to start in Liverpool's own half; a headed clearance from the second phase of a Liverpool corner (in truth, technically the *third* phase) falling to Joe Gomez some 45 yards from goal. He hit a difficult first-time pass out wide towards Roberto Firmino, which was about the only option to an 'open' player, aside from just hoisting it long and hoping; although the pass, along the floor, sent the Brazilian a little too wide. Firmino then twisted the blood of Mason Holgate so emphatically that the double-helixes of the defender's DNA entirely unravelled. Holgate, who had once dangerously pushed Firmino into the crowd leading to a heated exchange, found himself in the carpark, unable to work out how to pay to get back in, as the Brazilian laid the ball back to Gini Wijnaldum. The Dutchman cut across his shot so beautifully that it arced into the inside-netting of the far post. Job done, derby destruction complete.

Fast and Beautiful
Bournemouth away was up next, and the beautiful goals continued to flow. For the opener, a move from the Everton game was reprised – albeit with different participants: a simple but accurate long ball that drops perfectly for the striker; in this instance, Alex Oxlade-Chamberlain. The second came after more than a dozen passes and a third-man run by Naby Keïta, with the move ending as Mo Salah backheeled the midfielder in on goal. Keïta used the outside of his right foot in a strange improvisation to half-scoop the ball, with power, into the corner of the net. The third saw the same two players combining, albeit the move started all the way back with Alisson rolling the ball to van Dijk. Various players were involved in a slick passage of play, but the hosts momentarily regained the ball, but had it for such little time – one bad pass – that it felt like a continuation of the Reds' attack. Keïta sprinted forward and played the kind of inch-perfect through-ball that Mané had been almost trademarking in recent games, and Salah, without an away goal in the league all season, needed just one left-foot touch to divert it past the keeper. As with Shaqiri's goal days earlier in the derby, from much the same angle, it had just enough pace to entice the defenders into thinking they could clear it, but even a slow-rolling ball can easily clock up 20mph. Indeed, it was the second time in the game that Liverpool had scored a goal that was a near-simulacrum of one from the derby (almost as if these things are not just random).

Austrian Heights
The Reds were in Salzburg three days later, needing just a draw to qualify from the group, and a win against FC Red Bull to finish top. The first-half was intense and frenetic; almost like basketball in its end-to-end moves, with unconverted big chances at both ends. Ten minutes into the second half it was still 0-0; *twelve* minutes into the second half it was game over at 2-0. In a match that brought to mind the blitzkrieging Reds of Klopp's earlier seasons – given how the home team played – the converting of two chances in quick succession, to put the

Austrians to the sword, was reminiscent of how Liverpool used to overwhelm teams in short periods of play (back in the days when teams would still try and attack Liverpool with numbers).

Liverpool took the lead when their duo of African ex-Salzburg stars combined. The move started when a certain Takumi Minamino closed down Naby Keïta, who showed great feet to avoid the future Liverpool player's tackle, but the ball ran through to the Salzburg centre-back to clear long. It was heading towards the precocious Erling Braut Håland – soon to cause further sensations at Borussia Dortmund (after Manchester United passed up the option to buy him for relative peanuts) – but Joe Gomez read it well, and laid the ball back to Virgil van Dijk, who was a shade deeper than the centre-circle in his own half. The Reds' centre-backs moved the ball over to Trent Alexander-Arnold on the right side of the pitch, still deeper than the arc of the centre-circle. Liverpool's passing to get the ball to their no.66 was slow and steady, but he then launched a 60-yard cross-field pass to Andy Robertson – with a touch of spin that took the ball into the Scot's path – as the left-back, standing on the far touchline, ran into the space where the ball was looking to land. With it, five opponents were now out of the game. As Robertson fed the ball to Sadio Mané, Liverpool now had five attackers versus just six defenders. When Mané charged into the box and evaded a challenge, Robertson slowed down, and then it was five versus four – with two of the Red Bull midfielders quickly giving up, and another trying in vain to get back, as the keeper, Cican Stanković, also came flying out of his goal. Mané dinked in a cross, and by the time the ball reached the middle, Stanković had slid to the edge of the right side of his own area – totally out of the game – and the ball was dropping onto Naby Keïta's head, as one of three Liverpool attackers in front of a goal now defended by just two outfield players. Mané, back on his old stomping ground, had the assist, and fellow Salzburg alumnus, Keïta, did the rest with his head.

Next came the tenth consecutive free-flowing goal since the Reds' trio of headed set-piece goals by centre-backs that briefly allowed rivals to label Klopp's men a one-dimensional team. On the subject of dimensions, this goal was perhaps from the fourth or fifth; from the *hypersphere*.

It began from the hands of Alisson Becker, who set in motion a fast counter-attack after Håland had looked to get on the end of a Minamino flick. The Brazilian keeper rolled the ball out, and Liverpool were under way, keeping possession in their own right-back area. Four Salzburg players were trying to hem the Reds in towards the corner, with two more in that section of the pitch – in the Liverpool half, but behind the ball.

Within a second, the ball was behind *them*. It was one more example of how Liverpool reverted to the long pass to bypass the press, with skilful and accurate execution to pick out a teammate, rather than simply clearing their lines or hitting and hoping. Six players were taken out of the game as Mo Salah chased yet another inviting Jordan Henderson ball over the top, and a seventh – the defender, Jérôme Onguéné, who was now their last hope, with no other Austrian players within 30 yards – struggled with both his bearings and the falling ball; heading it wide of his own advancing goalkeeper. Henderson's ball had taken six out of the game, and now Onguéné was taking himself out, too. Eager to join the party, Stanković came rushing out of his area, and when Salah took it past him there was an open goal beckoning. In almost no time at all, Liverpool had bypassed the entire eight players that had, just moments earlier, blocked the route to goal. But of course, there was still a big problem.

Salah, who had already missed a hatful of chances, found himself arguably far too close to the byline, with Stanković stranded and Onguéné retreating in panic towards the goalline. It was an open goal, but even then, at such a narrow angle, it looked like there was no chance of scoring in that exact moment. With his unfavoured right foot, and as the ball ran towards the byline, Salah somehow stroked home the perfect first-time finish, improbably managing – with the unhelpful natural curl of the ball when kicked with the inside of the foot – to avoid the near post, as the ball end up nestling just inside the far post; a feat that seemed to defy the laws of physics. A left-foot shot from such an angle would allow the natural out-to-in curve to take the ball into the goal, but the Egyptian, who will sometimes spurn chances by trying to get the ball onto his favoured foot, went with the instinctive shot, and it was pure perfection. It was like trying to score direct from a corner with an *outswinger*.

Spanish newspaper *AS* ran a piece on their English website, looking at the geometry:

"The Egyptian was … about five yards from the goal line and on the edge of the penalty area, 18 yards from the near post and 26 yards from the far post. From those figures, we can work out that Salah had a target angle of about 4.3 degrees, meaning that the area that he had to strike for the ball to go in was approximately 1.3 metres wide, from a distance of around 18 yards from goal. And if that wasn't difficult enough, let's not forget that he had to do that almost at full sprint (he decelerated slightly before striking the ball) and under pressure from

Salzburg keeper Cican Stanković and centre-back Jérôme Onguéné. Even Reds manager Jürgen Klopp was lost for words when asked about it after the game, telling reporters, 'How do I explain it? Thank God I don't have to! A wonderful goal, one which shows all of the hard work with mini-goals on the practice pitches at Melwood was worthwhile'."

The game was as good as over, and Liverpool were progressing to the knockout stage once more. However, the smorgasbord of stunning goals continued. Up came two more beautiful goals, albeit in a somewhat ugly game spoiled by a strong wind.

Watford Awaiting

The eleventh and twelfth goals of the sequence followed a few days later, in windy conditions, at home to Watford. The first is worthy of specific attention. Gini Wijnaldum cleared a corner from the visitors, albeit not cleanly, and Will Hughes headed it back towards the Reds' box. The ball looped towards Firmino, who somehow played an overhead kick with one foot still on the ground; a different kind of no-look pass into the inside left channel, and right into the path of Mané. His ball – played from 10 yards inside Watford's half – was yet another in a growing list of perfectly-weighted inside-left assists from the Senegalese, although in this case Salah still had a lot to do. He chopped back onto his right foot, taking the defender by surprise – given that everyone knows the Egyptian's clear preference to get the ball onto his left foot, often at all costs (the goal in Austria notwithstanding). Salah took another touch, with the defender bamboozled, and before a recovering midfielder could get a block in, the Reds' no.11 curled a slightly surreal right-foot slow-motion shot into the top corner, possibly aided by the strong wind that, overall, had suited the more physical approach of the team in yellow.

(A few games later, Salah would be the one overhead-kicking a corner he was defending clear into the inside-left channel, and although Liverpool didn't score from the latter near-Xeroxed example at Leicester, it again highlighted the planning that goes into the attacking side of the game. There is room for improvisation and skill, but there are also set moves, where teammates can more easily read each other's intentions due to repetition on the training ground, but where opposition players won't have the same level of familiarity to quickly decode them.)

The twelfth goal in the run was up there with any of the others in terms of outrageousness, and it came as the result of yet another sensational breakaway – albeit this goal was slightly sullied in the aesthetic terms by the touch of an opposition player (the *swine*); a rarity within the dozen. A fast break ended with Salah, having moved wide of the goal to get out of the way of a Divock Origi shot, impudently flicked a backheel from an acute angle that fizzed through the desperately-closing legs of the hapless defender on the line. In five days Salah had scored three right-foot goals, and each of them – each radically different from the others – would arguably make his all-time top 10 in a Liverpool shirt.

In between these final two goals of the sequence was a Mané header ruled out for an offside where he appeared to be level, as the on-screen lines were drawn and redrawn by the VAR. In addition, the VAR *almost* took away Salah's sumptuous flick, but he was deemed onside by a fraction.

Perfect Dozen

As I have shown, virtually every goal in this run started in the Reds' own half, with just a couple of exceptions. And as stated earlier, not one header was involved in the moves (other than Naby Keïta's goal at Salzburg), other than to clear the ball before the moves really got started. Having powered home three headed set-piece goals within a few days leading up to the dirty dozen, the Reds' goals from corners and free-kicks dried up, but different types of goals emerged.

With Watford beaten, Liverpool departed to Qatar for the Club World Cup. What type of goals would they score there?

Why Liverpool Were One of the 'Cheapest' Champions

In these times of incessant opposition, conflict, trolling, denial and schadenfreude, giving credit where it's due is never to be fully expected – and where the 'game', in the 21st century, seems to be to make sure everyone else has their success sullied, like vandals who can only throw a can of paint over a masterpiece rather than create one.

Indeed, more fans seemed to get joy out of Liverpool failing to win the league in 2019 than anything their own club might do; although the Reds' success in Madrid three weeks later was a rather wonderful riposte to such bitterness. Many of those rival fans seemed fairly quiet as the Reds ran away with the title a year later, although the response of those who refused to be quietened by, or even concerned with *reality* – as they raged from their keyboards and on phone-in lines and video feeds – was to try and *discredit* this Liverpool side, through nonsense about VAR favouring Jürgen Klopp's team, or goals scored late in games (that therefore should not count, as if minutes 80-90 have never been a normal part of football), through to the idea of adding an asterisk during lockdown, to show that – despite being 23 points ahead with less than ten games to go, with the best points-per-game English football had ever seen – they would be illegitimate champions if the league title was awarded with three-quarters of the season already played. As it happened, Project Restart meant football resumed, and having played just two games the Reds were *legitimate* champions; and within just five games (including their game in hand) Manchester City found themselves on 66 points. With just another five to play, they could no longer catch the Reds' pre-lockdown points tally of 82. (Asterisk that!)

Critics also focused on the cost of players like Virgil van Dijk and Alisson Becker, to say that the Reds were just like their much-criticised petrodollar rivals, but rather than cheat or bend the financial rules, Liverpool *sold players to buy players*; the net spend was incredibly low – although for over a decade at *The Tomkins Times* we've been using a better method to assess the cost of a team.

Aside from Leicester's improbable triumph in 2016, Liverpool became the cheapest champions in terms of the average cost of the XIs they fielded (adjusted for inflation) – by some distance – since Roman Abramovich changed English football. (The oligarch arrived in 2003 but it was 2004/05 when his spending coincided with a league title and contributed to the demise of Arsenal, then the best team in the land, and a remarkable side whose achievements Liverpool have eclipsed, along with those of the Chelsea side that usurped the Gunners.)

And in *relative* terms (in relation to the gap to the most expensively assembled side) Klopp's men are the cheapest champions, aside from Leicester, since at least 1992, when, as we know, all records began.

Regular readers will know that back in 2010 I co-created the Transfer Price Index with football historian and statistician Graeme Riley. In 2008 I'd sought to devise a comparison tool to contextualise the spending of every Liverpool manager since 1959 for my book *Dynasty: 50 Years of Shankly's Liverpool.* The solution I settled upon was comparing all transfers to the record fee of their day (as a percentage), in order to work out how much Bill Shankly and Bob Paisley had spent when compared to the modern counterparts. Graeme (Riley, not Souness) suggested we work together to create a football inflation method, just like the retail price index but with players instead of a basket of shopping. We only covered 1992 onwards, in part because of the difficulty in researching all the required information prior to the formation of the Premier League (and we were just researching this in our own time, with no plans to specifically monetise it – just to use it in our football writing). And so, on the index, 1992/93 was 1; and for example, 2001/02 was 5.21, meaning that the average price of a player had risen by 5.21x in nine years. By 2018 the index stood at over *twenty-seven*, although there had also been years of deflation in between. Whatever the current index, we could therefore convert all player transfers into current day money. From this we were able to create the £XI, which is the average cost of a club's XI over all 38 league games (or 40/42 games in earlier seasons). This then enabled us to see the correlation between success and spending, even if *every single factor* in success will never just be financial. (As a note here, we don't use wage analysis, although £XI provides similar results; the one main advantage of £XI being that you are judging the players being picked and used by a club *in the current season*, and not what their overall wage bill was 12-24 months earlier when the last publicly available accounts were filed. And as ever, no model is perfect.)

Becoming the best team in the world on roughly half the transfer budget of Manchester City – and by spending far less on transfers than all the title-winning sides of Chelsea, City and Manchester United since 2004 – is an *incredible* achievement. None of which is to say that Liverpool are some backwater club achieving a total miracle on a shoestring budget, or some 5,000-1 shot like Leicester; but the spending, adjusted for inflation, is no greater than that which saw Arsène Wenger lead Arsenal to the double and then become Invincibles, all within seven years, and which people put down to canny player-spotting and radical new fitness and tactical ideas, rather than splashing the cash. Indeed, relatively speaking – in terms of the financial might of *rivals* – Liverpool's success has been achieved on a much smaller budget than the Gunners in 1998, when they won their first title with what was then, adjusted for inflation, the costliest side in the land – albeit by a narrow margin. By contrast, Liverpool ranked 3rd on £XI in 2019/20; Wenger's Arsenal not only ranked top, in a what was a much tighter financial field back then, but there was obviously no outlier at *twice* their wealth way ahead of them, as Liverpool faced with City. Of course, the swift decline of the Invincibles was partly linked to the new financial realities courtesy of a Russian in west London.

To take it further, the first time every club – bar Leicester (and this chapter could be called Bar Leicester) – became champions in the Premier League era they either had the most expensive £XI (Manchester United 1993, Blackburn 1995, Arsenal 1998, Chelsea 2005) or in the case of Manchester City in 2012, were within 10% of the cost of the most expensive team.

(As an aside here, I also noted 15 years ago that all champions since Leeds United in 1991/92 had finished 2nd – or equal with the 2nd-place team on points – the year before "first" winning the title, which I likened to a basecamp. In the 1970s and 1980s, teams could do what Leicester did, and come from nowhere; even winning the league in the first season after they were promoted, in the case of Nottingham Forest – although there were still plenty of examples of dominant teams like Liverpool finishing 2nd one year and winning the title the next.)

So, it's all *relative*. When Leicester miraculously won the title in 2016, with the 18th-cheapest side in the division, no one said that, actually, their team still cost three times as much as Bournemouth's, and twice as much as Watford's, so they were just benefiting from their wealth. At the same time, no one noted how unfair it was that Exeter City or Grimsby Town could not compete financially to build their way up from the lower divisions to become champions.

And, of course, there is also the way Liverpool have *raised* money, rather than relying on sugar daddy benefactors and/or financial doping. There is so much that sets Liverpool apart from the financially dominant teams that have ruled the roost in recent times. Indeed, when FSG – then NESV – bought the club in 2010, they were partly attracted by the idea of Uefa's Financial Fair Play (FFP), and how it would mean that, without oligarchical wealth, they could try and outsmart the system to make Liverpool champions (or least get the club back into the top four).

Before John W. Henry bought a football club he had previously never heard of, he went on Amazon and purchased some books, including the aforementioned *Dynasty*. As soon as the purchase of the club was complete he got in touch with me, via Facebook (which I initially dismissed as a hoax), but eventually we met and discussed ways in which Liverpool might seek to improve, as well as my take on its recent history. I made it clear that, due to chronic health issues, I wouldn't be interested in a role at the club, should one ever be on offer (but my statement obviated that; plus, having got to know Rafa Benítez and become embroiled in the vituperate club politics circa 2010 – even being placed on a blacklist by the club's paranoid executives – I was not keen to put myself in such a position). But every now and then Henry would phone or email, to chew the fat on an informal basis; and many years later I met others from the ownership group, which helped me to get a sense of where they were trying to take the club.

The aim was always to outsmart the field, and I probably wasn't a lot of help in that regard, other than to initially point out things like "no, Roy Hodgson *did not* win the league in Italy", and later on, to argue the case for keeping Jordan Henderson. (My suggestion via email, that Liverpool collect the DNA of John Barnes, Alan Hansen and Kenny Dalglish, mix it in a test tube with samples taken from a cheetah, a giraffe and a whale – and with what every scientist knows to be the vital addition of radioactive matter – in order to produce the quickest, tallest players with enormous lungs and superhuman strength, was strangely ignored. It was at this point I assumed they just weren't taking things seriously enough.)

Unfortunately, the initial money FSG raised by selling the want-away Fernando Torres was seen to have been badly reinvested, although as I discuss elsewhere in the book, it actually led to several major positive breakthroughs. (It's just that, alas, Charlie Adam was not one of them).

Being smarter, and applying more attention to detail to make marginal gains, is a *good* thing. Buying undervalued players, often from relegated clubs, and making them world-class is a *good* thing. Finding little-known coaches – such as Pepijn Lijnders – and analytics staff (who were initially ridiculed), and having them make a world of difference is a *good* thing. A policy of incentivising wages, and of only awarding the highest wages to players *once they have already proved themselves at the club* (and of limiting the wages of very young players to something like a tenth of what other clubs pay) is a *good* thing; so no one new rolls up in a Roller lording it over the rest of the players for earning half what he does, without having even kicked a ball for the Reds. Appointing a throw-in coach who has turned Liverpool from one of the worst at keeping possession from a throw-in in Europe to being the best is a *good* thing.

Yes, Liverpool had enough money to be competitive, but still lagged well behind the Manchester clubs in terms of resources. Of course, how Covid-19 changes this remains to be seen, but if Liverpool became the best team in the world without spending money they did not have, the obvious thing to expect is that the cloth will continue to be cut accordingly (whilst a temporary relaxation of FFP gives an advantage back to Manchester City and Chelsea in that regard).

Unlike Chelsea, Liverpool are not being propped up by an oligarch; with another £266m injected into Chelsea in 2019, Roman

Abramovich is now owed close to £1.4billion by the club he owns – and looks set for another big splurge in 2020. In contrast to Manchester City, Liverpool are not constantly being accused – and found guilty – of having breached FFP rules. And unlike Manchester United in the 1990s and 2000s, Liverpool initially failed to cash in on their domination of the 1970s and 1980s; indeed, until recently the Reds still lagged a long way, in monetary terms, behind the Red Devils.

In contrast to some accusations, the English league is not weak, as it might have been in the past when one side was so clearly dominant. Far from it. The Premier League in 2019/20 was extremely competitive; the financial rewards of broadcasting deals have boosted *all* clubs, to some degree, and recent seasons have seen English clubs perform well in the Champions League.

Spending

I've spoken for years about how gross spend is a terrible argument, and that net spend – while better than gross spend – is flawed for several reasons, not least the random start and end points, and also, the saleability of players at any given point in time. That said, in late 2019 ESPN published the net spend of clubs since Pep Guardiola arrived in England, and by using *Transfermarkt's* figures, Man City were at £527.8m since 2016, Man United at £432.3m and Liverpool miles behind at £75.3m, a mere fraction of a net spend.

Now, obviously Liverpool received (up to) £142m for the sale of Philippe Coutinho, so that affects the net spend (and shifting the net spend parameters to *just after* Coutinho was sold would alter the picture dramatically, but that would be misleading). Of course, Coutinho was seen by many as the Reds' best player – certainly the team's creative hub – and there was no little unrest at his departure. In hindsight it seems a masterstroke, but at the time there were accusations that FSG had lost the plot, and #FSGOUT was trending on Twitter (who is this FS, and why does he or she have gout?).

Now, what if Man City had been forced to sell Raheem Sterling or Sergio Agüero in order to buy Ederson and Aymeric Laporte? They'd still have two great players in Ederson and Laporte, but they would have lost key assets in order to procure them. (Indeed, City plucked at what resembled the carcass of Liverpool FC as recently as 2015 to land Sterling, as the Reds – prior to the arrival of Jürgen Klopp – looked about as far from title winners as they'd ever been.)

Despite things going exceptionally well for Liverpool *since* he was sold, it's easy to forget that there was still a huge risk involved in offloading a key asset in Coutinho (albeit once a player wants to leave it's often best to help him on his way, in the most financially beneficial manner you can muster), but that transfer fee essentially paid for Virgil van Dijk and Alisson Becker, with £1m in spare change. The difference with Liverpool – as seen in the cases of Fernando Torres, Luis Suárez, Sterling and others, in a situation mirrored at Arsenal and Spurs – was always that, unlike Manchester City, Manchester United and Chelsea, they often had to sell their best players, because they could not offer the Champions League and/or pay the highest wages. That was the trap FSG found the club in when they inherited (in addition to a big debt) a *Europa League side* in 2010, that was then performing so badly under Roy Hodgson that it was in a relegation battle, and at that point in no way likely to even qualify for the Europa League the following season. The virtuous cycle of Champions League participation looked a long way away, after the previous owners, George Gillett and Tom Hicks, assisted by Christian Purslow, made such a mess of running the club.

In the past decade, City never *had* to sell anyone. Not one single senior player left against the club's wishes, with the possible exception of Vincent Kompany – but he was 33 and out of contract, and Yaya Touré was phased out at a similar age; the same will happen this summer with David Silva, as he bows out after a wonderful decade in England. But interestingly, at the time of writing, for the first time they have been shorn of a massive talent against their wishes: Leroy Sané's refusal to sign a new deal meant he joined Bayern Munich in July 2020. And even that was only possible due to the contract issue, with his deal about to expire in 2021. Otherwise, in the past decade they have offloaded some costly flops, hit-and-miss players and/or troublesome characters, like Robinho, Jô, Jack Rodwell, Mario Balotelli, Emmanuel Adebayor, Javi García, Matija Nastasić, Roque Santa Cruz, Stevan Jovetić, Álvaro Negredo, Edin Džeko, Wilfried Bony and Eliaquim Mangala; but none was poached against their wishes by rival clubs, and the likes of Agüero, Kompany, Yaya Touré, Kevin de Bruyne, Fernandinho, David Silva *et al* were essentially locked into the club due to City's ability to offer Champions League football every season, and pay super-high wages. They created a virtuous cycle that, according to Uefa, involved breaking the rules. (City won their appeal to CAS to have their Champions League ban overturned, but much of that appeal success rested on the charges Uefa brought being over the time limit.) And if you break the rules to gain further financial reward and cachet – i.e. playing in the Champions League and challenging for the title – then it is not some fairytale story but an example of excluding others who played by the rules; after all, Cinderella was not the story of a woman having expensive surgery to remove her toes to make sure the glass slipper fit her foot.

Of course, there was one slight exception: the exit of James Milner – a player City wanted to keep, but who moved to Liverpool on a free transfer in 2015. (Whatever became of him?) But they had hardly made Milner the focus of their attention, and they let his deal expire. At Liverpool, Milner – despite turning 34 – had already played more games (over 200 in total) in four-and-a-half years at Anfield than he managed for any previous club, including five years at City; and of course, he has added a Premier League title to his Champions League medal with the Reds, having won the former (twice) with the Citizens.

Only by 2020 (at least prior to Covid-19) were Liverpool in a secure enough position – financially, as part of a gradual building process, with on-field success providing the money to compete and the regular qualification for the Champions League (and enhancing sponsorship and marketing deals) – to hold onto their main assets. And that included Milner, albeit now more of a utility squad-man; tied to a new deal in December 2019 that will expire when he's 87.

That doesn't mean players will no longer crave new challenges, or will be beyond being tapped-up by the Spanish super-clubs and their lure of sunshine, bigger stadia and perhaps a more familiar language and culture; but Liverpool, Covid-19 aside, are now in a much stronger position than at any point since the halcyon days of the 1980s. It could actually be argued that the Reds are stronger than even back then, given that *Serie A* was the dominant financial force 30-40 years ago, and able to snaffle away Ian Rush in 1986, ahead of a 1987 move to Juventus.

Any outbound transfers could be sanctioned as part of a rebuilding process (for instance, as the entire forward line simultaneously hits their late twenties), rather than the club being held at metaphorical gunpoint by agents and *La Liga* giants. And of course, the stars of this Liverpool team need only look at how their teammates have fared since leaving (it's not a good story).

In some senses Covid-19 comes at a bad time for Liverpool (indeed, it's not really great timing for anyone, except the makers of face masks), in terms of expanding and improving the squad; but equally, the stability of the club, built on FSG's nous, means few clubs will be as able to ride it out as well, unless they are getting their income from benefactors (with FFP relaxed for a short time, financial dopers benefit most). Indeed, if this pandemic broke out in 2010, or rather, if the 2009 H1N1 'swine flu' spread far and wide at a time when Liverpool were chin-deep in debt and wracked with infighting, the club's very existence could have been in question; after all, even without a global pandemic the club came close to administration in 2010, before Henry and co stepped in. Had Covid-19 instead been *Covid-17*, Liverpool may not have become European, World and domestic champions.

£XI and the Title Zone

While a lot gets made of it, a big net spend in one season doesn't really correlate with success in any given campaign, but it does seem to make success more possible *a further season down the line*. (The possible reasons why this happens are discussed in depth in a later chapter, on team dynamics.)

This is why I argued on several occasions in 2019 that Liverpool did not *have* to spend any money to improve, given the age of the squad, the growing cohesion, and the lack of any gaping holes in the XI. As seen with someone like Fabinho, it actually took almost half a season before he could start affecting results in a positive manner, and therefore, introducing new players can often see you suffer for a while, due to a lack of shared understanding; as has arguably been seen with Manchester City and their Fabinho-equivalent, Rodri, in 2019/20, as the Spaniard struggled at times to adapt. And of course, a big net spend is pointless if you buy all the wrong players, or don't have a plan to integrate them.

So, actually, if you follow the one-season net spend logic, Liverpool would *never* have been able to win the title based on their 2019/20 spend figure of around -£30m. Indeed, you might argue that -£30m would be relegation spending. The key is *the sum of the outlay on squad assembly*, when adjusted for inflation; and even more important than the cost of the squad is how much of that talent makes it onto the pitch (you can blow your entire budget on five expensive players and if they're all injured you won't get any of their influence, but you'll still be paying their wages. That said, what tends to happen is that the richest clubs have the bigger coterie of expensive signings, to absorb the shocks.)

For the past five or six years I've talked about the Title Zone, including in a rare talk I gave on the issue at an analytics conference in London in 2015, attended by analysts at Premier League clubs (a couple gave me their cards, but I did not respond); and it gets even more interesting in 2020.

Up until 2004 the title was won by a club that had an £XI between £200m and £400m in 2019 money (2020 money will only be calculated after this book is complete). So, even from 1992 to 2004 – pre Abramovich – there was still a clear Title Zone. After all, teams like

Swindon Town and Bradford City played in the Premier League, but never had a hope of competing for the title. Blackburn, for instance, fell somewhere in the middle of the Title Zone range: an £XI of nearly £300m in 1995 when, managed by Kenny Dalglish, they won the league. So, in 1992/93, for example, there was Norwich, finishing 3rd, and QPR, in 5th, with £XIs that cost about one-fifth of the eventual winners Man United – but obviously, despite doing well on a smaller budget, *they did not win the league.* Having a good season and winning the league are two entirely different things. Even runners-up, Aston Villa, had an £XI that was 76% the cost of United's, which put them in the Title Zone too. (QPR's was only 19% the cost of United's.)

The difference between pre- and post-Abramovich Premier League – as well as more than doubling the minimum cost of qualifying for the Title Zone – is the number of clubs that fall within the new range. The qualification figure rose markedly – and therefore the number of clubs able to field an £XI that could enter that hallowed zone fell dramatically. To contrast the before and after, at various points in the decade between 1992-2002, the clubs who had £XIs in the Title Zone for at least one season were Liverpool, Blackburn, Spurs, Newcastle, Arsenal, Aston Villa, Everton, Leeds United and obviously Manchester United; and so, theoretically, all nine were in with a chance of winning the title – and quite a few at least made title challenges. (Albeit Everton, Villa and Spurs only briefly had that kind of £XI, and never was it at the upper end of the limit.)

However, from 2004 to 2019, the only clubs to have an £XI in the newly established Title Zone were Man United, Chelsea and Man City: from nine clubs, down to three. If you looked at the cheapest champions in that time – bar Leicester – and the most expensive champions, the range in between was the Title Zone. And these three clubs were the only ones to fall within that range.

Now, admittedly the Title Zone has not been redrawn to include Leicester City, as they were such an inexpensive outlier that doing so would mean almost *any* Premier League team would stand a chance of being champions. And if it was a realistic possibility they would not have been 5,000-1 outsiders. (So, lightning struck, but it won't strike twice.)

So, excluding the single outlier of Leicester, we could say – based on £XI – that the only clubs who stood a chance of winning the title between 2005 and 2019 were Man United, Chelsea and Man City. And who won the titles? – in order: Chelsea, Chelsea, Man United, Man United, Man United, Chelsea, Man United, Man City, Man United,

Man City, Chelsea, Leicester*, Chelsea, Man City and Man City. (* Yeah, it still makes no sense.)

But then came Liverpool in 2020, winning the Premier League with an £XI that, like Leicester, ranked below the established Title Zone; albeit not outside it to such a remarkable degree. The Reds £XI worked out at roughly only 70% of the *cheapest* £XI inside the Title Zone (Chelsea's team from 2016/17), and not even half the £XI of the most expensive winner.

In 2019 money, Chelsea's 2005-2007 £XIs remain way ahead as the costliest in the entire 28-year period – more so than the recent Manchester City sides – and given that the Premier League itself increased spending power from the old football league days, we can comfortably call Jose Mourinho's Chelsea the most expensive side of all time. They got in before the financial regulation, spent wildly (which in part led to the financial regulation), won spectacularly (if a little mechanically), and then set about a period of general decline – interspersed with the occasional big success – that still saw their £XI rank in the Title Zone every single year, until 2019/20 saw them finally fall short. Interestingly, Manchester United were also due to fall out for the first time (in part due to the prolonged absence of Paul Pogba), but the January addition of Bruno Fernandes, the return to fitness of Anthony Martial and Paul Pogba, in addition to the new buys Harry Maguire and Aaron Wan-Bissaka, bumped them back up.

In the late 2000s there were just two teams in the Title Zone: Man United and Chelsea (which made life much harder for Rafa Benítez and Arsène Wenger, who both won a ton of major trophies between 2002 and 2005, just before the Abramovich effect really took hold). Then, from 2011 onwards there were three teams: Man United, Man City and Chelsea. But now the league, overall, is actually more condensed, with just City out on their own. Obviously this just makes Liverpool's season so far all the more remarkable. Unlike Leicester, you could now say that Liverpool have lowered the minimum limit on the Title Zone. But the Reds' £XI fell well short of the 2004-2019 Title Zone; and well below the average £XI of the champions in that time even if you threw in Leicester too.

The Premier League Is Still Elite

This was also a season where Leicester were at least challenging for the title when approaching the halfway point with an £XI that ranked 9th, and Sheffield United (the 2nd-cheapest side in the division) and Wolves were having seasons either comparable to, or better than, Man United, Spurs and Arsenal; much of which lasted well into the run-in. Plus, all of the English teams progressed past the group stages in both the Champions League and the Europa League, including newcomers Wolves. That's seven out of seven; on the back of a season when England had all four European finalists. This suggests that the league itself, despite some flaws, is in exceptionally good health and that – as the Club Elo index shows – Liverpool just happen to be the 4th-best team of all time, statistically speaking, having usurped the team currently ranked the 7th-best in the history of football.

That said, City, by 2019/20, appeared a shadow of that side, perhaps in part due to the pressure Liverpool had put on them for the final months of 2018/19 – which City celebrated gregariously after landing the title – but then immediately as 2019/20 began, with a five-point gap opened up within just five games. As the ClubElo website explains, their longstanding model "estimates the strength of a club based on the results against opponents and their strength. Every game's influence decreases when new games are played. In this way, a club's Elo rating is a combination of all its past results with games from the distant past having only a microscopic influence and newest games influencing the rating most. Elo does only consider results though, it completely ignores how the game went. When clubs play each other and win or lose, they exchange points, with home field advantage factored in. A win by a high margin is considered to be more significant than a win by a narrow margin. This is taken into account when the number of exchanged points is calculated.")

As Andrew Beasley wrote for TTT just before lockdown, "Based on the Elo average, this season is the second strongest Premier League season there has ever been. The median rating of the 20 teams was only higher than it is now in 2018/19 and in 2007/08. At the top end of the league, the average rating of the top six sides is currently at its fourth highest, with 2008/09 joining the previously two mentioned campaigns."

This not only shows what a force Rafa Benítez was dealing with against the best Manchester United team in the latter part of the 2000s (having had to battle Chelsea, the costliest ever side in his first three seasons at Liverpool), but it also makes sense that 2005-2010 was a period of great English European dominance – the first since the post-Heysel ban – and what was then a Big Four, before Spurs and Man City joined the party (albeit Spurs, new stadium notwithstanding, are starting to look cut adrift); all of whom reached Champions League finals in that time, with Liverpool and Manchester United reaching two – winning one and losing one – and Chelsea and Arsenal losing theirs.

Similarly, Klopp's Liverpool were at the forefront of the next really strong wave of European performance by the Premier League, which perhaps began with him leading the Reds to a Europa League final, but more relevant was reaching the 2017/18 Champions League final. From no Champions League finalists in years, English football suddenly had three in two seasons (and this book is being written before the 2019/20 Champions League resumes, with Manchester City favourites).

Clubs like Everton, West Ham, Southampton and Crystal Palace have never had so much money; and during the season these four clubs were at various points managed by: a man who has won three Champions League trophies and various league titles; a man who had won the Premier League as recently as 2014, who was replaced by the Manchester United manager of 2013/14; the boss who fairly recently finished 2nd in the Bundesliga with upstarts RB Leipzig; and the former manager of Inter Milan, Liverpool and England (which admittedly looks better on a CV than it worked out in reality).

With Mourinho also back in a job at Spurs, the 2019/20 Premier League had no fewer than *half* the previous 16 Champions League winners as bosses at their clubs (a shame Benítez had left Newcastle, or it would have been nine from 16). In part this incredible prevalence of highly-decorated managers was down to the decline of Mourinho and Carlo Ancelotti (who remained extremely well remunerated but were no longer going to win major honours) – allied to the rise of managers like Klopp and Guardiola. For Mourinho and Ancelotti to end up at Spurs and Everton would have been unthinkable just five years ago (ditto Benítez at Newcastle, at the moment he took the job at Real Madrid), but in addition to the natural decline of managers (which is also discussed later in the book), it was also indicative of the greater ambition of those clubs, and the ever-increasing wealth – at least until Covid-19 came along. Even allowing for the decline of Ancelotti as a European force, it was still a coup for Everton.

So, it's clear: Liverpool *did not* make a mockery of a weak league; they made a mockery of the strongest league in the world. This is one of the reasons why Liverpool rose to rank so highly in the ClubElo rankings: because the league itself was at an extremely high level, with even the poorest Premier League clubs richer, on paper, than some of the continent's biggest names. Statistically speaking, this Liverpool side – which peaked in February 2020 – is one of the best the world has ever seen, and it was built on smarts and mentality, not sugar daddies and petrodollars.

Qatar and Club World Cup: Liverpool, Champions of the World

You wait seven years for a trophy and then three come along in six months. While the Club World Cup may not possess the cachet in Britain that it has in other parts of the globe – and in particular, Latin America – the fact that Liverpool became the first English team to win it whilst also in possession of the European Super Cup (as well as the obvious initial requirement of having won the European Cup/ Champions League) befitted a 2019 in which Liverpool won an insane number of football matches; and when merely being 10 points clear in the Premier League, with a game in hand, did not feel like sufficient reward for the Reds' form going into autumn and winter. A couple of bad results in the league and the lead could quickly be slashed, and the season would have an entirely different feel.

Before the Reds entered the Club World Cup at the semi-final stage there was one other first-team fixture to contend with, although for the League Cup quarter-final at Aston Villa – scheduled just 21 hours before the match against Mexican side Monterrey in the Middle East – there were no first-team players to participate. Liverpool fielded a team at Villa Park with an average age of 19, which beat the club's previous youngest-ever XI by no fewer than *two full years*. It wasn't even a Liverpool "reserve" side, as some of the U23s were in Qatar, and others were out injured; it was more like the U19 side, and although – quite staggeringly – they matched Villa on xG, and actually outgunned them on shots and possession, the young side lost 5-0 due to the home side's superior goalkeeping and finishing, courtesy of bigger, stronger and more experienced players at the sharp ends of the pitch. However, it seems almost perverse to label this a senior game, particularly with the manager on another continent, and while it will live in the record books, and provided over half a dozen teenagers with their debuts, it was essentially just a way of not forfeiting the tie – which Liverpool could have done, and avoided the "defeat". Instead, they used it as an educational experience. There wasn't a goal scored, so it didn't affect the run of consecutive open-play first-team goals, which still stood at 12 since the three set-piece goals spread across the games against Napoli and Brighton.

Less than 24 hours later the real game began. A side lacking its four best aerial players (Virgil van Dijk, Joël Matip, Fabinho and Dejan Lovren), and shorn of a good dose of its pace, laboured a bit against a more cohesive and ramped-up Monterrey side – managed by a man apparently having a mid-life crisis and some kind of nervous breakdown on the touchline, dressed like a 17-year-old. The Concacaf champions threatened at set-pieces, where Liverpool were decidedly outgunned, but what Liverpool lost in understanding and physicality they made up for in freshness; the Mexicans tiring, as Liverpool's semi-B-team ended the game far stronger.

And so, to two more goals from moves that started in the Reds' own half, with skill, pace and absolutely killer assists that, for all the down-talking of Liverpool's qualities in some areas of the media, are about as good as you'll see anywhere in world football. That took the tally to 14 goals in a row scored with sensational open-play football, despite two of those games (Monterrey here, and Everton back home) seeing the Reds field what would otherwise mostly be their subs' bench.

Suddenly Naby Keïta and Mo Salah were an item; like Salah and Philippe Coutinho as soon as the Egyptian arrived, they share a wavelength, although Keïta adds more energy and pressing-power than the departed Brazilian, but where you'd expect fewer goals as part of a more rounded midfield skillset. However, after a stop-start time at Liverpool due to injuries (which, alas, would continue to stop and start), Keïta was on a run of six goals in a red shirt since the start of April, having *barely been fit since the start of April*. Excluding the League Cup, he had started just twelve games since April 5th, and scored six open-play goals. Along with Alex Oxlade-Chamberlain and Xherdan Shaqiri, Keïta could help the team to spread the goals a bit wider; although all three had experienced more than their fair share of injuries since arriving at Anfield. That said, all three starting in the same XI, as happened in Qatar, meant they couldn't all play their natural game; they cannot all make the same runs, after all.

The game had started well for Klopp's men, with Keïta putting the Reds ahead before the quarter-hour mark, although an equaliser was almost immediately conceded.

Liverpool were soon pegged back with a goal from Rogelio Funes Mori, the brother of the ex-Evertonian who broke Divock Origi's leg (and almost derailed the Belgian's career). Gary Lineker swiftly tweeted "Liverpool without @VirgilvDijk at the back look a bit like Liverpool used to look at the back before they signed @VirgilvDijk", which I ended up disputing and debating with him, given that a defence of James Milner, Joe Gomez, Jordan Henderson and Andy Robertson, backed by Adrián, and with *Adam Lallana* as the defensive midfielder, was about as left-field and untried as you could get. While van Dijk *obviously* massively improved the Reds (after a slowish start), and remains the best centre-back in the world, the entire structure of the team had improved radically by late 2019. Even so, this was not *that* team. Henderson is not a centre-back, and Lallana is not a holding midfielder; while Milner was probably too old to play at full-back (certainly against any winger with pace), and Gomez was returning to the side after a difficult calendar year, with his previous season – that saw him in imperious form alongside van Dijk – ruined by a broken leg, from which he seemed to struggle to recover, in terms of his playing rhythm (not least as Matip was impossible to shift until he too got injured).

The clock read 89:47 when the Mexicans made a substitution, taking off the impressive Rodolfo Pizarro, with the score at 1-1. Four minutes earlier, Divock Origi had been replaced by Roberto Firmino. Ninety seconds later the match would be won by the Brazilian.

The winning goal started with several Liverpool passes that moved the ball to Jordan Henderson – doing as well as could be hoped as a makeshift centre-back – who laid on a simple ball to Joe Gomez. Gomez advanced over the halfway line with pace and zipped in a lovely pass to Salah, who, rather than take it into feet with his back to goal, dummied it and span his marker. Closed down by three, Salah wriggled free and laid the ball back to Trent Alexander-Arnold who swished in a pass-cum-cross that was indicative of having his brain wired-up to Spidercam, such was the vision and spatial awareness, as if seen from high above the pitch. Firmino made the run across the defender and tucked the ball under the keeper – job done.

Flamengo Finalé

Having scored 14 consecutive open-play goals with flowing moves and beautiful passes (not a set-piece goal in sight), the Reds won yet another game with a goal that started in their own box. (Apologies if this is getting repetitive, but it does bear repeating.) It was *created* – as around half have been – with one of those inch-perfect longer passes, where the notion of "long ball" is instantly ridiculed by the angle, elevation and precision of what are essentially slide-rule deliveries that drop on the exact intended blade of grass. With the game in extra-time, after the 90 minutes ended 0-0, the move *began* with Flamengo on the attack: a deep cross into the Liverpool box headed back across goal, but Jordan Henderson was on hand to mop up on his own penalty spot.

By this point, Roberto Firmino had already lifted a first-half chance over the bar as the keeper advanced, and in the second half, after flicking the ball over a defender's head, hit a left-footed shot into the ground that bounced up and hit the post. Against his compatriots, and with a reputation that still saw him undervalued in the national side (despite leading the line on their way to a first Copa América triumph in over a decade), he resembled the "not quite" player the cynics in Rio and São Paulo mistakenly looked down their nose at. But for "Bobby" it was third time lucky.

Liverpool had thought they had a chance to win the game right at the death in normal time when Sadio Mané was brought down as he headed into the area; the referee was asked by VAR to decide if it was inside or outside and, utterly bizarrely, *decided it wasn't even a free-kick*. It was genuinely surreal. The VAR replay kept running back and forth without going to the next frame, which would have showed Mané's standing leg was clipped inside the box. The grossly inexperienced referee, Abdulrahman Al Jassim, had a nightmare, and so to extra time it went.

The 99th minute goal that sealed the win for the Reds began with a glorious curling forward pass from Henderson – after mopping up that Flamengo attack in his own box – that squeezed itself between two opposition defenders (one of whom may as well have been doing *flamenco* in a frilly shirt; such was his collapse to the ground that it was probably accompanied by the sounds of clacking castanets). Mané, receiving the pass, then swivelled on a sixpence to play it into the path of Firmino, who was presented with his third big chance of the game. This time he put both the defender and goalkeeper on their backsides, cutting onto his right foot, and while his shot took the slightest of nicks off the defender's shin – to slightly ruin the aesthetics – it was not a *meaningful* deflection, as it didn't affect the well-beaten goalkeeper. That said, it was a rare touch for an opposition player in the last 15 Liverpool goals, and even then it was merely slight and cosmetic. While Firmino may not be the most dead-eyed finisher in the world, few players seem as able to find "all kinds of time" in the box. Keepers rush out, defenders slide in, and there is Firmino, pressing pause.

Liverpool had won yet another final.

Oliver Kay, writing in *The Athletic,* noted: "In Madrid in June, it was the Champions League, their first trophy in seven years. In Istanbul in August, it was the Super Cup. This time, in Doha in December, it was the Club World Cup, secured with the type of gritty, resolute performance that has eventually become Liverpool's calling card under Jürgen Klopp. 'Our mentality shone through,' Henderson said after that gruelling 1-0 extra-time victory over Flamengo. 'We've found a way for a long time now.'

"He's not wrong. So often this season the talk has been of Liverpool digging deep and finding a way. In the 18 matches they have played since October 5, Klopp's team have scored equalisers in the 85th and 94th minute and winners in the 75th, 85th, 91st, 94th, 95th and now, in extra-time against Flamengo, the 99th minute. As Pep Guardiola has said through gritted teeth, 'If it's one time, two times, *We were lucky, we were lucky*, but it happened in the last two seasons many, many times. They have a special character to do that.'"

In a nice piece of symmetry – or circle completion – Mo Salah and Divock Origi scored the goals in the Champions League final, Sadio Mané in the Super Cup and now Roberto Firmino grabbed the vital strike in the Club World Cup. Alisson and Adrián also had big contributions, and there were two clean sheets in the three finals, lest anyone think it was all about the famous front three.

"The boys dug in again and massively put in a performance," Klopp said after the match. "They keep getting tested constantly - our life is like this. At the moment we pass test after test after test. We have to make sure we pass further tests as well."

The Halfway Point: Reds Rampage On

What was at the time deemed Liverpool's 2nd-toughest remaining away game – as the season reached the halfway point for everyone bar the Reds (who still had a game in hand after their trip to Qatar) – saw Liverpool travel to 2nd-placed Leicester, who hadn't lost at the King Power since February, and had only conceded five there all season.

After fireworks, a light show, and throbbing nightclub music blaring on the PA, Leicester ended up thumped 4-0. In truth, they were lucky it was that close. Liverpool's two most one-sided games in the first half of the season were against Brendan Rodgers' men. The first, at Anfield, "ended" 4-0 on xG to Liverpool after 18 shots to two, but it needed a last-minute penalty to seal the points. This time Liverpool finally got the goals their play deserved, and if anything it was even more one-sided.

Ex-Man United midfielder Darren Fletcher noted on the BBC in the build-up to the Boxing Day clash that Leicester "were unlucky to lose that day [in October], and had plenty of possession – 49.3% – but they did not create many chances. James Maddison's goal came from their only shot on target. They only had one other effort at goal, while Liverpool had 18 in total."

Which, of course, sounds like someone seriously contradicting himself. In the buildup to the Leicester rematch there was ongoing talk of how Liverpool "aren't that convincing". The Reds had beaten Everton 5-2, Bournemouth 3-0 (away), Salzburg 2-0 (away) and Watford 2-0, and yet a couple of tight wins – including the game against Watford, and the two in Qatar – seemed to instantly overwrite facts. And of course, even the tight wins *are still wins*, when other teams might draw or lose the inevitably tight games they face. Most other top teams would be "unconvincing" when losing four or five games a season, and drawing seven or eight. Even Arsenal's Invincibles failed to win 12 of their 38 games in 2003/04; yet few people thought them "unconvincing". (For comparison, Liverpool overtook the Invincibles number of league wins with a quarter of the season remaining.)

By this point the Reds had also been 3-0 up against Manchester City, Arsenal and others, but all those impressive displays seemed to get forgotten in the rush to reduce everything to its most simple conclusion: unconvincing and/or late winner (and late winners are somehow illegitimate). Even with half a dozen senior players out injured – with several big names missing for quite a while, including two centre-backs and the stand-in centre-back (who was also the league's best holding midfielder) – and fixtures all over the world in a crazy December schedule, the Reds' results were the opposite of *unconvincing.*

This game was essentially sealed with the Reds' first handball penalty in the league in over two-and-a-half years. While Leicester did everything to make it intimidating and noisy, by the 80th minute the stadium was emptying, with the punters perhaps taking the fireworks, flamethrowers, bugles, light-shows and deafening nightclub music with them. As kickoff approached, and the stadium's floodlights were strobed once again while the players stood in position, it felt more like a WWE SmackDown was about to commence. Although in many ways, that's *precisely* what happened.

As Leicester pulled out every electronic trick in the book, Liverpool, by contrast, were powered by the Qatari sun, with Roberto Firmino rediscovering his mojo in the Middle East, to rack up four goals in three games after a relatively barren season for the "false 9". While a striker's job is *partly* to score goals, his primary role – as it is for any player in any side – is to help the team win games. Firmino does that in so many ways: creating space, creating chances, pressing, flicking, feinting, dummying and no-looking the opposition into confused surrender. The next day, in the press conference for the impending Wolves game, Jürgen Klopp said as much: "When I think about Bobby, I don't think about scoring – I just think about how important he is. We had a little talk because, for the first time since I knew him, he looked a little bit concerned about that fact, and I told him I am not interested in that number because he is the connector for our team. He is so important for us. He is not the only one who can play the position but he can play the position in a very special way."

The winner against Flamengo, a club from his homeland, in a competition that is revered in Brazil, did wonders for his confidence; although an Anfield goal was still proving elusive (and things got very weird in March 2020, once one finally arrived). Never mind, though, as away from home he was utterly prolific, with important goals, too.

Liverpool had essentially conceded the League Cup a few days earlier due to facing an impossible two games in 21 hours on different continents, but returned from their week-long sojourn in Qatar – including extra-time – with a trophy and yet more self-belief. A year earlier, the Reds returned from a similar part of the world – purely as a warm-weather training exercise during some downtime – to face Leicester at Anfield; but arrived back stricken with a sickness bug, and then with a bizarre mix of snow and hail – which froze on the pitch and refused to be budged by the undersoil heating – halting the march towards the title. The Reds had to settle for being Champions of Europe instead. Any setback for this team, it seems, just becomes a motivation.

This was the 35th game in a row in which the Reds were leading at half-time and went on to win, in a run of over 60 such half-time leads without defeat.

Two weeks earlier Owen Hargreaves had told *BT Sport* that the Reds were his tip for another Champions League title, but while he got that wrong, what he said about Klopp's men summed up why they were running away with the Premier League title. "I think before everybody wanted to avoid Barcelona and Real Madrid, I think now everybody wants to avoid Liverpool," he said, but what he added was vital, "This team has virtually every style of play necessary, and for me they're the heavy favourites in this competition."

Has there ever been a more *rounded* side? There have arguably been more skilful sides, although not by much. But it seems that this team can do almost everything, having evolved from a counter-pressing team of inherited midgets who could not defend to a possession-dominating side that can still win without the ball if necessary, and happily racks up clean sheets. It is a team that excels at set-pieces, but scores a ton of open-play goals, mixing up long balls and short balls, fast moves and slow moves. It's even prolific from *throw-ins*.

The goals came courtesy of a far-post Roberto Firmino header in the first-half, followed by a second James Milner penalty against the Foxes within the space of a few months. Milner, who had missed the Reds' previous Premier League handball penalty in the league some 30 months earlier, and who had just come on as a sub, scooped the ball delicately into the centre of the goal after Schmeichel had dived to his left. (In total, the goal against Leicester took Milner to 19 scored for the Reds and just two missed, and this was his ninth consecutive success. Mo Salah, taken off just before the penalty, was on eight consecutive successful spot-kicks since the start of 2018, after he missed his first, against Huddersfield in late 2017.)

The third came when Alexander-Arnold fizzed a low cross to Firmino's foot like a preprogrammed missile, missing out all the other players who might have got a boot to it. The Brazilian's first touch was sublime, and, in the moments when he looked set to take his second touch – a shot – he did a strange kind of skip. Replays show that he was dummying the keeper and defender whilst also "giving them the eyes" – Schmeichel diving to the side the striker was looking – as Firmino, a heartbeat later, curled a no-look finish into the opposite top corner.

The fourth goal was another work of beauty; again – like so many the Reds score – beginning deep in their own half. In just five minutes the Reds took the scoreline from 1-0 to 4-0, to better reflect their utter domination. The move started with an Andy Robertson throw-in – yes, another *throw-in* – deep in his own half. The Reds broke at pace in a move that ended with a finish reminiscent of Carlos Alberto's for Brazil in the 1970 World Cup final. Mané's ball was laid beautifully into Alexander-Arnold's path – although at the pace he was running, the Reds' no.66 had no right to connect as sweetly as it rolled at an angle into the box. He cut across the ball with great dexterity, and it was past Schmeichel before he could blink.

Glass Is Half Full-Back
There were no fewer than 105 touches for Trent Alexander-Arnold in a title-race away game, in a match that ended with two superb assists and that wonderful goal, plus a brilliant piece of last-man covering to deny not one but two Leicester players in a rare attack; as well as two important back-post headers to clear the ball under pressure, and also another shot, inside the first minute, that set the tone. He moved to 20 Premier League assists since the start of the previous season, clear of the chasing pack, with Andy Robertson in third. The entire notion of what

a full-back is has had to be redefined, rather than people looking to redefine what role the young Scouser may play in the future.

It's bizarre that he "might be too good to be a full-back" – a common utterance – given that he has all the space that the team creates, especially when it so expertly and swiftly switches the ball from left to right. Would he get the same space in midfield? Would he be able to cross the ball as much? If you can have 105 touches as a *right-back*, score a goal and force another save, plus rack up two assists, is there anything to "fix"? After all, if it's not broken….

The only time you'd want to consider moving Alexander-Arnold further forward is *if someone better comes along*, or at the very least, someone who is good enough to ensure the right-flank can still be a potent weapon, with the current right-back then moved into midfield, if he is able to transition his abilities back into the role he enjoyed in youth football. And this *could* happen, further down the line, with Wijnaldum and Henderson joining Milner and Lallana (who will have left the club by then) in their thirties by November 2020, and a couple of the other midfielders struggling to get game-time or to stay fit. Welsh teenager Neco Williams excelled in the cups in 2019/20, and, with the title won, began to get some league minutes, too. He appears to have the requisite skillset to be a top-class right-back, but it seems premature to be thinking about that given that Alexander-Arnold helped lead the title charge from that very position.

Against Leicester, Alexander-Arnold wasn't the only English player excelling. Jordan Henderson did something that you normally don't see from any midfielder. Jonathan Wilson wrote in *The Guardian* that: "Nobody who started the game finished with a higher pass completion rate than Henderson's 93.4%, a stat that includes a remarkable 10 accurate long balls out of 11 attempted. He is not Xavi or Andrea Pirlo, and never will be, but at the King Power Stadium he had more in common with them than might ever have been expected."

The captain showed that he can mix safe and steady "recycling" passing with more elaborate rangefinders to put in a complete midfield display. The loss of Fabinho at the end of November was seen as a big blow – and understandably so – but Liverpool were keeping clean sheets with Henderson in the deep-lying role, and, most importantly, *winning games*; just as they did when Adrián replaced Alisson for eight league matches.

Liverpool's utter dominance was picked up by TTT author Andrew Beasley, who noted in his column for the *Liverpool Echo*: "*FiveThirtyEight* have an expected goal database containing over 15,000 matches. The expected goal difference in this match was just over four in Liverpool's favour, making this the joint-8th best away performance by this measure in the database, and the finest from the 1,328 Premier League matches in there. Phenomenal doesn't come close to describing it."

Ergo, evidence of Liverpool's era-defining brilliance.

It was also the biggest margin of victory in a Premier League clash between teams starting the day in the top two since Manchester City beat Manchester United 6-1 in October 2011.

Having sent a blunt, up-close-and-personal message to Leicester, Klopp's team seemed to send a psychic message to Manchester City too, as Pep Guardiola's men waited a day longer to visit Wolves – a team who had already beaten them earlier in the season due to stunning pace on the counterattack, as City's defensive woes were horribly exposed. Same opposition, same outcome. Such was the pace Liverpool were setting, any of City's shortcomings were ruthlessly punished – to the stage where, on December 28th, they stood 14 points behind Klopp's men, having played an extra game. City's defeat at Wolves felt *seismic*; the first moment the title really seemed *destined* for Anfield (even though destiny plays no logical part, unless the participants allow themselves to be adversely affected by the concept).

And Wolves, who came from 2-0 down to beat City 3-2, were up next at Anfield, in what would turn out to be another VAR-heavy game.

The Best 57 Varieties
Liverpool's victory over Leicester on Boxing Day meant that they had now gone a full season and a half with just one single solitary defeat: the controversial 2-1 reversal at the Etihad last season. That week I asked long-time resident TTT statistician Graeme Riley – whose records cover every single game in English football history – to see if a team had ever suffered so few defeats in a run of 57 league games (in Liverpool's case, 38 in 2018/19, 18 in 2019/20, and beginning with one at the end of 2017/18).

"The answer," Graeme replied, "is *no*. No-one else has achieved it. There have only been four discrete runs of over 40 games in which a team has suffered as few as one defeat." The four teams to lose only once in at least 40 league games were Arsenal between 2003 and 2004 (one defeat in 55); Chelsea, between 2005 and 2006 (one defeat in 54); Leeds, starting in 1969 (one defeat in 53); and up to the end of 1978, Nottingham Forest (one defeat in 46).

Liverpool eventually stretched their run to a staggering single league defeat in 66 games, before the 3-0 reversal at Watford could be added to the 2-1 defeat at Manchester City just over a year earlier.

So, going into the game against Wolves, the Reds had already set a new kind of record. And despite some controversial moments, Jürgen Klopp's men were worthy winners (all the xG models suggested as much), even if the visitors were feisty and clearly hyped-up by what they felt were unfair VAR decisions – but where, in truth, VAR was simply overturning tight – but *incorrect* – decisions.

Liverpool's first free-kick of the game – deep in their own half (and won as late as the 41st minute) – was put into touch in Wolves' half for a throw-in to the Reds. From that point, Liverpool never lost possession, working the ball forwards and backwards, side to side, until it ended up with Virgil van Dijk in his own half. His perfect long ball found Adam Lallana, whose chested touch fell to Sadio Mané to sweep home, only for Taylor to initially disallow the goal; VAR then concluding, correctly, that it was off Lallana's chest and shoulder, rather than his upper arm.

It was yet another goal that came from keeping the ball from a throw-in; and another goal that came from a long forward pass designed to drop around the edge of the opposition half – the opposite of long-ball hit-and-hope.

Just before the halfway point of the season, the Reds were ranking 3rd on longer passes, up from 15th the season before. It was only actually a rise of 6.79 per game, but that meant almost exactly 10% more than in 2018/19, and if you alter anything in football by 10% – be it possession, shots or saves – you will probably see a marked difference.

And yet Liverpool hadn't actually added any taller players; indeed, their entire summer business involved bringing in a tiny 16-year-old prodigy who would initially compete at the fringes of the squad, and an admittedly giant 17-year-old defender – who was only initially destined for the U23 team. Plus, a back-up goalkeeper. So it's clear that it was even less of a case of hitting hopeful long-balls to colossal strikers, and more a case of quickly switching the play from one flank to the other, or hitting either long diagonal passes behind the opposition full-backs or, in the case of the Wolves game, one direct forward pass that, all the same, was designed – like the ones in recent games against Everton, Bournemouth and others – to fall nicely in the box, rather than be contested aerially.

In February 2020, in attempt to legitimise his own tactical approach – which had seen him deservedly labelled a dinosaur (having once been much closer to the cutting edge) – Sam Allardyce made some erroneous observations about Jürgen Klopp's Liverpool. While Allardyce was right to say that Liverpool *use* the long ball, this is no more than the way players like Jan Mølby, Glenn Hoddle and Ronald Koeman used the long pass in the 1980s and '90s, to great acclaim. Indeed, Bob Paisley famously said "It's not about the long ball or the short ball, but the *right* ball".

If ever a team used the *right* ball it was this Liverpool side.

"Liverpool play long ball very well indeed from right to left, and very quickly," Allardyce had noted, correctly. "But nobody will say Liverpool play long ball," he added, as his paranoia started to creep in. "You wouldn't hear Martin Tyler saying it," he added, "because it would be frowned upon." And yet plenty of commentators frequently noted the way Liverpool can switch from short to long passing, and hit beautiful raking rangefinders that take out half a dozen opposition players in an instant, either from flank to flank, or back to front. It was a recurring observation.

"You've got to be careful about saying they play long ball," Allardyce said, sounding like someone about to make an off-colour comment. "But that's the way it is. They play long ball exceptionally well and better than anybody else. And that's why they do it."

At the time Allardyce made those statements, Liverpool had fallen to 4th in the long-pass rankings, with 1,636; but they ranked way down in 16th for the *percentage* of long passes made during a game (10.7%), compared with Burnley and Newcastle – with one in every five passes a long one – at that twice that percentage. Manchester City, at 7.5%, were the only team to play a significantly lower proportion of their passes longer.

Indeed, in a strange quirk of tactics, Liverpool have dual defensive quarterbacks, which must be a first in world football. For all the pressing, and the pace and movement of the front three, it is arguably this tactical quirk in the back four that could define how the team is seen by future generations. We've all seen pressing before; and a fearsome front three is not a new concept. But the way this Liverpool team is *knitted together* is revelatory.

Trent Alexander-Arnold is essentially a quarterback full-back, while Virgil van Dijk's passing is similarly sublime. That's two defenders who are up there with the best passers in the world, as part of a defence that is also notably parsimonious (so it's not like they were playing in defence but unable to defend, although Alexander-Arnold has had to learn on the job). Not far behind comes the vision of Henderson, who perhaps doesn't ping a pass as effortlessly as those two defenders, but whose range is still mightily impressive; while Andy Robertson has become adept at the quick switch from one flank to another.

Barcelona in the 1990s, in a team that contained Pep Guardiola, famously had Koeman in their defence; the player who scored the only goal of the 1992 European Cup Final against Sampdoria at Wembley Stadium, to make Barça European Champions for the first time in their history. His long-range passing from centre-back was outstanding, although he couldn't match van Dijk for pace, size and strength. Koeman was a ball-playing centre-back (who scored a ton of free-kicks and penalties for the Catalans – 72 in total), and so it's possible to recall a centre-back who had a similar *passing range* to van Dijk; but it's hard to think of many *full-backs* who pass like Alexander-Arnold. Even more remarkable is to have two such players in the same defence.

Part Two

Sgt. Pepijn's Jürgen Klopp Club Bond: The Brilliant Team Behind The Brilliant Team

The genius of *Sgt Pepper's Lonely Hearts Club Band* – objectively the greatest album of all time (based on any number of polls, and also, of course, a product of Liverpool) – was down to two men: John Lennon and Paul McCartney, the songwriting geniuses of their age, and the two lead singers. Okay, to be more specific it was down to *four* men: John Lennon, Paul McCartney, George Harrison and Ringo Starr, aka The Beatles (you may have heard of them? – four Scouse lads, mop-tops, but by 1967 some rather wonderful moustaches).

Okay, *five* men: John Lennon, Paul McCartney, George Harrison, Ringo Starr and producer extraordinaire, George Martin.

Now I come to think of it … *six* men: John Lennon, Paul McCartney, George Harrison, Ringo Starr, George Martin and pioneering sound engineer, Geoff Emerick, who helped turn the aural ideas into stereophonic reality.

A small number of key players, but look further and the group gets bigger.

The saxophone sextet Sounds Incorporated, who lent their horns to *Good Morning Good Morning*; Neil Aspinall, credited with tambura and harmonica. Mal Evans, noted for "counting, harmonica, alarm clock", and the famous final piano E chord, which followed the forty-piece orchestra in *A Day in the Life*. Not all of these contributions *defined* the album, but they were still part of the mix.

Then, what about all the other support staff at the Abbey Road studios, from the technicians down to the tea lady or tea boy? Next, what about all the key players' partners and families, supporting the band during its most creative – but also fracturing – phase? Or the pop artists, Peter Blake and Jann Haworth, who designed arguably the most iconic album cover of all time, as would befit the most iconic *album* of all time. Then, the record company, EMI and Parlophone, and all the executives who years earlier took risks on a gang of raw scallies with some promising tunes, funny haircuts and enormous chutzpah; and even the workers at the famous EMI vinyl factory in Hayes, which I could see from my bedroom window when growing up (and which, as an aside, is more or less where Stockley Park – of VAR infamy – is located).

And so, if you follow the analogy, Liverpool Football Club's success these past couple of seasons is still all down to Jürgen Klopp, right?

Okay then, so maybe not *all* down to the German genius. You get my point.

He is perhaps the George Martin of it all: the facilitator; although obviously Klopp is himself a very public figure, whose personality is that of an A-list star. By contrast, even though he received recognition as the 'fifth Beatle', Martin was not one of the glittering stars of the enterprise – they were Lennon and McCartney – and nor was he even one of the less-heralded players, Harrison and Starr. But he was the man responsible for bringing it all together. (You could argue that the Beatles would have been just as good without Starr, but nowhere near as good without Martin.)

Not only was Martin's job to produce the most innovative sounds and to shape the tempo of songs, or to sense where an instrumental break might best be placed (and indeed, whether that instrumental break should be cut up into pieces and played backwards), he had to hold together the egos; at a time when Lennon and McCartney, as the world's most famous songwriting duo, were starting to mostly write alone. Klopp is to Mo Salah and Sadio Mané what Martin was to Lennon and McCartney: the man to get them to produce their best, to fire their imaginations, to have them excel as individuals but also create harmonic beauty. Obviously the metaphor falls over in certain senses, but the general gist remains applicable.

But then Klopp, as surrogate for Martin, also has *his* Geoff Emerick; indeed, it's Liverpool's own Sgt. Pepijn (to Colonel Klopp).

And beyond Pepijn Lijnders are a whole host of vital lesser-seen contributors that underpin the unprecedented success.

Teams of Teams

There are essentially two types of team that support the players at Liverpool: the ones who have direct contact with the players, such as the coaching and medical staff; and the unseen analytics department, akin to some top-secret laboratory, where some very smart people work on theories and analyse both data and video, some of which then gets presented to the coaching staff, who in turn translate it into an understandable and digestible format for the players, so as to not overwhelm them.

(Or, if Liverpool were, for some bizarre reason, employing Proper Football Men at the coalface rather than erudite coaches, they'd tell the players: "This is a load of fucking old shit, ignore it. Forget all that fancy bollocks and focus on getting it into the mixer early doors, and get in their faces, they don't like it up 'em. And hit Les, over the top. Can we not knock it?")

Pep Talk

If it seems impossible that there could be *another* Jürgen Klopp, then it's worth looking at someone who could essentially be the Liverpool's manager's son; or at the very least, at the age of 37, a much younger brother. Much was made when fitness specialist Andreas Kornmayer arrived from Munich of him being a 'mini Klopp' on account of a few physical similarities, but Pepijn Lijnders is starting to look like a closer clone.

When Klopp's erstwhile sidekick Željko Buvač left Liverpool under a cloud on the eve of the Champions League semi-final second-leg in April 2018, it appeared that the manager had lost what he often called the "brains" of the operation. However, after 17 years together, it could be argued that Klopp – via daily discussions, and hundreds upon hundreds of matches – would have assimilated all his assistant's ideas via osmosis, if not by direct education. Buvač may well have been the brains way back in 2001, when Klopp was first trying to get his head around the idea of coaching, but a guy as smart as Klopp will have imbibed much of that knowledge; after all, we all learn and develop, if we are open to doing so.

At the point Buvač left, Liverpool's football was still largely rooted in Dortmund's style. But Lijnders – originally brought to Liverpool from under the noses of Manchester United in 2014, to work with the youth team – was one of the brightest young minds in football; not to mention being from the next generation to Buvač, as 20 years his junior. If Klopp already had Buvač's ideas, Lijnders could bring fresh impetus.

Speaking on the *BT Sport Football Writers'* podcast in 2020, football writer Mike Calvin talked about people in the game who had told him of Lijnders many years earlier. "Premier League and Football League managers went to a masterclass organised by the Welsh FA with Lijnders, and they said he was *sensational.*"

Lijnders had actually left Liverpool a few months before Buvač, to take a managerial job in the Dutch second tier, but with mediocre results in a short spell at ambitious NEC, was sacked before the Reds loss to Real Madrid. As such, he had already agreed to return to replace Buvač; indeed, Lijnders later admitted that Klopp began trying to convince him to return as soon as Buvač departed. And so, Liverpool had a new 'brain'. So close have Klopp and his new sidekick become that they seem to share the same ebullient *joie de vivre*, and play paddle tennis most days in an indoor glass court at Melwood, specially built for the pair to challenge each other.

And while Liverpool were progressing steadily with the Klopp and Buvač axis (including the recruitment of players like Sadio Mané and Mo Salah, followed by Virgil van Dijk in January 2018), Klopp and Lijnders – along with the third member of the team, Peter Krawietz, who has worked with the manager for almost 20 years – took things stratospheric. Lijnders added fresh ideas and fresh energy, at a time when Buvač was starting to seem a bit stale and sour. Two key players – third and fourth captains, van Dijk and Gini Wijnaldum – now had a compatriot in a key role, and young starlets from Holland were making the move to Merseyside.

If the cycle of management and players often stales within three years, as many experts note (and if the period is *intense*, it can hasten the ennui, if physical and mental exhaustion plays a factor), the simplest and cheapest solution is often to replace the manager; but who would want to get rid of Jürgen Klopp in his pomp? That would be madness, unless there were signs that the cycle really was moving towards an end, as started to happen in his *seventh* seasons at his only two previous clubs. Another response is to overhaul the squad; but that's often costly (which is why the manager usually gets sacked instead), and can destroy the unity and discard the specialist long-term education and shared understandings those players have developed. Alex Ferguson's solution was usually to replace his assistant, albeit that often happened when the assistant was headhunted for, or opted to try, a managerial position elsewhere; but Ferguson did often find a fresh approach with his replacement assistants, rather than just trying to replicate what he lost.

And in fairness, Klopp seems hard to tire of, unless you cannot stand smiles and bearhugs, and winning football matches; but Buvač was a more dour character, who might be more grating. Lijnders wasn't needed to offset Klopp's weaknesses, but serves to multiply the overall cache of skills, and provide fresh ideas.

Another reason why the return and promotion of Lijnders was inspired is because he did not need to get to know the players or the other staff members. He was guaranteed to fit in with the ethos of the coaching staff, as he had already been a member. In a tight-knit group, any outsider may take time to settle, or to be accepted.

And while Lijnders' first – and so far, *only* – six months as a manager was unremarkable (just as the early tenures of Ferguson, Rafa Benítez, Jose Mourinho and even Klopp himself were unremarkable), it was a chance to better understand what support a manager needs; and all experiences, good and bad, can be educational. Not only was Lijnders closer to the age of the players (just three years older than James Milner, himself a potential future coach), but years earlier he had worked with Trent Alexander-Arnold, and others, with the youth team. Lijnders also had a chance to observe Buvač at close quarters for a couple of years, to take on his better ideas and update the coaching process with his own fresher take; knowing enough of the existing structure to integrate his ideas, rather than come in anew and possibly clash with what was already being done. Also, perhaps Lijnders' education in Dutch football, and several years as a youth development coach in Portugal, helped Liverpool evolve the possession side of their game, in a way that Buvač may not have managed.

Identity
Speaking to Arthur Renard for *The Guardian* in late 2019, Lijnders explained: "Jürgen [Klopp] is the leader and face of the team, the one who defines the character and who stimulates everyone. Pete [Peter Krawietz] is responsible for the analysis and prepares everything in

regards to videos which are shown to the players. I'm responsible for the training process.

"Together we decide what kind of aspects we want to develop for the team and then I create the exercises. It's quite simple; it's just about the continuing stimulation of our mentality to conquer the ball as quick and as high up the pitch as possible. That element comes back in every exercise. We as staff always try to find ways so the players can be more spontaneous and more creative."

The high counterpressing has become the identity of the modern Liverpool. Lijnders works to refine its model and creates exercises which help players master the system. For example, in training a rule can be that a goal counts only when all the players have crossed the halfway line. Training exercises are designed to create challenging situations that test the players, and enable them to think quickly and instinctively under pressure. He explained that the exercise where a goal only counts if all the players are in the opposition half is, "Purely to stimulate the team to push up quickly and be ready to counterpress; counterpressing is only possible when you are together at all times. People say Liverpool are good at this or at that but I always say the main thing we are good at is that we are always together."

This is perhaps why Liverpool's midfield was clearly underrated for so long, and in many cases, remains unsung: its role is often to help the team shape, not to create moments of individual glory. They had to get up to support the attack, but also get back to support the defence, while providing support behind the overlapping full-backs; whereas some elite ball-playing midfielders will just play a nice pass and stand to admire it, or let a runner sprint past them as they lazily walk back. They may get more plaudits, but right now they are not getting more of the major medals.

Lijnders talked through other routines with Renard. "Let's take the five-v-two rondo, which in fact is a pressing rondo. Our game is about movement and speed, and with only five players those five have to run non-stop. The two guys in the middle are encouraged to make an interception within the first six passes. If they succeed, they can go out both at the same time, otherwise only the player who intervened is allowed to leave the middle. This all stimulates our counterpressing vision where we try to disrupt the buildup of the opponent inside their first few touches."

Indeed, Lijnders explained, this is now known as 'Milly's rondo', such was (and maybe *still is*, even at 34) Milner's ability to win the ball back within the first six passes.

"…. When a team lose the ball in training, you will hear me, Jürgen or Pete screaming: 'Go! Get it back! Don't stop!' It's so loud they'll even hear that in Manchester, haha. They have to understand why it's so important. That power and emotion is our game. Because our identity is intensity. That comes back in every drill. And that's what I like about coaching: that you can stimulate certain common behaviour and create a lot by specific team training. That's what I live for."

"… We always focus on ourselves, attack the opponent with – but especially without – the ball; a chasing attitude over 95 minutes.

"So our way of playing is the central element in our training sessions. But I also look to details of opponents which can give us an advantage, like spaces they might leave open or other weaknesses which we can exploit. I always try to interweave those elements in our sessions without the players noticing it." However, "75% of the opponents we've played against so far in the Premier League changed something in their formation beforehand".

In January 2020, Lijnders told James Pearce of *The Athletic*, "The passion and ambition of these players is from another planet. Their self-confidence, their self-criticism, that is what makes us consistent. These boys have the ability to make even a simple rondo competitive. People talk about going game to game – no, we commit session to session. Small things make big things happen. You have to focus on doing the small things right constantly. The passion and ambition I see, especially on the rainy and windy days here, that for me is what separates us from the others."

The Secret Lab

While I will also touch upon it here, the transfer and analytical side of things at Liverpool is assessed more thoroughly in *Mentality Monsters*. I will go over some of the ground again (and include a few paragraphs from that book), but there's no point going into the same level of detail, not least because 2019/20 owed little to *new* transfers. The new arrivals were limited to two teenagers not expected to go into the first team for at least a year or two (and who would play in the League Cup), a free-transfer backup keeper and a cut-price attacking player who arrived midseason from Salzburg after a month of inactivity, and as such, was always going to find it difficult to get up to super-speed right away.

Behind the scenes, albeit not in a bunker deep under a mountain wearing white lab coats and protective eyewear, are people like Michael Edwards and Ian Graham, who won't be found on the training pitches, but whose work feeds into the matrix.

Klopp, who worked alongside a sporting director at both Borussia Dortmund and Mainz, expressed his support for Edwards' promotion to Sporting Director in November 2016, saying: "This decision is hugely positive for us. It will make us better and stronger in managing the process of building and retaining playing talent at all age groups. Development is so important and it makes sense to have a position, within the football structure specifically, that focuses on where we can improve.

"It's no secret I like the concept of a sporting director and having worked under this model previously I have found it to be nothing but positive and forward-thinking. Michael is absolutely the right person for this. He has the knowledge, expertise and personality to flourish in the role and I was delighted when he told me he would be accepting the position. Importantly, he also has a fantastic team of people around him, who have all played a significant role in putting together the talent we currently have in the first team, development squad and at even younger age levels."

Everything he said has rung true.

Prepare, Perform, Reflect and Refine: How Liverpool's Backroom Staff Helped The Reds Dominate At Home And Abroad

A football team is an ever-evolving creature. When Jordan Henderson captained the Reds to Champions League glory in 2019, it was the final match of his eighth season at the club. Many players had been and gone from Anfield since he joined, but the team improved along the way with a key new signing or two embedded into the starting XI and squad each year.

It's a similar tale with the backroom staff at Liverpool. If a club appoints a new manager, the media stories will usually explain how the man in charge will be bringing his staff with him. And while that is true of Jürgen Klopp, he also made use of existing coaches at the club, as well as having seen his assistants change during his five seasons on Merseyside.

Take John Achterberg, for instance. The 48-year old is a rare example of someone from the first team staff who has been at the club longer than Henderson. When Achterberg initially joined the club – first as coach of the reserve and academy goalkeepers in 2009 – Klopp had only just finished his first season in charge of Borussia Dortmund, never mind Liverpool.

At times when goalkeepers such as Simon Mignolet and Loris Karius were struggling, Achterberg faced fierce criticism from the club's fans. Achterberg was blamed every time a goalkeeper dropped a clanger, as if the coach could control every situation on the pitch; and when, in fairness, he'd only been given "pretty good" keepers to work with, rather than anyone at a truly elite level. And no matter how good a goalkeeping coach is, if the player makes mistakes then those mistakes can start to permanently erode his confidence; even once apparently forgotten, they can be dredged up following a further mistake.

And if Klopp wasn't satisfied with Achterberg's work, he'd be gone. In reality, the Liverpool manager is impressed by his ferocious work ethic. "He's one of the hardest-working people I've ever met, he works as a coach 25 hours a day," said Klopp.

For Achterberg, a certain style of goalkeeping, which tallies with Klopp's vision, is vital: the ability to be a *proactive* keeper, who enables a team to play a high line. That won't have worked for every Liverpool manager who has been in the hot seat in his time at the club – and it's hard to do without pace at the heart of the defence (otherwise the defence just drops deeper and deeper) – but it certainly aligns with Klopp's philosophy.

"I always thought, and how I learned in Holland – if you can play high lines and defend the space behind the defenders, you can also play for a team that plays with 11 in [defence] because you only have to be in the right position to make the save," he said.

But despite that, it's also important for a goalkeeper to be aware of their surroundings, as Achterberg explains. "My thinking is always teaching the goalkeepers in the goal as much as we can because that's how they learn the angles, the body positioning, the feet positioning, shoulder positioning and the hands."

Speaking to the club's official website, Achterberg was quick to praise Klopp and the staff he brought with him. "When the boss came, he had a massive input in what happens now, in the way he manages, in the way he created the team and created the environment, and way the boss makes things happen in the club in a professional way.

"He got Mona [Nemmer] in, and Andreas [Kornmayer], to make the food and physical sides more professional. Pep [Lijnders] was brought back because he could help, he already had Peter [Krawietz], who helped him a lot with all the stuff he needed for the games. The boss created the team himself around him that he is happy with.

"Then Vitor [Matos] came in later, Jack [Robinson] is helping me as an assistant now, which is great. Also because I'm getting a bit older so you need a younger guy, and to help him again to develop as well. That is the way the boss has created this situation in the club."

Many of the names Achterberg mentioned will be familiar to most Liverpool fans, though the name Jack Robinson may stir memories of the club's forgotten one-time youngest ever player (although he returned to the Premier League with a January 2020 move to Sheffield United) rather than a recent addition to the goalkeeper coaching team.

Robinson, who holds a Uefa A licence in goalkeeping, joined the club in a newly created role in September 2018, having previously worked with Manchester United, Crystal Palace, Leeds United and the FA. In a 'Behind The Badge' feature article on Liverpool's official website, he gave an insight into the three things he and Achterberg consider when planning training sessions:

One: What are the individual needs of the four first-team goalkeepers at the current time and how can the next workout improve them?

Two: What specific threats will the Reds' next opponents pose? Robinson explained the sort of things they look for. "Do they press us from goal-kicks? Do they press high when we're in possession? How do they want to try to score, is it crosses, is it through balls?

And three: How must the goalkeeper adjust to the tactical requirements of the whole team for the next match?

The layout of Liverpool's training complex illustrates how seriously they take goalkeeping, as the same article noted: "Robinson and Achterberg are based in a room directly adjacent to Klopp's office at Melwood, shared with assistant managers Peter Krawietz and Pepijn Lijnders, where the manager and his coaches coordinate training, swap ideas, consider tactics, analyse opponents and problem solve."

It sounds like it's the very nerve centre of football operations, and Krawietz – nicknamed 'The Eye' by Klopp, due to his expertise in scouting and video analysis – will clearly be a key part of the activity there. Krawietz was deemed largely responsible for the incredible improvement in Liverpool's set-piece threat from 2018/19 onwards, amongst many things he offers. "Even now I am still amazed at the things he spots during a game," Klopp said. "He's always been essential to me but his personal development since arriving at Liverpool has been outstanding. He is so smart, so insightful and so important to us."

Being prepared is everything to the 48-year old German, who once memorably described football as "like chess, but with dice." Strategy is important, but the random nature of the sport can lay waste to even the greatest manager's best laid plans. How a team responds and reacts is of paramount importance. During a match, Krawietz can often be spotted jotting down notes in a journal. A key part of his job is highlighting key points from the first half to Liverpool's players during the interval, as he explained to the club's website in April 2020.

"With around 35 minutes played, I try on the bench, together probably with Pep and Jürgen as well, to get an idea on what are the talking points for half-time. Always the question is: 'How can we help our players? What is necessary to do in the second half?'

"Three or four minutes before half-time, I leave the bench and go to the dressing room. I meet there Harry [Harrison Kingston] and Mark [Leyland] and I try to choose the right clips I noticed during the first half. My colleagues Jürgen and Pep come in and I present the clips and tell them what I think could help.

"Then we make a decision together, if we want to show it or not, and the question behind this decision is always orientated on the solution, or one solution, for the second half and if it is helpful for the players that we show it.

"We make the decision 'yes' or 'no', and if we decide to show the one or two or three, maximum, clips, then we are going to present and show these pictures to the players. This is the process that goes on."

In an article on *liverpoolfc.com* back in 2016, Mark Leyland – who was at Burnley prior to joining up with his boyhood team – spoke of Klopp's strength in these crucial moments.

"The manager is unbelievably good at reading the situation at half-time. His decision-making is one of the things that I think stands him apart – no disrespect to other people I've worked with, but his decision-making and the way he relays information at half-time is so good. He's really clear, he's obviously really passionate, but his knowledge of when to give information and when not to, of what to give and what not to, is just at a different level."

The duo of Leyland and Harrison Kingston aren't just kept busy at half time during games, as they are also post-match analysts. The former explained how they work well as a pair. "Harrison focuses more on team style presentations – anything to do with defensive shape, offensive patterns, transitions – whereas I deal with individual player performances."

The analysts will no doubt be guided by Greg Mathieson, Liverpool's head of opposition analysis, who arrived in 2015. He told the club's official website: "Another key role is attendance of live matches – an important component in our understanding of the opposition." Where Bill Shankly would dispatch Reuben Bennett to far-flung corners of Europe to learn about teams because there was no alternative in the pre-digital age, Mathieson still undertakes the same task even though footage is widely available at the click of a mouse these days. But Mathieson also helps out on other areas of analysis, such as working with other coaches to identify ways to hurt the opposition from corners and free-kicks. In 2019, after yet another successful set-piece routine, Klopp said, "Pete Krawietz, Greg and James [French], our analysts, what they do around set-pieces is unbelievable."

The Reds are arguably the fittest team in the Premier League. A lot of this can be put down to Andreas Kornmayer, the club's head of fitness and conditioning who they poached from Bayern Munich in 2016. Kornmayer – the aforementioned Klopp clone – was at Bayern for over 15 years, meaning that as well as working with Klopp, he has assisted Louis van Gaal, Jupp Heynckes and Pep Guardiola. Many of the best managers of his generation have trusted him to ensure their squads have reached peak physical fitness. Working well as a unit is clearly the key, as the former Bayern man once told the official Liverpool website: "I try to get everything fixed, done and in motion so that everybody is really clear on what they have to do. We have to put things together – we have several connecting points with each department, so we have to put them together to get the best out of the squad."

One key section of the backroom team looks after the players' food. Mona Nemmer, Liverpool's head of nutrition, joined the club from Bayern Munich at the same time as Kornmayer. "Mona is heart and soul, she is everything," Klopp said of her. On another occasion in late 2019, he added: "We are a good team in many areas, but Mona is our only really world-class player". Sky-high praise, all things considered.

"She is so smart. Not one player is in doubt about her – that's outstanding. Nobody likes it when someone tells you what you're eating is not good, but Mona is really strong in this," Klopp said. "In this department we have changed pretty much everything and the players like it because they know Mona is just there to help them and make their lives easier, at Melwood and at home because she works with their better halves." Nemmer conducts individual consultations with players, offering them or their partners cooking lessons. She is in no doubt about the importance of her work. "We try to accentuate certain aspects of nutrition, such as boosting the immune system or supporting regeneration," she said. "Eating properly is a kind of legal doping."

With a team of 26 cooks who work under her, Nemmer is able to guide the player's diets before and after every match, be that at home or abroad as she explained to *Four Four Two* in October 2019: "We're lucky enough to have separate teams of home and away chefs, and that includes two away teams – one for European matches and one for domestic away matches. You need this, really, to achieve some form of work–life balance. "Take a Wednesday Champions League game. The chefs fly out on Monday, preparing to feed the players who arrive on the Tuesday. They'll feed them again on Wednesday, the matchday, but with the evening kick-off, inevitably the chefs don't fly back until Thursday. If you're then playing away on the Sunday, you'd be driving off again on Saturday and that's too much. So the domestic away team take over."

It's a demanding schedule for staff and players alike. For the squad, people inevitably think of the physical demands from Klopp's high-pressing football, but the mental toll taken by playing for one of the world's biggest football clubs shouldn't be underestimated either, especially as the pressures associated with media exposure has grown exponentially over the years.

Enter Lee Richardson. The former player and Chesterfield manager – who was once scouted by Kenny Dalglish early in his playing career in the late 1980s – was appointed as Liverpool's sports psychologist in June 2019, and as such is one of the newest additions to the team; arriving in time to help lift the players after the disappointment of finishing 2nd with 97 points, and also to process the emotion of winning the Champions League in Madrid. The club had been searching for someone to fill the role for nearly two years, but Klopp knew it required the right type of person (which seems similar to how he waited for Virgil van Dijk to become available, rather than bring in a substandard player and a substandard person). Richardson fitted the bill, and now works with the players, usually on a one-to-one basis. He has been very impressed with their attitude toward his work, as he told the club's website.

"I have to say, the lads at Liverpool have been the best in terms of being open to chatting and discussing anything. That's a sign of people who have what I call a 'mastery approach'; they just want to get better," he said.

This is along the same lines as 'growth mindset' versus 'fixed mindset', the work Carol Dweck pioneered in the mid 2000s, which she further explained in 2012: "In a fixed mindset students believe their basic abilities, their intelligence, their talents, are just fixed traits. They have a certain amount and that's that, and then their goal becomes to look smart all the time and never look dumb. In a growth mindset students understand that their talents and abilities can be developed through effort, good teaching and persistence. They don't necessarily think everyone's the same or anyone can be Einstein, but they believe everyone can get smarter if they work at it."

The same is surely true in sport: those who reach a certain level and then think they've made it; that their talent is god-given, and they no longer have to work hard. These are the types of players Liverpool have looked to weed out in the scouting process. The mental culture is already spot-on; it doesn't need too much revelation from a sports psychologist, but one can still be on hand, to provide further guidance, or to offer support during any player's inevitable loss of form.

Liverpool reserve keeper Andy Lonergan, speaking to Dominic Fifield of *The Athletic* at the end of the season, said "Here at Liverpool, you can't fail to improve in this set-up. Not unless you were too arrogant or ignorant, and closed to it all. If you listen, you'll learn. It's just the perfect environment. I wish I could have had this chance to experience it when I was younger because my career would have worked out very differently."

Richardson, when asked by Jonathan Northcroft of *The Sunday Times* where Liverpool's incredible form during 2019/20 came from, said: "A psychology and a performance cycle of readiness, that you see from the best in all sport. It's prepare, perform, reflect, refine. Prepare, perform, reflect, refine. And that matches up with efficacy.

"Momentum, in sport, is a psychological not physical state because winning builds self-efficacy, which is belief in yourself, and co-efficacy, which is belief in each other," he added.

It's worth interjecting here to say that several studies suggest that the existence of momentum is actually overstated, but self-belief, and a belief in teammates, *is clearly better than the opposite*; however, winning runs can end due to overconfidence and complacency, which is where 'momentum' – statistically, at least – can often fall down. Thus, successful teams need a lot more quality overall to sustain domination, and are more likely to bounce back from a setback. Momentum, as it is often described, can end during a couple of bad results – by definition, the momentum is lost; but the best teams will go back on a new winning run, or a run with a lot of wins interspersed with the occasional setback – not because of momentum, but because they are an elite team who find ways to win games, and part of that is due to a particular mindset. And the best teams will use winning as a source of positivity; while flawed teams will see their momentum, should they gain some, as proof they are now *perfect*, and grow complacent.

Liverpool have clearly amassed an incredibly impressive staff, all of whom – from the outside at least – believe greatly in one another and the lofty goals they are collectively aiming for. Their common goal is to help the main man, as analyst Mark Leyland explained: "The manager is the figurehead to everything we're trying to achieve. Everything that he does is with the right things in mind, and as a staff member that's all you can really ask for. He's always very honest with you, whether he wants more or less. Our relationship with him as a staff and a playing staff is unbelievable. You do get that feeling of 'We all want the same things, we're all striving to be the best' and that's something he believes we can be. His belief filters down through everyone else, and you're starting to see that in the confidence and attitude of everyone."

Leyland was speaking over three years ago, before the processes put in place were reaping dividends; and it's safe to say Klopp's belief has turned both the team and its supporters from doubters to believers in that time. He couldn't have achieved it on his own though.

It has taken a blend of world-class experts in their respective fields to coalesce, in order to prepare the team to be the very best they can possibly be. The continual evolution of personnel both on-and-off the pitch has enabled the Reds to reach the footballing apex of European, world, and Premier League football.

With talent at every level of the club which is the envy of most others, Liverpool look well placed to prepare, perform, reflect and refine at the highest level possible for a good while longer yet.

Majestic Recruitment

On February 16th 2020, back in those heady days when people could still gather around a table, football writers Martin Samuel and Mark Ogden – amid the bagels and orange juice – discussed the Reds' transfer record, and progress as a team, on Sky's *Sunday Supplement*.

Samuel: "The recruitment [at Liverpool] is the greatest I've ever seen by any club. Because everybody they have bought fits in, everybody they have bought buys into what Klopp wants to do. And what Klopp wants to do is not normal."

Ogden: "The mark of greatness is winning the Champions League, and Liverpool have already done that. Arsenal's 'Invincibles' didn't do that, Mourinho's Chelsea didn't do that, Man City haven't done it."

Samuel: "They were one of the greatest teams we'd ever seen last season. They were the best team never to win the league. All the records we are talking about now started last season."

Obviously Liverpool went on to secure the league title four months later, and in the process became the first English team to do things back to front: champions of Europe and the world, and only then *champions of England*. But it was interesting to hear how widespread the praise for Liverpool's recruitment had become, after previously being seen as a laughing stock. Indeed, as soon as Brendan Rodgers was sacked in early October 2015, Neil Ashton, writing for *The Daily Mail*, published a now infamous attack piece on Michael Edwards – headlined "Liverpool's head of technical performance Michael Edwards is the laptop guru who did a number on Brendan Rodgers", with the line that has dated least well of all, "The committee have yet to explain how they came up with the figure of £29million to sign Brazilian forward Roberto Firmino from Hoffenheim, who finished eighth in the Bundesliga last season."

Just in case you're wondering, that's in relation to £29m *being a waste of money*, not an absolute bargain. We all make bad predictions when writing and talking about football – it's a constantly shifting game that sees fortunes reversed all the time – but that always seemed like a mean-spirited hatchet job. (Ashton, the erstwhile host of the aforementioned Sunday brunch, is a Crystal Palace fan who now works for Manchester United on their public relations.)

Lots of Smart People in the Room

At this point it's worth re-running a section of a dozen or so paragraphs from *Mentality Monsters,* which covered the backroom innovation, with much of it quoting an in-depth *New York Times* article about the largely unseen recruitment team, with the main focus on Ian Graham.

In late May 2019 Bruce Schoenfeld of the *New York Times* wrote about the time Ian Graham – one of Liverpool FC's many PhDs, with a doctorate in theoretical physics from Cambridge – first met Jürgen Klopp.

"Jürgen Klopp was in his third week as Liverpool's manager, in November 2015, when the team's director of research, Ian Graham, arrived at his office carrying computer printouts. Graham wanted to show Klopp, whom he hadn't yet met, what his work could do. Then he hoped to persuade Klopp to actually use it.

"Graham spread out his papers on the table in front of him. He began talking about a game that Borussia Dortmund, the German club that Klopp coached before joining Liverpool, had played the previous season. He noted that Dortmund had numerous chances against the lightly regarded Mainz, a smaller club that would end up finishing in 11th place. Yet Klopp's team lost, 2-0. Graham was starting to explain what his printouts showed when Klopp's face lit up. "Ah, you saw that game," he said. 'It was crazy. We killed them. You saw it!'

"Graham had not seen the game," Schoenfeld notes. "But earlier that fall, as Liverpool was deciding who should replace the manager it was about to fire, Graham fed a numerical rendering of every attempted pass, shot and tackle by Dortmund's players during Klopp's tenure into a mathematical model he had constructed. Then he evaluated each of Dortmund's games based on how his calculations assessed the players' performances that day. The difference was striking. Dortmund had finished seventh during Klopp's last season at the club, but the model determined that it should have finished second. Graham's conclusion was that the disappointing season had nothing to do with Klopp, though his reputation had suffered because of it. He just happened to be coaching one of the unluckiest teams in recent history."

Schoenfeld details how, in that first meeting, Graham spoke to Klopp about various games where Dortmund had lost, but on pretty much every measurable aspect, deserved to win. Klopp, who had not studied data at Dortmund, was converted to these new ideas. Indeed, Klopp observed that it was Ian Graham who got him the job at Liverpool in the first place (although Graham was just part of the process).

"'I don't like video,' Graham – a Liverpool fan born in Wales in the 1970s – told Schoenfeld. "'It biases you.' Graham wants the club that he works for to win, but he also wants his judgments to be validated. 'All of these players, there has been discussion of their relative merits,' he said. 'If they do badly, I take it as sort of a personal affront. If I think someone is a good player, I really, really want them to do well.'"

Schoenfeld explained that Graham often eschews the most basic, widely-available stats in favour of his own models. As explained in the mammoth *New York Times* article, one such model calculated "the chance each team had of scoring a goal before any given action — a pass, a missed shot, a slide tackle — and then what chance it had immediately after that action. Using his model, he can quantify how much each player affected his team's chance of winning during the game. Inevitably, some of the players who come out best in the familiar statistics end up at the top of Graham's list. But others end up at the bottom."

Despite what might be inferred from the *New York Times* article, Liverpool do not treat Graham's model as an omnipotent god, to which they are subservient; they still use traditional scouting, in person and on video, to assess players. Graham's model is an incredibly important tool in the process, but it's just one facet of the operation. Graham himself would not like to think that he is the secret to the Reds' success – as that would go against the club's ethic of teamwork and humility, as well as not being strictly true. Right now, the club has so many vital cogs, rather than one genius or magical computer model running the show. (But the idea of a magical computer model makes for better copy.)

Graham, like Michael Edwards, was working at Spurs a decade ago. Ahead of the final, the Reds' erstwhile director of football, Damien Comolli – the man who brought both Graham and Edwards to Liverpool – told *The Independent*: "I met Ian when he was working for Decision Technology," Comolli says. "I appointed them as our data providers, data analysts at Spurs. So I go back a long time with all those people.

"… We took two of the most advanced individuals in terms of analytics in the Premier League, if not the world of football, in Ian Graham and Michael Edwards. I knew they were incredibly smart, and they could take any clubs to the next level. Ian and Decision Technology helped Spurs get there and they are obviously doing it at Liverpool as well."

In his *New York Times* article, Bruce Schoenfeld detailed the group of men who could probably start a fight over who is the smartest in the room, were they so inclined. "Tim Waskett, who studied astrophysics, sits to Graham's left. Nearby is Dafydd Steele, a former junior chess champion with a graduate math degree who previously worked in the energy industry. The background of the most recent analyst to be hired, Will Spearman, is even less conventional. Spearman grew up in Texas, a professor's son. He completed a doctorate in high-energy physics at Harvard. Then he worked at CERN, in Geneva, where scientists verified the existence of the subatomic Higgs boson. His dissertation provided the first direct measurement of the particle's width, and one of the first of its mass. Another club might conceivably hire an analyst like Graham, or Steele, or Waskett, and maybe even Spearman. But it's almost impossible to imagine any but Liverpool hiring all of them."

Spearman's job, however, is not to analyse Liverpool's football; it's to try and think of a totally new way to play football. As such, his results – if successful – could still be years away.

Eddie The Eagle-Eyed

By all accounts, Michael Edwards is known as Eddie; something that was somehow used as further evidence by Neil Ashton in his 2015 attack piece to sneer at him, as if most people in football didn't have their surnames shortened in such a manner. (Eddie also drinks coffee, and has an air-conditioned office, *the utter bastard*.) Daniel Taylor and Adam Crafton, writing about Edwards for *The Athletic* after the Reds landed the league title in June 2020, recounted a recent story from Harry Redknapp, the man who gave Edwards his first break more than a decade earlier.

"I'd met a guy who had only a few weeks to live," Redknapp said. "This poor guy was in his early 40s. He had been married only a couple of years and he knew he was dying. Someone had got in touch and said, 'Harry, he'd love to meet you. He's football mad.' So I went round to his house […] and he told me it was his dream to go to Liverpool.

"I rang Michael Edwards and, straight away, he went, 'Harry, not a problem'. I arranged a car, I got a driver. Eddie sorted everything else. There wasn't any of the, 'Oh, Harry, I'm sorry, mate, you know how busy I am', that you can get sometimes.

"He put himself out, he organised the full day and treated him incredibly. We have to remember we are in a position where we can make a difference to people's lives. Sadly, this guy died four or five weeks later. Eddie had got him into the directors' box, introduced him to everybody – Kenny Dalglish, Jürgen Klopp – the boy had the best day of his life. Loved every minute of it."

Edwards, it seems, is a nice guy. Nice Guy Eddie. (Not to be confused with the far less-Nice Guy Eddie from *Reservoir Dogs*.)

"It is a very good relationship," Klopp said of Edwards. "He is a very thoughtful person. We don't always have to have the same opinion from the first second of a conversation, but we finish pretty much all our talks with the same opinion. Or similar opinions."

Divisions

In *Mentality Monsters* I assessed, in depth, the deals that were down to the transfer committee and those personally driven by Brendan Rodgers. It did not look pretty to the manager from that time. Even a year on – and now five years down the line from Rodgers' sacking – many of the committee signings that failed under him, or were not given a chance, continue to shine elsewhere. Spaniard Luis Alberto, signed as a 20-year-old in 2013, is now one of *Serie A*'s genuine shining stars, leading the way with assists in the league, and voted the league's player of the month twice before lockdown. Compatriot Iago Aspas, signed that same summer and now aged 32 (and also perhaps not quite ready for the move to Anfield back in 2013), has scored 101 goals in Spain since returning to *La Liga* in 2014; Rodgers' pick a year later, Christian Benteke, who cost the Reds almost four times as much as Aspas, has scored five goals in all competitions *in his last three seasons.*

One deal that never really made sense to attribute to either party – such was its bizarre nature – was that last-ditch signing of Mario

Balotelli, a player Rodgers had earlier said, quite passionately, that he had zero interest in. Equally, it didn't feel like a call by the committee. In the end, Balotelli scored one sad and solitary league goal for Liverpool. While he scored goals in France, at the time of writing has scored just six league goals in *Serie A* across two spells back in his homeland in 39 games.

According to Daniel Taylor and Adam Crafton in *The Athletic* "'He [Rodgers] was wielding his veto power a little bit,' one person with knowledge of the deal recalls. "So Liverpool said to him, 'Okay, fine.' That [Balotelli] was not a deal Liverpool wanted to do but he insisted on it. Basically, it got to the point where there were a few transfers in which Brendan said, 'It is my way or the highway. I need this player and you need to back me as manager. We have lost Suarez, so this is what we need to do.'

"'They [Liverpool] said, 'Okay, that is fine, but under our model if we all fuck up together on a few transfers, it is everyone's responsibility and we share that. If you tell us you want to take the decisions, then you will have to take the responsibility for that.' He went, 'Yep, fine, I will do that.' The next season was not great and he ended up getting sacked.

"Some extremely senior sources were pretty adamant they would not have sacked him for the results that season if they had shared the responsibility more for transfers."

This is the same situation that saw Roberto Firmino, who between 2013 and 2015 had the best goal-involvement stats of any Brazilian playing in Europe bar Neymar, unwanted by Rodgers; Benteke was his man. But for the arrival of Klopp, Firmino could have gone the same way as other half-ostracised committee signings.

And so, no matter who the committee recommended, if those players were not given the chance by the manager (for legitimate reasons, or something more petty), then it was hard for the committee to succeed. All that in-fighting went out the window with the appointment of Klopp, whose ego is so in-check he doesn't need to prove himself to people within his own organisation, or harbour petty feuds and seek oneupmanship. His aim is to make use of all the brilliant people at his disposal; not to try and prove he's smarter than them.

David Sumpter, a Professor of Applied Maths and author of football analysis book *Soccermatics*, told Melissa Reddy of *The Independent:* "In terms of using analytics in the transfer market, Liverpool are some distance ahead of their competitors. What you need and what they have is a team with a full understanding of the club, working towards the same goal through use of a variety of data and knowledge to make informed decisions.

"Liverpool are well run, properly structured and have a clear identity. Without this, it wouldn't matter how brilliant Ian Graham's work is. Not only do they have the right platform for their data scientists to work, but they've empowered them and have great synergy in decision-making. There is no sole genius at Liverpool. It is not Graham or Klopp or Edwards – it is collection of all these superb minds coming together to meet objectives and generate success."

It's not widely known that Edwards was initially a data sceptic, even after working with ProZone in his early days at Portsmouth, where he also focused on video analysis. At the south coast club, the players would be eager to take kickoffs, just so they could pass the ball back and instantly improve their passing percentages, in order to make their way onto the published ProZone leaderboards. The data was therefore often just numbers, with no relevance to winning or losing football matches; whilst the manager, Harry Redknapp, was not the kind to ask meaningful questions and prod and poke the data – instead choosing to lightheartedly mock Edwards and, perhaps parodying the *Little Britain* sketch, ask what the computer said. When he met Ian Graham at Spurs, Edwards was taking Decision Technology's superior statistical information and feeding it to chairman Daniel Levy (a man who knows how to drive a hard bargain, and who may have taught Edwards a thing or two about the art of the trade); and so Edwards had to understand Graham's model. In the process, he was learning from Graham, and learning from Levy.

In November 2010, Spurs' director of football Damien Comolli moved to Liverpool as FSG's version of the sport's Billy Beane, with the Frenchman soon taking Edwards with him. But Liverpool had no access to the impressive Decision Technology model due to their exclusive deal with Spurs. After two years working with Graham, Edwards knew the importance of the model – something that restored his faith in analytics, after the largely meaningless stats generated elsewhere – even though it was still nowhere near perfect. As such, unable to get Decision Technology, he recommended FSG just go and get Graham instead.

According to *The Athletic*, "Daniel Finkelstein, who collaborated with Graham and Decision Technology for his analytical newspaper column the Fink Tank, explains how Liverpool's owner and Edwards centred their plans on recruiting Graham: 'When John W. Henry of FSG bought Liverpool, he came to the offices of Decision Technology. John wanted to hire Decision Technology for Liverpool but he could not do that as they had a contract with Tottenham. Ian took the job himself with everyone's blessing. Ian had been working on modelling for 10 years before he joined Liverpool and they secured an amazing talent'."

Now reunited at Liverpool, Edwards and Graham travelled together to the 2012 Sloan Analytics Conference, at which Graham spoke to Tom Tippett and the legendary Bill James in a conference suite overlooking FSG's Fenway Park. One of the things baseball was trying to solve was weighting certain stats across different leagues, and Graham explained to James and Tippett how his *football* model already addressed such issues; and in that moment, a nascent data sport had – in one area at least – eclipsed the sport of *Moneyball* and sabermetrics. At the home of the Boston Red Sox, in the presence of the man who pioneered baseball analytics, it was perhaps the start of the Liverpool revolution that saw FSG eventually conquer *both* sports, having ended, back in 2004, the Sox' 86-year wait for the title (a wait so long it was called the Curse of the Bambino). In 2018 the Red Sox landed their fourth World Series title of the millennium, whilst in the same year the Reds lost the Champions League final; in 2019, the Reds won the Champions League (and the Club World Cup), and in 2020, became champions of England. That is one extraordinary level of success for *any* ownership.

But Graham's model was still flawed. After two years working together, Edwards and Graham had frequently discussed all the model's shortcomings, and the lack of context to some of the data; and thus, at Liverpool, were able to build a *better* model from scratch, which they continue to develop and hone to this day. Edwards remains incredibly proud of the teamwork that has gone into building the data analysis tools the club now uses, but it would be far less powerful if the manager had no interest in its findings. For someone as talented, intelligent, passionate and charismatic as Klopp to trust in the data is the reason it then gets turned into something meaningful, which in turn led to the club becoming the champions of Europe, the world and then finally, of England.

The Future

In the aforementioned in-depth article by Daniel Taylor and Adam Crafton in *The Athletic*, the authors state: "It has been a remarkable success, underpinned by this extraordinary statistic: Liverpool's net transfer spend of £92.4m from the last five years is less than Watford's, not even half that of Brighton & Hove Albion or Aston Villa and a fair bit behind Mike Ashley's Newcastle United. There is only Crystal

Palace, Sheffield United, Southampton and Norwich City with a lower net spend in that time. Manchester City's total is £505.6m. Manchester United's £378.9m."

(It's worth noting here that the Reds' net spend on transfer fees has been incredibly low during Klopp's time, but obviously the money the club makes has been pumped more into wage rises for players, that are themselves heavily bonus-related. It's not like the owners are removing the profits.)

"'Their [Liverpool's] recent record is ridiculous, really,' one person with inside knowledge of analytics says. 'They have barely had a failed signing. I don't think that can continue, I don't think anyone is that good. If you get 15 out of 15 transfers right, it can't always be that way. He [Edwards] is over-performing and it will regress to a mean at some point'."

The truth is, that run *has* to end. However, it doesn't make it any less impressive. Using the Transfer Price Index I'd co-created with Graeme Riley in 2010, through which we calculated the current day prices for all Premier League players by working out seasonal football inflation, I devised a separate coefficient to judge the best signings of the entire Premier League era; with the model looking at how much was paid (adjusted to modern day prices); how much the player was later sold for (if applicable, and also adjusted to modern day prices); the profit or loss as both a percentage of the fee paid but also as the net figure in millions, adjusted for inflation; and crucially, how many league games the player started.

(I initially thought about working in other metrics for success, like goals scored, but what if the player was a defensive midfielder? Equally, who do you decide merits a clean sheet? – wouldn't the defensive midfielder also contribute, if not the entire XI? Similarly, it didn't seem fair to award points for trophies won, as most players will be moving to clubs that won't win trophies. Perhaps such a comparison would work between the Big Six, who usually contest these titles, although even then, the budgets of the Rich Three – both Manchester clubs, and Chelsea – often dwarfed the budgets of Liverpool, Arsenal and Spurs, and as such, the Rich Three won all but one of the league titles between 2004 and 2019; and so, someone moving to those clubs, even if a mediocre transfer, could have a winner's medal. For instance, Xabi Alonso, Fernando Torres and Luis Suarez, to name just three, were fantastic signings for Liverpool but didn't win a title; Massimo Taibi was an absolute car-crash of a keeper at Manchester United but the season in which he played four times – sharing duties with the almost equally bad Mark Bosnich and Raimond van der Gouw – saw them crowned champions. As such, I just tried to keep it simple, with the number of games played being a proxy for success on the pitch, in that if a player kept getting picked he must mostly be doing something right.)

So, someone bought for £1m in current day money and sold for £3m would be an inflation-adjusted profit of £2m, and it would be three times the original fee; which might be seen as better, in some sense, than buying someone for £25m and selling them for £29m, although the pure profit from the latter is greater, at £4m. To make it fair, playing hundreds of games had to be as important to the coefficient as selling a player for an incredible profit; although the ideal scenario was to buy young and cheap, see the player make 300 league starts, then sell him for an astronomical fee to some overly rich club just as his legs were about to go. (We stuck only to the Premier League era with all the data, as it proved harder to find accurate transfer information before 1992; and it is not an assertion that football only began in that year.)

When I last updated the coefficient in 2017, Cristiano Ronaldo's move to Manchester United came out top (on account of the sale fee then equating to over £200m, after six years of service to United), but to show the contrast, also in the top 10 was Kolo Touré's move to Arsenal, which was ludicrously cheap, and saw him play quite a lot of games (including winning the title), before he was sold for an incredible profit in relation to what he cost (almost 100 times the original fee when adjusted into what was then 2017 money). The model only really looked at players who had been sold on, or who had retired; anyone still playing was *technically* eligible (and included in the list), but unlikely to rank in the highest positions due to a lack of a sale fee and also, unless they were 35, a lack of time to rack up an extremely high number of appearances (so, for example, Jordan Henderson now, aged 30, compared to where he could rank aged 33; and more on him in a minute).

Liverpool's two top signings, as of the 2017 version, were ranked 13th and 14th out of the 4,379 player-transfers that were included (so, the same player might appear five or six times, and in some cases even more, if he had five or six moves within the Premier League; and to clarify, each *transfer* is what is ranked, not the player's overall career. So, James Milner's time at Liverpool is one entry; his time at Man City is another; and so on, back to all his previous clubs). At no.13 overall was Luis Suarez, and at 14 was Sami Hyypia – two very different players who had very different careers at the club, and succeeded in different ways. One was younger, more explosive and controversial, and left after less than four years for a phenomenal fee; the other was older, cheaper, and left for free when well into his thirties – but started over 300 Premier League games, for a transfer fee that, 18 years later, still only equated to £15m. (Imagine getting a world-class centre-back for that now.)

By 2017, the fee Liverpool received for Suarez equated to £127m, and as such, it gave an idea of why, soon after, Philippe Coutinho fetched £142m from the same Spanish club. Fernando Torres' move to Liverpool ranks 29th, on account of the sale fee equating to £117m, but his move to Chelsea – the club who *paid* that £117m – comes out as the second-worst, at 4,378th, one place ahead of Andriy Shevchenko (cost £134m, released for free) at the foot of the table. Interestingly, both Torres and Shevchenko were utterly proven superstars that Chelsea purchased as reigning champions; perhaps highlighting the difficulty of improving on successful teams, but also, the hubris wrapped up in those deals, with the owner desiring superstars rather than hungry players on the rise.

The coefficient – albeit any adjustments to its weighting could alter the results – suggested that maybe only 40% of transfers (aka Tomkins' Law) were *by some definition* successful. Most deals were neutral or failures, based on the different criteria (and that's without factoring in the wage drain). Only 40% played enough games, and/or made enough of a resale profit, to be called worthwhile, even if this would be harsh on the squad player who didn't get much game-time but scored some *priceless* goals (such as Divock Origi, for example – although his fee was not steep; but even if Origi had cost £50m, would his goals not still be worth their weight in gold?) Sometimes mediocre signings played a lot of games, and thus fare quite well in the coefficient, merely because all the other signings made by whatever mid-table club it was, to play in the same position, were even worse; and so the player got to start regularly by virtue of the fact that he was the least rubbish. But it's really difficult to make buys who either make a huge profit or play a ton of games. Equally, at any one time, about 60% of any playing squad (of 25) won't be in the XI, so that could also explain why there is a similar ratio in the findings, although the 25-man squad is more of a recent development, rather than something seen in the early Premier League years (and the coefficient covers the earlier Premier League years too). The best signings, and the best homegrown players, tend to get more games, and the worst signings often get pushed to the fringes of the squad, before being sold.

In addition, a signing like van Dijk, bought by Liverpool at the age of 26 in early 2018, for a hefty fee (albeit not quite in the top 10 for centre-backs when adjusted for inflation), would leave little scope to succeed in the model, as he is unlikely to play 400 games for the club (although he might manage 300 like Hyypia, who arrived at the same age, albeit van Dijk was five times the price in 2017 money), and it seems unthinkable that the Reds would cash in on him at any point soon while his value is sky-high. (Which is another bonus of being champions: it becomes harder for other clubs to poach your best players, in contrast to when Liverpool were finishing 5th and 6th, and unable to retain their key assets. Liverpool's own increasing wealth – prior to Covid-19 – meant it could increase wages for its successful players, whilst refusing to bring in anyone new on more than what the proven stars were already earning.)

As such, the model, like any other, is not perfect; but by the time he hangs up his boots it also wouldn't label van Dijk a flop. The coefficient was designed to reward value for money, and as much as that's still been the case at £75m, it's not the kind of objective bargain that I was trying to identify (i.e. Hyypia; and now, you'd expect Joe Gomez and Andy Robertson to be able to rise high in the rankings). So while the model is not perfect for assessing Liverpool's recent transfer activity – not least as enough time hasn't passed – it still provides some insights.

Indeed, one single early committee signing arguably helped turn Liverpool from a top four team into the best team in the world, *purely by being sold.*

Philippe Coutinho was the first big success of the then-transfer committee, which had just been given the power in January 2013 that Brendan Rodgers squandered after his utterly chaotic first transfer window as manager six months earlier. Along came Coutinho and Daniel Sturridge; the latter a clear success on the pitch until injuries diminished his talents. Where Sturridge's legs went, and his force faded, Coutinho was sold at the peak of his value, and his career – while still ladened with league titles every season in Spain and Germany – has not been as successful.

It occurred to me that Coutinho would now feature quite highly in the coefficient, when I next update it; but a provisional check* would place him way up in 4th place, behind just Ronaldo, Gareth Bale (Spurs) and Nicolas Anelka (Arsenal), and just ahead of Kolo Touré. What's interesting here, as an aside, is that Damien Comolli scouted Touré, signed Bale as director of football for Spurs, and of course, Comolli also brought Suarez, ranked just outside the top ten, to Liverpool (and indeed, took Luka Modrić, ranked 24th as a deal, to

Spurs). Along with Suarez, Comolli also gave the Reds both Edwards and Graham. Plus, of course, Jordan Henderson.

(* Coutinho would *provisionally* rank 4th, but this is without working out if other recent developments would also send other transfers into higher positions, which would almost certainly happen – although it's hard to think of anyone bought for what was £22m in 2017 money and sold for £142m in 2017 money, representing both a £120m profit *and* a markup of more than six times the fee paid when adjusted for inflation, after as clocking up almost 150 league starts. As such, Coutinho represents the perfect deal: cheap, impactful, and offloaded for a massive profit that meant losing one potential world-class player resulted in *two* soon-to-be-confirmed world-class new ones – van Dijk and Alisson – arriving.)

Indeed, even Henderson would now rank just outside the top 50, even when considering his fee was not exactly cheap; and just two more seasons of regular league football for the Reds, or a sale fee of just £20m, would promote his move to Liverpool – so mocked on many occasions – into the top 25 (assuming that countless other players are not projected upwards by a similar amount). Again, a cold coefficient cannot capture the qualities Henderson has brought to Liverpool, or cover the myriad challenges he has faced over the years, but along with Suarez and the procurement of Edwards, was one of the major things Comolli got right, that set the club on the path to glory further down the line. While Liverpool and FSG wasted plenty of money between January 2011 and January 2013, the signings of Suarez, Henderson, Coutinho and Sturridge were all huge steps in the right direction; and that includes the process of *selling* them.

Right now, there simply isn't room for a 100% success rate in transfers for Liverpool, given that the team has become almost too successful to add to; and with no regular first team players ready to be phased out. New players are still needed – albeit less urgently in 2020 after the pandemic – but any new centre-back would have to displace Joe Gomez and Joël Matip, which would not be easy, let alone ousting Virgil van Dijk. It's one thing to buy van Dijk when you have recently offloaded Martin Škrtel and Mamadou Sakho, but how do you improve on the best centre-back in the world, and his supreme young apprentice, or the increasingly important Matip? Quite frankly, you can't. So any new centre-back – if one is even sought (and someone like Fabinho isn't instead used as the fourth choice) – would almost certainly be a squad player who wouldn't get much game-time; and if thrown in on occasions, might struggle, due to lack of playing time, and no real understanding of the team dynamics. After all, even the

Reds' existing centre-backs struggle for a few games when they return to the side.

This is part of the issue facing Takumi Minamino, in addition to arriving midseason after a month of inactivity in Austria: he has to usurp one of Sadio Mané, Mo Salah and Roberto Firmino. Three years their junior, that won't happen overnight, as all three are still at the absolute peak of their physical powers, with no signs of slowing down (and elite fitness measures could keep them going a little longer, such as with Ronaldo in Italy); although Firmino could perhaps drop to his old attacking midfielder role, or Minamino might prove himself in that position. But for every game someone like Minamino plays in midfield it lessens the chances of Naby Keïta or Alex Oxlade-Chamberlain – two attacking midfielders whose success at Liverpool has been limited by both injuries and indeed, the existence of the other – less scope to prove themselves. Based purely on playing time, it's hard to see all three of these signings being labelled as successes, unless they all force their way into some new-look XI. Their talent and hunger is not in doubt; but due to previous transfer successes, there is simply less scope for all three to thrive. Despite a year out with injury, Oxlade-Chamberlain is seen as the most successful of the three right now, but a run of games for either Keïta or Minamino might diminish the view of Oxlade-Chamberlain as a successful buy. All three could end up being absolutely brilliant, but it's unlikely that all three *will* end up being absolutely brilliant.

And with every new signing, that new buy will either become a squad player (and fare badly in the coefficient) or nudge a hitherto successful buy into a more neutral ranking, as his game-time gets severed. (Of course, there can still be those non-coefficient successes, like Origi, who don't start many games but provide big moments, or who prove solid understudies.)

All this said, the advent of Covid-19, and the massive reduction of money flowing around not just the Premier League but in leagues across the world (and in global economies in general) means that there will likely be fewer transfers; and as happened following the collapse of ITV Digital in 2002 and the financial apocalypse of 2008, the average price of a Premier League footballer will fall. Back in 2017, the average price of a player had risen to 18 times what it was in 1992; and then, by 2018, it rose massively again, to 27 times to 1992 level. Now it seems likely that the average price of a player will have its sharpest Premier League-era fall, at possibly half the peak of 2018. As such, a £50m transfer in 2015 (such as Raheem Sterling's to Manchester City) had become the equivalent of a £100m signing in 2018, but is now back to £50m or so in 2020 (based purely on his value as of 2015, and not what he would be worth as a more established player in 2020). This is perhaps why Leroy Sané, with a year left on his deal, joined Bayern Munich for just an initial £44m in July 2020, and why, at around £50m, Liverpool backed out of the race they led to sign RB Leipzig's Timo Werner, given that in the current market that could now equate to £100m. (The idea with Werner was that £50m was a *reasonable* release clause for a player of his ability, but if the value of all players ends up halving, that £50m is what you would now expect to pay for a player valued at £100m a year earlier, and Werner, for all his potential, was not that man.)

And as of early July 2020, Liverpool had still not resolved a pay cut with its playing staff. As such, Klopp said it would not look good to spend £50m on a new player whilst trying to negotiate with the existing players to put some kind of scheme into place whilst the club's expected income had fallen so dramatically – as it had for all Premier League clubs – due to having to refund season ticket purchases, loss of sponsorship money, and, more pertinently, having to join all the other clubs in paying back their share of over £300m to the TV broadcasters (a situation that could apply to 2020/21, too).

While the current Liverpool squad would start to look fairly old in the summer of 2021, it should still be within peak range in 2020/21. And even in 2021, the only regulars to be in their 30s would be Jordan Henderson (31) and Gini Wijnaldum (30), and perhaps by then one of those would become more of a squad player. And with Adam Lallana leaving, and Dejan Lovren unlikely to be around in a year's time, the only other player *in the entire current squad* who would be in their thirties, aside from whoever the backup goalkeeper might be, would be James Milner.

Assholes! AKA: You Can Only Have Good Training With Good Trainers

There are many ways to make a team exceed the sum of its parts, but this chapter will focus on just a few, including some methods Jürgen Klopp adheres to. Because one thing about Liverpool's meteoric rise under the German is that none of the players arrived as world-class, and by the end of 2019/20, you could say that *at least* seven or eight now had that standing within the game. While not exactly plucked from obscurity, many of them, just a few years earlier, had barely played Premier League football or represented their countries on more than just a handful of occasions.

(Note: a few small sections of this chapter are repeated from *Mentality Monsters*, simply because they still apply – the science remains the same – although I have mostly used new examples, and added further insights. As before, see *Mentality Monsters* in full for alternative insights.)

Assholes!

While the recruitment at Liverpool has been sensational (as it was during Klopp's time at Dortmund in a way that it was not before and after), one area where the manager has taken the data and the video analysis provided by smart people at Melwood and made the process more successful is with his insistence – dating back to those jobs in Germany – of signing "no dickheads". By this, a player need not be a total nightmare to be classed a dickhead; but it's a way of weeding out the time-wasters, the bad trainers, the egotists, and those who care only about the match (the end goal) and not the *process*.

"He showed little mercy when berating co-workers. He seized on their setbacks and scoffed at their maladies. He punched at least two in the head," Noam Scheiber wrote in May 2020 for the *New York Times*. "The office etiquette in question did not belong to a swashbuckling bond trader or adrenaline-addled bouncer. It belonged to Michael Jordan, a six-time National Basketball Association champion and pop-culture icon widely regarded as the game's best player ever. As Jordan himself said of his teammates in *The Last Dance*, the 10-part documentary about his career whose last two episodes will be shown Sunday night: 'I'm going to ridicule you until you get on the same level as me. And if you don't get on the same level, then it's going to be hell for you'."

The article also quotes Robert Sutton, the Stanford University management professor, from his 2007 bestseller *The No Asshole Rule:* "Every organisation needs the 'no-asshole rule' because mean-spirited people do massive damage to victims, bystanders who suffer the ripple effects, organisational performance, and themselves."

The article continues: "According to the studies Mr. Sutton cites in his book, the problems with toxic workers range from the obvious to the subtle. Their belligerence creates costly distractions. Their treatment of co-workers increases turnover and absenteeism. When the demoralised colleagues do show up, they perform apathetically.

"One classic study of Sears employees in Chicago from the 1970s found that workers with widely disliked supervisors came to work at about the same rate as their colleagues on typical days, but that their attendance dropped significantly during a snowstorm, when they had an excuse to stay home. The study suggested that poor morale tended to destroy the so-called discretionary effort that often abounds in a healthy organisation."

In stark contrast to Mario Balotelli – the perfect example of a problem at Liverpool, because of the uniquely unprofessional way he trained, and issues such as poor timekeeping – Michael Jordan was a perfectionist, who wanted to win so badly, and who trained so hard himself (and reached such incredible heights), that he could not handle others falling short. Will Perdue, one of the players Jordan punched, is quoted in the article as saying "I started to go back at him and Eddie Nealy grabbed me from behind. Then it was abruptly over. We kept practicing." Perdue notes that Jordan got the most out of teammates by setting super-high expectations; the implication being that they felt driven towards, or perhaps shamed into, meeting them. However, it's probably not a wise tactic to deploy; and perhaps only someone of Jordan's exceptional gifts could get away with it. Obviously basketball is different from football, in that a star baller comprises 20% of his team's total, due to only five players being on the court at any one time, whereas a star outfield footballer is exactly half that, at 10%, as one of ten on the pitch. You can therefore rely on the asshole elite baller to win you games more than you can the dickhead footballer.

A genius basketball player can have more influence in a game, but also, due to being 20% of the team, perhaps also be more disruptive. The *New York Times* articles adds, "Jeff Van Gundy, who coached the New York Knicks during Jordan's last three seasons in Chicago, said most players who doled out such lashings 'would be marked with resentment' … 'You'd have to be that level of great to lead that way,' said Mr. Van Gundy, adding that the approach would probably backfire even for an excellent but not transcendently gifted player."

"… More than 15 years after Jordan retired from professional basketball – for the third time – the mix of power and grace he displayed on the court remains a breathless thrill. But his leadership style, such as it was, feels outdated.

"In the intervening years, a chorus of experts has warned employers, investors and board members against tolerating such cruel or demeaning behaviour. Academics and government officials have used terms like 'toxic worker' or 'superstar harasser' in preaching vigilance against flawed if seemingly talented performers."

Why Klopp Didn't Even Consider Balotelli

The Athletic's Liverpool FC experts, James Pearce and Simon Hughes, wrote about Mario Balotelli in late 2019, as part of an examination of what went wrong for Brendan Rodgers in his final 15 months at Liverpool: "By Christmas [of his debut season], some of Liverpool's players were shocked to find that Balotelli was still learning the names of some of his team-mates, though whether he was bothering to learn them at all was up for debate. Players who lived close by in Formby initially offered to take turns in giving Balotelli lifts to training after he was banned from driving. One of those tells a story about him not recognising Joe Allen when Balotelli sat in the passenger seat one morning and Allen was in the back even though he'd been at the club for several months.

"[Steven Gerrard] recognised his talent and the potential to be 'world class' [but] he described him as 'unmanageable' because of his mentality and the people around him. He was regularly late for training and always wanting attention [...] Though Liverpool's players didn't mind him and sometimes his antics provided light relief in the stresses of a football season, for Gerrard, he simply 'didn't train hard enough – you were always fighting a losing battle. He did too many things wrong'."

As such, even though Liverpool didn't have many striking options when Jürgen Klopp arrived in 2015, and were in the market for attacking options in 2016, the manager barely acknowledged the existence of the Italian striker when he returned from loan at AC Milan. Balotelli wasn't allowed to train with the players, and did not go on the preseason tours. There was simply no point in entertaining the circus that was Balotelli; and instead, Klopp purchased Sadio Mané. Unlike Rodgers, Klopp didn't have the hubris to think he could be the one to *finally* steer the Italian striker onto the right path; the time, the effort, and the distraction, in addition to the damage failing to correct bad habits would cause, were just antithetical to the ethos he wanted to engender.

Eden Hazard's move to Real Madrid provides another interesting example of how superstars can do more harm than good. Hazard seemed to spend his entire Chelsea career aching for the chance to go to the *La Liga* giants, albeit – as arguably the most individually gifted player in the league – he had a habit of taking entire seasons off, and failed to score half the goals of which he appeared capable. Costing up to £150m with clauses, and almost 29, Hazard turned up to Real Madrid in the summer of 2019 *seven kilos* overweight; an even more startling amount when you consider his short stature. The pictures were shocking; he was carrying more timber than a gang of lumberjacks. "If I'm on vacation," he said, "I'm on vacation … I'm someone who puts on weight very quickly but I can lose it fast as well." Various former Chelsea players have stated Hazard often dined on hamburgers and pizzas.

Alas, a year into his stay in Spain (as of July 2020) he'd scored a single league goal, albeit the season had obviously been delayed by Covid-19. He admitted he had been a flop, but that he'd be better in his second season, albeit by then he'd be in his thirties. All of which leads to the conclusion, *why not turn up in good shape to start with?*

Neymar is another superstar who has not turned his ability into the sustained success of Lionel Messi and Cristiano Ronaldo; like Hazard, the Brazilian was supposed to be an heir to their thrones, but he has largely wasted his talent in the past few years. While it could be argued that Mo Salah is another heir to the thrones who hasn't pushed on to the levels expected after his frankly ludicrous 2017/18 – when he got 44 goals in the season – it's worth noting that Salah, rather than being the standout star, has become a vital cog in the ultimate machine; and has gone from winning nothing in 2017/18 to winning the Champions League, Club World Cup and Premier League across 2019 and 2020. Thankfully he has swapped simply winning individual awards to winning the biggest *team* awards, in an age where the individual is still ludicrously fetishised (and individual awards are proliferating to a nauseating degree, to the point where there seems to be an award ceremony each week). In terms of raw ability and even pace, Neymar outstrips Salah. In terms of who had the world at their feet at 21, it was Neymar. In terms of who you'd want in your team – who is not a dickhead – it's Salah.

Now 28, Neymar, in three years in France, has played 20, 17 and 15 league games respectively, albeit with the season prematurely ended in 2019/20; poor "attendance" figures from a player in a team designed to win the Champions League, on account of petrodollar PSG being so financially far ahead of everyone else that they win the French title almost by default. What a great superstar he is, with his entourage, his *couture du jour*, at the club that claims it wants to turn itself into the most fashionable in the world, due to its location in Paris.

But seriously, *what a load of utter bollocks*. These are the superstars that Liverpool, and Klopp, look to avoid like the plague (a phrase that, alas, hits too close to the bone in 2020).

The BBC reported in February – before Covid-19 had torn through Europe and then his native Brazil – that Neymar had taken to

Instagram to declare that, this year, "he would not – repeat NOT - be attending the Rio Carnival."

"Every year, since 2014," they reported, "he has been either unfit or suspended around this time of year – which coincides closely with the carnival and his sister's birthday. This year was to be different. Until the inevitable happened. A second yellow in the 92nd minute of Paris St-Germain's 4-3 win against Bordeaux on Sunday means the Brazilian will now be suspended for Saturday's home game against Dijon.

"In 2015, he was suspended from action for Barcelona, around his sister's birthday in March. In 2016, the same happened. In 2017, he had a muscle issue, which saw him ruled out around his sister's birthday. And in both 2018 and 2019, he was at home, recovering from metatarsal injuries. However, we are not for one moment suggesting Neymar purposefully got himself sidelined so he could attend the carnival.

"There was some speculation last March when he chose to return to Brazil and go to the carnival, rather than recovering in Paris and he responded by saying: 'I do not think that my social life hinders my performance on the pitch'. Either way, this latest incident – a seemingly quite unnecessary second yellow in injury time – has sent the rumour mill into overdrive once again!"

In 2019, the Brazilian national team – for almost a decade built around the Neymar myth – finally won their first Copa América during his career; indeed, the first in 12 years, since two years before he first played for Santos. Perhaps tellingly, however, *Neymar was not part of the successful squad*. Some guy that the Brazilians don't seem to revere anywhere near as much – some unfashionable oik – was the lynchpin. And that lynchpin spent 2019 and 2020 winning every trophy imaginable, for club and country.

Bobby Dazzles
Gary Neville, speaking on Sky after the Reds' 1-0 win at Spurs in January, said of Liverpool: "The whole defence is outstanding, the goalkeeper is brilliant. They are doing everything a championship [winning] team should be doing. They're brilliant to watch."

But he singled out Roberto Firmino, adding: "Any manager in the world would have him in their team. I think he's absolutely incredible, Firmino. He's selfless, brilliant, scores goals, sets things up. They can link off him, makes all the right runs, just an outstanding player."

Writing that week in *The Guardian*, Barney Ronay stated: "Firmino is a relentless presence on days such as these, a monster of the decisive away goal. This was his ninth goal this season, all of them away from Anfield. Five have been winners, a big-game, daddy-goal, title-driving level of efficiency.

"He has never been a poacher. There was some talk last summer that Liverpool might even buy a new star centre-forward, someone to pump up those numbers. But Firmino's lack of starriness disguises the fact he is the perfect part in this team, with the ability to press, to hold possession, to drop deep and sweep the ball either way, a player who has proved almost as revolutionary to the frontline in this Liverpool era as Virgil van Dijk has to the back.

"What is he anyway? Firmino has been described as a false 9, but this doesn't really do justice to it. If you want to go down the numberwang route he's a bit of everything: 9, 10, 8, 11, even 4; a post-modern kind of striker for a disruptive age. Twice here he produced that swooping Capoeira-style trap, pulling a long pass out of the air. Nobody else does this. It's his move, the Firmino Sweep, his own cross-cultural take on the long-ball flick-on."

Firmino, perhaps more than anyone, represents Kloppian football. Yes, he does the occasional fancy flick and kung-fu kick, but he is defined by his work-rate, his professionalism, his desire.

A couple of years ago I publicly stated that Pep Guardiola would prefer Firmino to Sergio Agüero at City, and while that obviously drew some derision, I feel it remains one of my better assertions based on the passage of time – despite the Argentine's undisputed greatness *as a finisher*. (Certainly better than my wild assertions that Sean Dundee would eclipse Maradona, that Torben Piechnik was the new Alan Hansen, and that Neil Ruddock would be able to run 10 yards.)

Agüero obviously scores the greater number of goals (although also takes penalties), and in fairness, started to work harder under the Catalan manager after looking like he'd get cast aside, but even so, Firmino works *much harder still*, and links play in a superior manner. Plus, he's less prone to injury. Strangely, Firmino still isn't adored in Brazil, in part because he never played in their top division, moving to Germany in his teens; and so there are few local advocates. But with Firmino up front and Alisson in goal, Brazil won that Copa América, for the first time in a dozen years. For all Neymar's showboating, Firmino *gets results*. And he doesn't go missing for months on end.

And that's all you can ultimately judge any player on. Does the team win when he plays?

It also comes back to how good players are in training, and how they help with the social multiplier effect. In Germany, when interviewing potential new signings, Klopp used to ask strikers if they'd be happy coasting in training as long as they got two goals at the weekend; and if they said yes – as many did (after all, wasn't the point to do it in games?) – they were instantly dismissed as candidates. To me, this sounds a bit like Sergio Agüero. It might be fine for some teams, but not for a Klopp team; and Klopp is all about improving players, and training as hard as you play. And training as hard as you play *is the very thing that improves players*. After all, after inflation, not one of them arrived at Liverpool for the kind of money Agüero cost City; nor did they have such a stellar reputation.

When, in 2019, Agüero became the leading overseas scorer in English football, Micah Richards, who was at City when the Argentine first arrived, said: "Looking back now it seems crazy, but when I first trained with Sergio Agüero after he joined Manchester City in 2011, I did not instantly think 'superstar'. Sometimes when a new player arrives at your club, you see him in action with your own eyes and just think 'wow'. That was happening a lot at City at the time, because of the kind of big signings we were making that were transforming the club, but it was not the case with Sergio. When I first saw him, I didn't actually think he was that good … It is not as if I was expecting him to be dribbling past four or five players or anything, but I was marking him a lot of the time and he did not really do anything at all."

You cannot doubt Agüero's finishing, albeit in a team that dominated the league most during in his time in England. But the one thing City have struggled with over the past decade is individual defending, despite spending absolute fortunes on defenders. Perhaps they don't do as much back four work as other clubs, and obviously full-backs these days are required to attack more than defend in the elite teams. Since 2014, City have spent over half a billion pounds (*without* the adjustment of inflation) on defenders and goalkeepers: João Cancelo, Angeliño, Aymeric Laporte, Danilo, Benjamin Mendy, Kyle Walker, Ederson, John Stones, Oleksandr Zinchenko, Claudio Bravo, Nicolás Otamendi and Eliaquim Mangala.

In 2017/18 money – at the time when Virgil van Dijk cost £75m – Mangala cost an eye-watering £106m, and was still on the staff when Guardiola took charge (Mangala finally left in 2019), even if it wasn't the manager's mistake in the transfer market. But Stones, at £74.3m, was virtually the same price as van Dijk; while Otamendi, at £62.1m, was very expensive too. Then come Cancelo, Laporte, Mendy and Walker, all signed by Guardiola for between £50m-£60m. Laporte aside, who has markedly improved? (Walker has also been a good signing.)

By contrast, Liverpool's best back four under Klopp cost less than £100m when adjusted to 2017/18 money, the year it was fully assembled; while you could replace Joe Gomez with Joël Matip and shave another few million pounds off.

So why have so many City defenders regressed? Could it be at least partly linked to Agüero being a bit of a lazy trainer?

In *Mentality Monsters* I wrote: "In Scotland, Virgil van Dijk used to train on a daily basis against Teemu Pukki and Georgios Samaras, while the top scorers outside Celtic – the strikers he faced on matchday – were Kris Boyd, John Sutton, Billy Mckay, Adam Rooney, Nadir Çiftçi, Anthony Andreu, Greg Stewart and Niall McGinn. It's clear from that list of mostly *who the hell are theys* that this was hardly the most testing of environments for the giant Dutchman, with such players unlikely to be household names outside of Scotland. (Occasionally van Dijk may have played against a team like Barcelona, but they'd ship seven goals in a serious mismatch – even if, as an individual, he'd win plaudits.)"

Obviously Pukki has gone on to have a pretty good late-blossoming career with Norwich (another who took his time to reach the very top), but he scored just seven goals in his one full season at Celtic in 2013/14. It was a gradual process for van Dijk, improving steadily with every step up in quality he has faced, including only becoming a regular for the Dutch national side shortly before joining Liverpool. Even when he joined the Reds, few in the media thought he was a world-class superstar; indeed, many questioned the fee. With hindsight, everyone agrees that signing him was a no-brainer. (Personally speaking, I was very much behind the signing at the time, having been mightily impressed with his full range of abilities in the cluster of games the Reds played against the Saints in his final year or so on the south coast, including the League Cup semi-finals. His pace, and his reading of the game, stood out, but also his technical skills. But even so, his *stature* has seemed to exponentially expand.)

People attribute playing alongside van Dijk as the reason why Gomez, Matip and even Dejan Lovren have improved, and the fear is that it would all collapse if the big Dutchman was out injured. But in that same period of time, Trent Alexander-Arnold has matured, Andy Robertson has improved, and in Alisson and Fabinho, Liverpool added protection in front and behind the centre-backs (Fabinho has even deputised successfully for van Dijk). In addition, all of those players now train on a daily basis – in intensive sessions – against Mo Salah, Sadio Mané, Roberto Firmino and various tricky midfielders; and that will surely improve those defenders more than – to go back to the Reds' options of just a few years earlier – training against Rickie Lambert, who wasn't very mobile (and not that special), and Mario Balotelli, who liked to do things like score own goals in practice matches.

When I hear players talk about other players improving in training, it's usually framed as a younger player learning from an older one who plays in the same position, often by *watching* them. This is true, of course, but playing intense training matches against other elite players is perhaps even more of a development tool. A striker can learn from watching Salah in finishing practice (and Salah himself was a notoriously poor finisher as a younger player, who had to spend extra training time focusing on improving), but how much does someone like Gomez or Alexander-Arnold improve by facing Salah, Mané, Firmino *et al* in fiercely contested encounters at Melwood?

The Flynn effect only made sense to me – as a possible explanation about why so many cheap, low-key signings turned into superstars – after reading about how intense training was under Klopp at Dortmund. As such, I discussed it in *Mentality Monsters*, but it bears repeating. The Flynn effect dates back to 1998, when James R. Flynn, an Emeritus Professor of Political Studies at the University of Otago, noted that the IQs of certain societies improve due to the way knowledge is shared. (This has essentially become the basis for what's also known as the social multiplier effect.) An example Flynn used in his work related to basketball, and how the sport changed rapidly with the onset of regular televised games. It led to an increase in kids playing the sport, and of course, they would try to emulate what they were seeing on television. Angela Duckworth discussed the Flynn effect in her seminal book *Grit: Why Passion And Resilience Are The Secrets To Success*: "The kids started trying left-handed layups, crossover dribbles, graceful hook shots, and other skills that were routine for the star players on TV". As each individual improved, so did those they played with and against. They learnt from watching, but then took those skills out onto courts, where *everyone* had the chance to improve.

In this time of coronavirus, a parallel would be the notion of a dose-dependent contagion: the more of the virus you are exposed to – the more *intense* the exposure – the more likely it is to seriously affect you; just as a more virulent strain would also have a greater impact than a weaker version. (So, a mixture of time and intensity.) In the case of football training, the better those around you, and the more time you spend in their company during practice (but also, around their general professionalism away from the pitch), the more you can improve – providing you are giving your all in the process, rather than just being passive. If a player just messes around in training, no one improves. Perhaps it could be argued that those on his side during the practice match (or various drills) have to work harder, and exert themselves more to compensate; but certainly the defenders facing Balotelli, if all he was trying to do was score an own goal (and admittedly, this wasn't all he ever did), won't have gained a thing. And so, even if Balotelli was then sensational on match days (which, alas, he largely wasn't, but potentially *could* be), the entire preparation wouldn't have been as good. The team would not be improving both in its shared wavelengths in an attacking sense and also in the process of testing and improving the defence (and after all, a training exercise is essentially like a scientific experiment – albeit one where the variables can never be identically replicated in the way that you can control for everything in a laboratory – in that the idea is to see if it fails, and where it fails, and why it fails; and if you don't test it properly, you'll never know). Another analogy is sparring partner in boxing: if you have someone who just stands there and lets you punch them repeatedly, and never throws a punch back, you may feel good about yourself, but will not be prepared for a proper fight. The better the sparring partner – as long as he doesn't crush you to the point where you are a physical and mental wreck incapable of entering the ring (in which case, *he* should be the professional boxer) – the better you become. As such, players will learn from watching their teammates; but more pertinently, from testing themselves *against* them (and again, as long as those training opponents don't crush them to the point where they are physical and mental wrecks; or just go around breaking legs from being too hyped up).

Defender Neven Subotić, talking about training a couple of seasons into Klopp's reign at Dortmund, told Rafael Honigstein for the book *Bring The Noise*: "Training felt like war. The starting eleven playing v subs. By the middle of the week, you sort of knew the line-ups. You can't imagine how difficult these games were. You were used to having a bit of space and air to breathe but that was all gone. Everyone attacked the ball, everyone defended. Everyone pressed. These games were as hard as the real ones, perhaps even harder."

Legendary Liverpool coach Ronnie Moran used to bemoan "Monday to Friday players", who'd then go missing in the game at the weekend; an understandable gripe. They were excellent in training, but either couldn't handle the occasion of the game, or maybe were more suited to smaller-sided games, around which Liverpool's ethos was built. (As an ex-semi-pro, I have some sympathy: I was always much better at five-a-sides, as I was two-footed, had good touch and a turn of pace with speed off the mark, so could operate in tight areas; but was average in height, and so longer sprints on bigger pitches were harder work, and I was not the strongest or bravest, and was absolutely rubbish in the air. The "not above head-height" rule helped me a lot. Also, in five-a-sides you didn't face studs-up flying tackles – usually just fair block-tackling – so the emphasis was on skill and technique.) In the late 1980s and early '90s, Mike Marsh was often highlighted as being the best player in training with Liverpool, almost as a criticism; but looking back he seemed suited to five-a-sides: technically excellent, but not very big and not very fast. Obviously this is not ideal for match days. But perhaps players like Marsh, and others before him, were part of the Flynn effect at Liverpool: almost like sparring partners, who tested the others during the week, even if they themselves, for whatever reason, never quite made the grade on match days (particularly in an era when smaller technical players were not in vogue; someone like Peter Beardsley had to be truly brilliant to succeed, and even then, he sometimes got left out against the brutal teams like Wimbledon).

By all accounts, training at Manchester City is also pretty intense. Thomas Müller told *The Athletic*'s Raphael Honigstein in February 2020 about what it was like to train under Guardiola at Bayern Munich. "To exert the kind of dominance we had under Guardiola for most of the time, you need to work extremely hard in training. That's the problem. It's incredibly exhausting mentally. You need to repeat things – repeat, repeat, repeat, until they're second nature. For Pep, it was normal to push his players that much. Other coaches have different ways of working […] I understand why some found our extreme dominance under Guardiola boring but that sort of total control can't be reproduced as a carbon copy. You can't say, 'They've learnt all that stuff from Pep. They simply have to keep playing that way.' That's not the issue. You have to work at it every single day."

Under Klopp at Liverpool it's much the same, albeit with more light relief that can make such intense training *fun*. (Just not the light relief that Balotelli used to provide, that undermined the entire endeavour.) The coaching staff at Liverpool are hard taskmasters; but they can smile, too.

Not only was someone like Agüero lazy (if perhaps less so more recently, once Guardiola got to him), but with his age and injury issues he's probably unable to train at full pace, even if he wanted to. Training is the absolute bedrock of a football team; and in addition to technical and tactical improvements, a player who is *fitter* can cover more ground, and therefore sprint harder for longer, and more easily appear to be in two places at once. This is another area where Klopp has turned Liverpool from below-average into elite.

Having super-fit players is indeed like fielding 14 or 15 at times, if they are prepared to make the forward runs *and also get back*. A player who does only one of the two will be less effective for the team overall, unless others seriously compensate for his "half" game. Someone like Gini Wijnaldum will burst forward for Liverpool, but in keeping with Klopp's old adage, he will only do so if he knows he can get back again (which, almost always, he does). And of course, this ties in with versatility too: there's less point Wijnaldum bursting forward if he wasn't a player with over 100 career goals to his name, other than to provide passing options. The fact that, if the game calls for it, he'll sprint even further forward, deep into the box, means that Liverpool suddenly have a midfielder who can finish like a forward. Without elite fitness, he cannot make such a run; and if he tried, he'd be unable to get back if the move broke down.

If Wijnaldum sprinted all that way forward but then only walked back, Liverpool's midfield could be more easily overrun. The quicker he gets back to make up the numbers, the harder it is for the opposition to make any brief numerical advantage count. And it's one thing having the *desire* to do these things (which is essential), but you also need Olympian conditioning. You can then outnumber the opposition when you attack but also outnumber them again if you get back quicker.

There are further examples of problematic issues from training across Manchester, at the red half. In Mark Ogden's detailed ESPN article from December 2019 about what was going wrong at United, there was an interesting insight into how the decline started so rapidly: "It was chaos under David Moyes," one former United player told ESPN FC, about the manager that replaced Alex Ferguson in 2013. Another recalled how the "training was shit in Australia" during the early weeks of the Scot's reign.

"'He told us that he would make us fitter. We had just won the Premier League by 11 points, but we were a group of players who would always strive to be better, so we bought into it,' said a former player. 'But training ... was boring and unchallenging. Under Sir Alex [Ferguson], we would warm up in boxes, with one-touch passing, and it was intense and competitive. Under David, it became two-touch and our technique diminished'."

Most importantly, it sounds like it was no longer *competitive*. If competitive, the technique is honed and the fitness partly takes care of itself.

United's fitness also diminished over the coming seasons, to the point where Jose Mourinho – once a trailblazer – left a team that looked stuck in the past. In December 2018, following the Portuguese's dismissal, *The Times* ran a piece about how Mourinho's United were simply not as fit as other teams. United ranked 16th out of 20 for total kilometres covered, and 16th again for total sprints. (Or, if they *were* as fit, they simply weren't showing it.)

Indeed, two players from United's history show the talent myth to be just what it is – a myth. When the work – and desire – required to stay at the top wanes, players can resemble amateurs. Between 1970 and 1971, with George Best approaching his mid-20s, he registered his fifth consecutive season scoring more than 20 goals, although the off-field issues started to arise. He was still making 40 league appearances a season, although he failed to turn up for training for a whole week in January 1972, as he instead spent his time with Miss Great Britain 1971, Carolyn Moore. (And let's face it, which of us delusional straight males hasn't spent a week with a Miss Great Britain at some point? It's a common problem we all face.) He stopped training regularly, and went missing – as in *genuinely AWOL* – in December 1972 to party at various London nightclubs, while the club had no idea where he was. Still only 26, the goals dried up, and he played fewer and fewer games, until he finally left United. His next stops were the Jewish Guild in South Africa, Stockport County, Cork Celtic, Los Angeles Aztecs, Fulham, Fort Lauderdale Strikers, Hibernian, San Jose Earthquakes, Bournemouth, Brisbane Lions and Tobermore United. He was supposed to be one of the most talented British players *ever*, but without training regularly, and lacking motivation – in addition to the blight of alcoholism – he was washed up before even hitting his potential peak. Mere talent alone got him nowhere, once the hard work stopped.

A decade ago, Ravel Morrison was touted as the most talented player to come through the ranks at United since Best, yet he never played a league game for the club, with Alex Ferguson offloading him, having previously called him the best young player he'd ever seen. Morrison has been at West Ham United, Birmingham City, Queens Park Rangers, Cardiff City, Lazio, Queens Park Rangers again, Atlas, Östersund, Sheffield United and now Middlesbrough. Between 2011 and 2015, Morrison found himself entangled in various legal proceedings relating to acts of abusive behaviour, albeit he was cleared of some of those charges. Having turned 27, Morrison had just 100 league games to his name, across all those clubs, in various countries, often in weak leagues or divisions.

Back in 2012, when offloading the player to one of his fawning coterie, Ferguson had told West Ham manager Sam Allardyce that Morrison was "A brilliant footballer. Brilliant ability. Top class ability. Needs to get away from Manchester and start a new life."

"The genius of Ravel Morrison," Allardyce drooled, after the player scored against Spurs. "That's a genius goal for me. You'll struggle to see a better goal than that this season." It was one of only three he bagged for the club.

Five years later Allardyce described Morrison as "the biggest waste of talent" he had worked with. Yet even in 2019, Chris Wilder at Sheffield United was prepared to take a punt on him. However, Morrison then left for Middlesbrough on loan, without playing a single game for the South Yorkshire club. So many football people seem in awe of Morrison's 'natural ability' – even now – yet for all the attempts to get the best out of him, he's had a few good games in a decade, that suggest he's now just a *myth*. Had he not been so fêted in his youth, would anyone care? At the very time he was extolling the virtues of Morrison, Ferguson turned down the chance to sign Jordan Henderson, a player with far less 'natural talent'.

But talent is not a constant.

Joe Cole was similar to Morrison, albeit someone who achieved far more in his career. But by the time he turned up at Liverpool he was not physically able to do the things that saw him labelled England's most gifted young player, again by Ferguson. Cole, a fading force, scored just four goals in his final two seasons with Chelsea, and yet in 2010 Liverpool paid him a massive £100,000-a-week to tap into that famed natural ability. But if the body can no longer respond, or the heart isn't there to keep training to elite levels, what good is the talent? The overriding memory of Cole at Liverpool is of a player hunched over, looking like he might puke. (As an aside, he seems a surprisingly good pundit for someone who never seemed very articulate as a player; proof that people can grow more intelligent with time and effort, if in possession of a growth mindset.)

Henderson has eclipsed Morrison to a *staggering* degree, but also arguably eclipsed Cole at his best, too. Yes, all three are different types of players, but essentially all are midfielders who attack, with all three starting off as wingers or wide midfielders. Henderson has spent a decade as a Premier League player; but crucially, the past few years have seen him training at an elite level, playing at an elite level, and now aged 30, has over 450 club career appearances to his name, and over 50 caps for England. All that physical and mental *testing* – day after day, game after game, allied to a fantastic attitude – all adds up to the reason why he got better as he approached his thirties. Can you just plug a 'natural talent' like Morrison back into a Premier League team aged 27 and expect them to suddenly find that old magic? No. Because Morrison has lost out on a decade of additional elite education. If talent was all that mattered, it *would* be possible. Indeed, if talent was a constant, then it would be *automatic*. But across the world, players with a quarter of Morrison's ability at 19 have developed far greater abilities than him by the age of 27. How good you are at 19 only matters if you continue to work at your game; you have an *advantage* at that stage, but staying at that level, let alone improving, is not a divine right.

In 2008, Nathan Luscombe was the cocky kid who showboated and lorded it over another young player from the same Premier League academy in the north east on Sky's *Soccer Am Skill Skool*. (A show that obviously needed avoiding due to its oh-so-cool spelling, but now provides some fascinating reminiscences via YouTube.) Three years later the skinny loser in that battle of free-styling was getting a big-money transfer, while the victor – Luscombe – was released by his club and ended up at Hartlepool United, where he turned up for preseason training several stone overweight; even later describing himself as a "sumo wrestler". He made five starts for Hartlepool, before again returning after preseason grossly out of shape – think Neil Ruddock doubling his daily calorie intake – which left the manager, Neale Cooper, "raging" and "unable to speak to him". By 2012, aged 23, Luscombe was a non-league player. The player who lost that battle of skill, as all the others mocked him (albeit in the name of 'banter'), was Jordan Henderson.

While issues with alcohol, eating and discipline can be due to underlying mental and emotional issues (and even footballers often have things more important than *football* going on in their lives), it also requires a special kind of mindset to rise to the top and stay at the top. What would psychiatrists say about Hazard turning up to his dream move in terrible shape, as if to self-sabotage? Could you imagine Henderson or Firmino doing the same?

Lonergan On Again
One great story from the Jürgen Klopp era is how Andy Lonergan somehow ended up a Liverpool player at the age of 35, to fill the position of third choice goalkeeper. After spells at Preston, Darlington, Blackpool, Wycombe, Swindon, Leeds United (twice), Bolton, Fulham, Wolves, Middlesbrough and Rochdale he joined Liverpool to provide back up on the pre-season tour of America, before injury to Alisson – after Kamil Grabara had just gone out on a season-long loan to Huddersfield Town – turned it into a permanent move. Unlikely to ever actually play a meaningful games for the club, he still provided an insight into just how good the attitude is in training.

"I don't want to say just being among this group is enough because if I don't train well I am disappointed and I want the next day to come around so I can put that right," Lonergan told Paul Joyce of *The Times* in February 2020. "A 'well done' from the lads, a 'you're on fire today' shout … that's the reward for me.

"It could be from Mo or Millie [James Milner]. That is another motivation because if you are on their team, say Millie, Hendo [Jordan Henderson] or Virgil [van Dijk], you don't want to let them down. You have to perform because they are not shy of giving you a rollocking.

"That is just the standard. If Mo gives the ball away, they are going to be onto Mo. That is why they are doing as well as they are. The standards are ridiculous."

In terms of what Klopp insists on when signing players, Lonergan proves the point. "You get people and players at clubs who say: 'See him, he's not a trainer, he doesn't fancy it, he just plays on a Saturday.' Well, here, if you don't train [well], you don't play. Simple. The professionalism is unbelievable. I have been guilty in the past of thinking: 'They've got it easy those Premier League boys. They are not playing every midweek, they have the best travel etc.' But the schedule is absolutely relentless and add to that the training is never less than 100 per cent. The training pitch is where they make the Saturday easier. It is like the boxer who says hard work is the camp, the enjoyment is the fight. It is the same here.

"My friends will say: 'Who is not the best person? Who is this or who is that?' I mean this: it is the most honest, down-to-earth squad that I have ever been in. People might find that hard to believe, but they are such genuine, good lads. There is just one goal for all of them."

In other words, there are no dickheads, no assholes. Just English, European and world champions, everywhere you look.

Part Three

Injury-Ravaged Reds Rack Up More All-Time Records

Liverpool's resources were so stretched after a ludicrous December schedule that the bench against Sheffield United contained a 16-year-old, two 18-year-olds and a young centre-back recalled from a loan in the German second division, with a combined total of *zero* league starts for the Reds. The result? With the first XI likely to be tired due to no possible rotation, they still ran up the fourth-highest number of completed passes ever seen in a Premier League match (since Opta began recording data in 2003), and a thumping 2-0 victory when Jürgen Klopp's men possibly didn't even get into third gear.

In total the Reds made 969 passes, at an accuracy rate of 90.1% – not quite enough to overtake the 1,015 played by Manchester City against Swansea in April 2018. Duncan Alexander of Opta noted that Liverpool made more passes in the second half than they managed in 14 of 20 *entire* league games under Roy Hodgson. Suddenly, a mere decade felt like a lifetime.

But this was one more statistic that showed that the massive possession advantage City used to have over Liverpool – with Pep Guardiola's men masters of keeping the ball – had been whittled away, so that Liverpool's different strengths could help them to overtake City on the whole. Liverpool were now the more balanced of the two teams, with far superior physicality allied to all the skill and guile.

On the injury list along with Fabinho were Joël Matip, Dejan Lovren, Alex Oxlade-Chamberlain, Naby Keïta, Xherdan Shaqiri, Rhian Brewster and Nathaniel Clyne, while new signing Takumi Minamino was ineligible. So that made nine senior players absent; Keïta's injury occurring in the warm-up, to further disrupt Klopp's plans.

Liverpool's Defensive Brilliance

When he had his leg broken at Burnley by Ben Mee in December 2018, Joe Gomez was in the best form of his nascent career; arguably the best young centre-back in Europe (and I'd include Matthijs de Ligt as being his inferior). While Matip then had an outstanding 2019 from an individual point of view, and the team still won games, the defence was never as resolute as when Gomez was in the team. After 15 matches of 2018/19 the Reds had conceded an almost impossibly low total of just six goals – yet 16 were conceded in the next 23 games after Gomez's injury; still impressive, and title-winning numbers, but the absence of the young central defender, with quality on the ball and pace to burn, had a big impact.

Gomez returned to the team at the start of 2019/20 but lacked the confidence and rhythm he'd displayed the previous season. It's always a worry when a young player has a long-term absence, and then when they return looking a little shaky there's the worry that the self-belief will be drained for good; but after returning to the side on a regular basis following the injuries to both Matip and Lovren, Gomez helped the club to match its best clean-sheet sequence in 14 years, with seven in a row.

He was possibly Liverpool's best defender in the first half of 2018/19, with Matip the best across the calendar year of 2019 – then Gomez arguably took the crown back in late 2019 and early 2020. A big part of the reason is the one constant in all this: Virgil van Dijk, who is simply *the best defender on the planet*.

I'd argue that it was only in his first six months at the club that van Dijk actually shone head and shoulders above everyone else, albeit after a shaky few first games where the Reds conceded goals, and he conceded a costly late penalty against Spurs. His quality was apparent from day one, but he was rusty after several weeks without a game for Southampton, which followed half a season out with a serious injury in 2016/17.

Within six months at Liverpool he'd dragged everyone else up towards his level, but since the start of 2018/19 he has been the one giving 8.5/10 displays *every week*, without fail – no matter who has partnered him – while Matip won the man of the match award in the Champions League final, as part of a run of standout displays; and Gomez excelled before and after his broken leg. Even Dejan Lovren had games where he was Liverpool's best defender. And of course, in all these conclusions I'm referring purely to the *art of defending*, and at Liverpool it's about so much more than that. What van Dijk provides transcends mere defending, in that he projects calmness to the whole team.

On the more proactive side of the game, Gomez gives the team the pace and composure to bring the ball out of defence and clear the first line of opposition press. Unlike Matip, Gomez tends to stop there, after a short but devastating burst; the ex-Schalke man will tend to go on fantastic mazy dribbles that often end on the edge of the opposition area (sometimes – purely due to the length of his legs – looking as coordinated as a baby giraffe encountering an improbably copious spillage of Swarfega, but almost always incredibly effective, and with plenty of skill). By contrast, Gomez brings the ball out of defence to zip a pass into midfield or the forwards (at which he is improving all the time), almost in the same way Alex Oxlade-Chamberlain makes 10-yard gains towards the edge of the opposition area.

Aerial Is A Key Point of Difference

Obviously Matip, as the Reds' tallest player, has the biggest advantage when it comes to height and aerial dominance. Based on a minimum of six Premier League appearances in the 2019/20 season, calculated at the two-thirds juncture, Matip was the most successful Premier League player for winning aerial duels, at a whopping 89%; with only one other player above 80%. (To qualify for all these lists, I set the minimum requirements at six games played, and having contested at least 20 aerial duels.) It's impossible to overstate the improvements Liverpool have made in the aerial side of the game, without resorting to adding big full-backs or giant target-men. The front three remain fairly diminutive, and the full-backs are of average height (although Trent Alexander-Arnold now looks closer to 6'0" than the 5'9" he has been listed at since he was 18.)

During the early days of Klopp's tenure, as he worked with a series of aerially-challenged players, I analysed the heading success rates across the entire Premier League, and there was – as expected – a clear correlation between height and the number of headed duels successfully won. This was to counter those who insisted to me that small players can be just as good in the air, if they are good jumpers. But for every inch in height over 5'9", the average aerial duel success rate increased; after all, it's about *probabilities*. Small players have to be able to time their jump perfectly, and while attackers can obviously do that on occasions, it's not so easy for small defenders – especially at set-pieces, and especially if they get caught wrong-side. Players can of course try to improve their leap, their timing and their strength in holding off an opponent. But if a taller, stronger player matches the jump of a smaller player, he almost certainly wins the ball. In 2015, with the squad the German inherited, Liverpool were the smallest team in the division, and statistically, the worst in the air. I go into all this in more detail in *Mentality Monsters*, and about how the recruitment specifically addressed and rectified this problem. But for now, it's worth looking at the improvements made in this area by existing players in 2019/20; as it's one more area that Liverpool have clearly worked on at Melwood, once that clever recruitment was in place (and the inferior small players despatched).

At 6'2", Gomez is fairly average height for his position – the general range for centre-backs is 6'0"– 6'4", with a few outliers at either end – but in previous seasons his aerial win rate was always below average for the position. This seems fairly common for young defenders. Gomez had the power to go with his reasonable height (although a couple of years ago Klopp had to tell him to stop hitting the weights so hard, in order to not lose his explosiveness), but not the experience, nor the ability – honed over time – of levering wily attackers out of the way, or knowing the precise moment to jump. If an experienced defender like Martin Škrtel, at 6'3", could struggle against a battering ram like Troy Deeney (and sadly, Dejan Lovren too, in February 2020), it wouldn't be easy for a mere rookie. By the peak of his career, Jamie Carragher, at 6'0", was a tough competitor who was strong in the air; but in his earlier years, despite not being a shrinking violet, he got bullied to the point where he had to be recast as a full-back for five seasons. Young centre-backs are also prone to costly mistakes, given their proximity to their own goal, and will also tend to rush into situations where they'd be better off holding back; but a lack of physical imposition also lets them down. While you'd expect them to improve in all those areas with time, it's not a given; however, it's hard for young defenders to dominate, and even van Dijk was an unremarkable player in his late teens and early twenties, and like so many central defenders, was another relatively late-bloomer. By contrast, Gomez is an outlier, as a rare central defensive prodigy.

After matchweek 25 in 2018/19, Gomez was averaging just 55% of aerial duels won, below the two-thirds average expected from centre-backs, but up on his previous best, where he was below 50%. However, a year later – in 2019/20 – he was up to 71%, level to within a tenth of a percent with a player who cost £80m, in part because of his aerial ability – Harry Maguire.

Maguire had contested three times as many duels as Gomez, but had also played more than twice the number of minutes. However, Maguire's success rate ranked him 15th, just ahead of Gomez in 16th. Virgil van Dijk continued his staggering consistency by ranking in the top 10 yet again, although this time he was *just* in, at 10th, with a fraction over three-quarters of his aerial duels won (identical in number to the success rate he had in 2016, when I first ran the figures, and noted that he might be a solution to Liverpool's woes).

Interestingly, Matip, despite being nearly 6'6", was only winning 59% of his headers in his debut season; showing that, as well as having the height, he needed to add both bulk and *nous*, in the more direct English game. He was too lightweight. But by game 25 of 2018/19, Matip, now physically stronger, had narrowly overtaken van Dijk in the aerial stakes, up to 77%, albeit from roughly half as many games. And with an albeit even smaller sample in 2019/20 of just six games up to mid-February, he was up to an astonishing 89%. (In his seventh game, at Everton post-lockdown, he won all three of his aerial duels, to further improve his success rate.) It's another example of year-on-year improvement of a player's game under Klopp.

Back in 2016/17, Dejan Lovren was the Reds' best aerial player, winning a fairly mediocre (for his position) 63% of all duels, which ranked him outside the top 60 across the whole Premier League. (At the very least you'd expect 67% for a centre-back.) If you look back at the Reds' central defenders and holding midfielders (so not even including the aerially hopeless Alberto Moreno and Nathaniel Clyne), the players in those key central positions had won just 250 of 447 aerial contests in Klopp's first full season in charge. Lovren and Matip were joined by Emre Can, Jordan Henderson, Lucas Leiva, Ragnar Klavan and Gini Wijnaldum in posting that combined 55% success rate.

Contrast that to the figures three years later, with Matip, van Dijk, Gomez, Lovren, Henderson and Fabinho: six players who contested 374 and won 273, at a success rate of 71%. This improved further after the Goodison derby, where Fabinho also won all three of his aerial duels, and Lovren and van Dijk won two out of three.

(And while not looking at full-backs in this section, Alexander-Arnold – due to age, size and build – has never been very good in the air, but he is still improving, as he grows and fills out; up from 21% of aerial duels won in 2018/19 to 36% in 2019/20. And Andy Robertson offers some aerial solidity that neither Moreno nor Clyne were able to get close to: roughly 48% in each of the past two seasons. Clyne was surprisingly bad in this respect, winning just 17% of his headers in his final full season in the team.)

Liverpool, with those six central "defensive" players, were now averaging an increase of roughly 10% on the best that any *individual* was managing in 2017. Three years ago Liverpool had no one in the top 50 out of the entire Premier League for aerial duels won; by 2020 the Reds had *five in the top 30*. While Fabinho wasn't winning headers as frequently as he had in his debut season, Jordan Henderson had risen from his annual 50% success rate – year after year, as regular as clockwork – to suddenly rank 27th overall, above even the majority of

Premier League defenders, with 68% successfully dealt with (winning 21 of 31). He had even *scored* with a header, albeit deflecting off his shoulder.

If there was one key area where Liverpool could look to continue to find some gains on Manchester City it was in this regard. Being better in the air won't win you the league; but a succession of marginal to *major* gains in various metrics all start to add up.

At the end of 2018/19, Pep Guardiola mentioned that City were too easily beaten in the air; it was one area where they could improve, he felt. It was why he went out and bought Rodri, although he also lost Vincent Kompany – a player who in 2018/19 ranked just ahead of Matip and van Dijk in aerial duels won, at a little over 77%, as he came into the side to help Guardiola's men pip the Reds to the title (and the City club captain ranked 4th overall in the entire league). After 25 games a year later, Rodri ranked 24th in the Premier League in the metric, one place behind John Stones, who was marginally City's best player in the air – but with an unremarkable 68% success rate. (Aymeric Laporte had not played enough games by this stage to qualify, but he was at "just" 63% in his five games, which was well below average for elite defenders.) By contrast, Liverpool now had the players ranked 1st, 9th, 16th and 22nd – all above any City player. City's third-best aerial player, Nicolás Otamendi, ranked 63rd; good for a player who stands just 6'0" tall, but not what you really want from a centre-back (particularly as heading is supposedly one of his stronger suits). Frequently selected ahead of Stones, Fernandinho's 59% is exceptional for someone who is 5'9", but … he's *five-foot-nine*. So City's main centre-back combination as 2019/20 unfolded had a combined aerial success rate that was below Jordan Henderson's.

Indeed, City's five players who regularly played central defence or holding midfielder – Stones, Rodri, Otamendi, Fernandinho and İlkay Gündoğan – had a combined average of less than 60%, whilst the Reds' aforementioned six averaged out above 70%. (Indeed, if you added a sixth player – any midfield player – to balance it out as six versus six, then City's average falls further still.)

So, for all the talk from some neutral fans about how much "better" City's football was, they had a clear weak link at the heart of their defence, which stretched beyond panicky clearances and a lack of leadership. And of course, Liverpool's aerial prowess reaped dividends in *both* boxes.

Like the Liverpool team that Klopp inherited, City in 2019/20 – once Kompany was gone – simply could not contest aerial situations well enough, and in Ederson, they had a below-average height keeper

(6'2") whose excellent distribution and sweeping, and reasonable save percentage, could not overturn a lack of aerial prowess. So even if City weren't conceding a *ton* of chances, given that they still dominated the ball, they had a reasonable chance of conceding goals due to a shambles of a defence. When Guardiola identified the problem in 2019 he probably didn't expect it to get even worse.

And this is the balance you have to try and strike when buying superbly gifted technical players who are below 5'10" in height. When I identified Liverpool's height issues in 2016 and 2017, the worry was how expensive it always seems to be to sign taller players who are also excellent on the ball; if they have pace too, then you have the full package, but it usually costs even more. That's why the investment of £75m in van Dijk was so necessary – *complete* players cost a lot of money – along with a more commanding goalkeeper and a defensive midfielder who could drop into the back four area when the team was under pressure.

Fabinho and Matip add aerial stability, although the big surprises are the quantum leaps (no pun intended) made by Henderson and Gomez. Despite all that, van Dijk is the one who contests the most aerials at both ends of the pitch; indeed, you could add Matip's 45 in seven games to Gomez's 49 in 16, and Lovren's 58 in eight games (31 games combined), and still not quite reach the total of 158 that van Dijk had contested in 25. Indeed, with 119 *won*, the Dutchman had connected with more successful headers (in total) than all but four players in the Premier League, and some of those were strikers who had contested over 300. (Matip, as the tallest, also contested the most aerial duels *per game*.)

The beauty of van Dijk is that he can *do it all*. He can bring the ball into midfield and look as comfortable as anyone who starts games in that position – although when Gomez or Matip plays he tends to be the one who stays back, to provide the mixture of pace and experience to see off any potential counterattack. But what the Dutchman can do that the others can't – in addition to a zen-like ability to remain unruffled – is twofold: score a lot of goals; and hit passes from the back that the league's most creative midfielders couldn't even dream about *thinking* about attempting, even when they might be at their most expressive and arrogant, and in the mood to dream the kind of dreams a real dreamer might dream. Matip can match van Dijk's defensive aerial stats, but his goalscoring record is far inferior. (In Germany, Matip's record was more similar to van Dijk's, with a goal every ten games. For Liverpool, it's a goal roughly every 20 games.)

As of March 2020, Liverpool had still done well in the major games they had played without van Dijk, but the sample size was tiny. He remained the one constant at the heart of the defence, albeit as part of a team that was improving in pretty much all areas of the game.

A Key Reason Why Liverpool Were Better Than City

All of this leads to an area of great difference between the two clubs, with Liverpool exceptional in the air and City below average. The gulf can be seen not just in the aerial duels – many of which can lead to goals at both ends – but in the number of actual headed goals scored and conceded.

As of mid-February 2020, Liverpool ranked only 7th for headed attempts at goal, with 61. Everton had the most, at 85, but even Man City were ahead of Liverpool, having had 70. So for all the talk of Liverpool *relying* on set-pieces and headers – or being crudely "direct" – City were actually having more attempts via that route. The difference is that their attempts were often useless. From just 61 attempts, Liverpool got 27 on target (44.3%) and scored 14 times (23%). The contrast with City is staggering: they managed just 18 attempts on target from their 70 headers (25.7%), and scored seven times, at a success rate of just 10%.

And while City had actually conceded fewer headed chances than Liverpool – 38 to the Reds' 40 – they'd found six of those headers nestling in the back of their own net, whereas for the Reds it was only three. (Of course, two of the goals City conceded to headers were from Mo Salah and Sadio Mané, albeit both were unmarked and stooping, rather than classic aerial challenges).

And so while City fractionally edged the possession stats in the Premier League in 2019/20, with Liverpool ranking 2nd, the Reds were miles ahead in terms of dealing with anything in the air.

Keep-Ball

As mentioned at the start of this chapter, Liverpool beat Sheffield United in the first game of 2020 with an amount of possession that even City struggle to match. Goals from Mo Salah and Sadio Mané clinched a 2-0 win. The second is worthy of analysis.

Halfway through the second half the visitors decided to try an attack, which can often be akin to hari-kari against Jürgen Klopp's men. Two Sheffield United players worked the space to cross down their left flank, as three in white awaited near the penalty spot. Alisson, under pressure, collected the cross, and Chris Wilder's men were mere seconds away from disaster. The goalkeeper threw the ball to Robertson near the flank, and the Scot played a delightfully weighted pass down the line to Mané. Such simplicity, but with a perfect throw and a perfect pass the Reds had Mané running at the backpedalling Blades' defence. When the Senegalese entered the box he played a square ball to Mo Salah inside the D, and at that precise moment it was two in red surrounded by six in white, all of whom were about eight yards away from Salah at all points of the compass. To look at a still image at that precise moment would be to see no clear chance of a Liverpool goal; but Salah, stretching, played a delightful reverse pass that took all six defenders out of the game. Mané, seeing the ball speed towards the six-yard box as he arced his run, lunged to shoot from eight yards out, as the goalkeeper spread himself to block with whatever part of the body he could muster from point-blank range. It hit his arm, and bounced kindly back to Mané, who still had to show brilliant athleticism and composure to bounce quickly up – in a situation where you will often seen strikers unable to regain balance in the panic of seeing the ball rolling before a gaping goal; and, with a defender running onto the line, scoop the ball into the net. His 74th goal for the club (and his 99th in English football), it was Mané's 100th goal involvement in 151 Liverpool appearances in all competitions, with 26 assists added to those 74 goals.

Meanwhile Alisson, in his 50th Premier League appearance for the Reds, kept his 26th clean sheet – to leave him ranking third behind only Petr Čech (33) and Liverpool's own Pepe Reina (28) in terms of most shutouts in their opening 50 starts.

The plain-speaking opposition manager was in awe. "Both parts of the game we couldn't lay a glove on them," Chris Wilder told BT Sport. "I thought they were outstanding, but they didn't have to get out of second or third gear.

"They won every first ball, every second ball, dropped on every second ball, ran forward and ran back, and they did that miles better than us … They still had the humility and the desire to do that as world champions, as European champions, and obviously well on their way to being Premier League champions."

Wilder added, "I wish Jürgen and Liverpool all the best, I love everything about them: the way they go about it, tactical and technical players, but the top bit, the physical and mental part of it, is amazing. And if that's good enough for them, it's certainly good enough for anyone else."

Liverpool Break All-Time Record: Klopp's History Boys

With a 1-0 victory at Spurs' shiny new stadium, Liverpool became the first team *in the entire history of the major European leagues* to win 20 of their first 21 league games (and of course, the other match was a draw, so it was also part of an *unbeaten* run). This came on the back of nine straight league wins at the end of the previous season, and the unbeaten Premier League run – stretching back over a year – was supplemented by winning the Champions League, the European Super Cup and the Club World Cup.

Oh, and in the midst of it all was the greatest-ever European comeback in a semi-final (the greatest comeback in a final still belongs to Liverpool, at Istanbul). The records were racking up at such a rate that it became difficult to keep track. (Indeed, you could probably write a book on the statistics alone.)

While they would continue to add to them, the records that Liverpool broke, domestically and in Europe, with the win at Spurs can be seen in the two tables below:

Best points totals after 21 games of an English top-flight season
Team – Season – Points – (Record)
Liverpool 2019/20 – 61 – (W20 D1 L0)
Manchester City 2017/18 – 59 – (W19 D2 L0)
Chelsea 2005/06 – 58 – (W19 D1 L1)
Tottenham 1960/61 – 56* – (W18 D2 L1)
Preston 1888/89 – 55* – (W17 D4 L0)
based on 3pts for a win

Best points totals after 21 games in Europe's top leagues
League – Team – Season – Points – (Record)
Ligue 1 (France), PSG, 2015/16 – 57 – (W18 D3 L0)
Serie A (Italy), Juventus, 2018/19 – 59 – (W19 D2 L0)
Bundesliga (Germany), B. Munich, 2013/14 – 59 – (W19 D2 L0)
La Liga (Spain), Barcelona, 2010/11 58 – (W19 D1 L1)
La Liga (Spain), Barcelona, 2010/11 – 58 – (W19 D1 L1)

It's worth noting that Tottenham in 1960/61 and Preston in the 19th century were not necessarily financial powerhouses; my own financial figures don't go back that far, but obviously transfer fees have been around since the earliest days, with a whopping £100 the record way back in 1893, paid by Aston Villa for Willie Groves (a player Roy Hodgson apparently tried to bring to Liverpool in 2010, before someone informed him that Groves died 102 years earlier. That said, Groves still might have been more mobile than Christian Poulsen).

But Manchester City and Chelsea, along with PSG, Barcelona, Bayern Munich and Juventus, were either the richest or second-richest club in the league when setting those previous high-water marks, and far ahead of the rest of their leagues in terms of spending. By contrast, after 21 games, Liverpool ranked 3rd in the £XI rankings in the 2019/20 Premier League, just ahead of Chelsea, but with a team that cost just over half that of Manchester City's.

So, this was an all-time record *set without financial doping*.

According to *LFCHistory.net* and TTT writer Terry Dolan, Liverpool's previous best points tallies after 21 games, adjusted to three points for a win, were 54 (2018/19), 53 (1987/88), 49 (1990/91) and 48 (1878/79). Now the record stood at 61.

Yet More Records

But it got better. Another new and scarcely comprehensible record was that, based on a rolling 38-game tally, Liverpool had overtaken the all-time record jointly held by Chelsea and Manchester City of 102 points, to register 104, with 33 wins and five draws. Now, this was obviously not the same as *finishing* a season with 104 points – the Reds ended 2019/20 with 99, one shy of City's record of 100 – but the games at the end of 2018/19 were not a case of coasting in mid-table security with zero pressure and the freedom to just enjoy playing; they were ultra high-intensity, high-scrutiny, knife-edge games, in a battle to the wire with Pep Guardiola's men – whilst simultaneously playing a total of six Champions League games, two apiece against Bayern Munich, Porto and Barcelona; with the Reds' 38-game league run of 104 points commencing just before the mighty Germans flew to Anfield in February. (And the record would get better still.)

While Jürgen Klopp was correct in quickly pointing out that you don't get trophies for records (in order to play down the achievement – after all, the work was not yet complete), such accomplishments are nonetheless staggering; and when it comes to analysing how good a team is, they are absolutely vital.

Also, after going almost 140 years with a best-ever winning streak in the league of 11, Liverpool posted winning sequences of 12 or more games twice in quick succession.

Give the Ball to Bobby and He Will Score

With Sadio Mané in Africa midweek to accept the African Footballer of the Year award – and thus only at 90% awesomeness in north London (as part of a trend where Liverpool's players keep winning awards and therefore spend half their time jetting around the world to receive them) – it became Roberto Firmino's chance to take centre stage; although the entire front three were a constant menace in terms of creating chances and testing the Spurs keeper. It's actually quite rare for all three of the triumphant trident to fire simultaneously, just as they never all seem to have a bad game on the same day; usually one or two will coruscate, and the other one or two will be below par, or merely providing a support role – with the occasional addition of Divock Origi to the equation. Here the Belgian came on as a late sub, danced past three defenders and fired a fine low shot towards the corner, but not quite far enough away from the long reach of the giant Paulo Gazzaniga; while early on, Firmino had hit the post with a fine effort. At the other end, Alisson Becker's handling – on the four occasions he was called upon – was yet again as if there was velcro on both the ball and his gloves.

The game was won following a throw-in. As Mané drifted down the touchline towards the corner flag – taking advantage of the lack of offsides from throw-ins – he drew two defenders, including Aurier. Firmino – as is so often the key movement – had gone towards the taker, Andy Robertson, but then span in behind, arcing his run into the box. To highlight the work of Thomas Grønnemark, Robertson's throw landed just inside the box; it wasn't a *booming* delivery, but a fast, low throw that, rather than looking for a head, was looking for *feet,* or space. By the time it bounced – unexpectedly high – three Spurs defenders had managed to close off some of the space, as Firmino leapt to kick the ball (and if Spurs have any gripes, it is that this could have been a free-kick for a high boot, although that particular law only seems to be enforced if someone gets caught). Toby Alderweireld managed to half-clear the ball, towards the edge of the box, and again there was an awkward bouncing ball to contest. Jordan Henderson, as the attacker, was perhaps able to be braver than Dele Alli, the defender in the situation, in that the worst that the Liverpool captain could concede was a free-kick; for Alli, taking out Henderson would result in a penalty. Henderson went in hard, and the ball bounced up off Alli's hand, and fell to Mo Salah. With great vision Salah, with his back to goal, helped the ball towards Firmino, who was to his right, on the left-side of the area. As 20-year-old debutant Japhet Tanganga looked to pounce, Firmino allowed the ball to roll across his body, and the rookie defender was rendered an irrelevance. Firmino's fulminating left-foot drive flashed past the statuesque Gazzaniga, who had no chance other than to stick a hand out – somewhere, anywhere – in the hope of getting a touch. (The slo-mo from behind the goal is a work of art. He didn't even *smell* it.) The Brazilian reprised his one-eyed celebration that followed Jan Vertonghen gouging his cornea in the same fixture early the previous season.

The rest of the match saw the Reds totally boss possession, with two-thirds of the ball, but towards the final fifteen minutes – having failed to run up the comfortable lead their first-half play deserved – they began to turn actively down chances of promising breaks in order to pass the ball backwards, in an attempt to kill the game with keep-ball; a tactic improved by the introduction of Adam Lallana from the bench, although Wijnaldum, Henderson and Joe Gomez were all caught in possession. Spurs pounced on those late errors, but Son Heung-min blazed a shot over, and substitute Giovani Lo Celso slid in to smash a shot wide from close range, with the goal gaping.

Meanwhile, Alisson, as he did in Madrid last June, comfortably held all four of Spurs' shots on target – to cap a record where the keeper, in mid-January, hadn't conceded a goal in the league since 23rd November, saving every shot on target in that time. (Liverpool conceded one after he was sent off against Brighton, and two against Everton when he was suspended.) The rest of the team began their clean-sheet streak in early December, and since the return of Gomez it was now 585 minutes since the Reds' defence was breached.

Indeed, since van Dijk and Gomez were first partnered together at the start of 2018/19 – before the younger man had his leg broken at Burnley at the start of December – the duo had played 15 full Premier League games together as centre-backs (with various other games where Gomez played right-back or part of the game at centre-back). In those

15 games the Reds conceded just five goals, with ten clean sheets and five single-goal concessions against Chelsea, Leicester, Norwich, Arsenal and Spurs. That's an average of a goal against every 270 minutes, or, pro rata, just under 13 goals a season, which would be an all-time record if extrapolated to 38 games. (Chelsea, in 2004/05, conceded 15 in a season, and Liverpool an even better – pro rata – total of 16 in the old 42-game format back in 1978/79.) Also, the average fixture difficulty was fractionally higher than normal, as the 15 league games where the two were partners included four Big Six clashes and a game against Everton. (In total there will be 12 such encounters in a season – ten Big Six games and two feisty derbies – occurring at a rate a bit below a third of all fixtures, whereas, to date, Gomez and van Dijk had faced such games in exactly a third of their pairings; plus, of course, two games against Leicester, one of which was with Brendan Rodgers' men in the top three.) The list – at that point – did not include a game against Manchester City, however (one later followed, after the title was won, when the Reds were not at the races), although Gomez had played right-back when keeping a clean sheet in the Anfield clash in 2018/19.

In total the 15 games resulted in 13 wins and two draws. Their record together in the Champions League is not as impressive, conceding two at home to PSG and one away in a defeat at Napoli, plus three at home to Salzburg, as well as one against Genk, with the only clean sheet against Red Star Belgrade; but the pair kept out South American champions Flamengo for 120 minutes in the Club World Cup final. (And of course, there were still many more clean sheets for the pair still to come in 2019/20.)

Every game someone different stepped up to be the man of the match. Prior to the Spurs game it had been Jordan Henderson and Naby Keïta, but at Spurs, possibly just edging out Roberto Firmino, it was Gini Wijnaldum, who was absolutely everywhere, bossing the midfield (five dribbles but also a staggering *twelve ball recoveries*) as, with just 33% possession and six at the back, Jose Mourinho tried to "Inter Milan" his way to another fortunate result, as if this was still 2010.

It proved an excellent day all-round for Liverpool, with 2nd-placed Leicester – who beat Southampton 9-0 earlier in the season – losing at home to the Saints in a 3pm kick-off (how often does a team thrash someone *twice* in a season? – almost never, it seems), which meant the gap stood at a staggering 16 points *with a game in hand*;

Man City were 17 points back, on the same number of games. Liverpool were now beyond of the biggest lead ever blown, but no one could quite relax … *yet.*

Changing Times

Ken Early, writing a withering assessment of Mourinho for the *Irish Times*, noted how the Portuguese's old mantra of waiting for the opposition to make mistakes was in full effect:

"For the first time since Mauricio Pochettino arrived at Tottenham in the summer of 2014, a Spurs home crowd got to watch the opposing team pass the ball 796 times. In all that time the closest any team playing away at Spurs has got to Liverpool's Saturday total was the 684 passes recorded by Barcelona in their 4-2 win at Wembley in the autumn of 2018.

"[…] Spurs made 388 passes on Saturday. Pochettino's Spurs made fewer than 388 passes only 10 times in his 293 games. These performances mostly happened away from home at difficult grounds – twice at Liverpool, twice at Manchester City, twice at Arsenal and once at Real Madrid."

But of course, there should also be praise for Liverpool – in another high-possession match – making 100 more passes than any visiting team at Spurs' two stadia since 2014, even if Mourinho is happier than Pochettino to cede possession. Ken Early noted that Mourinho got a couple of decent results against Liverpool earlier in Klopp's tenure, as manager of Manchester United (one of which was a victory – one of only two he has achieved in what is currently 11 games against the German).

"But Liverpool have changed," Early noted. "A defence that used to include names like Clyne, Moreno, Mignolet, and Karius is now based around Van Dijk, Gomez, and Alisson. The goalkeeper is better on the ball than some of the defenders Jürgen Klopp inherited from Brendan Rodgers. These players have the technique and confidence to run the game from the back, and they no longer make many mistakes."

There was also the fact that, in the first half, no Spurs player had an average position in the Liverpool half – bar one, who was about an inch over the halfway line. Mourinho deployed what some pundits called a "double right-back" formation, while Son did not have a single touch in the Liverpool half between minutes 30 and 60.

Mourinho, who used to mock managers like Rafa Benítez and Arsène Wenger for not winning the league when lording it over them as Chelsea manager in the mid-2000s, seemed to forget his own rules about what constituted success and failure; although by the time he was labelling finishing 19 points behind Manchester City as one of his greatest achievements in football you knew he was radically lowering his own bar.

Shelf-lives and Zeitgeists

While Jose Mourinho no longer seems important enough to worry about in the grander scheme of things, it's worth pointing out that he gets jobs, even now, because he is a "winner". That's the phrase everyone in the game seemed to use, and still used when he took charge at Spurs. While you can never totally write off managers, the fact is that most have a shelf life that is lucky to extend beyond ten years. Mourinho used to guarantee 60-70% win percentages at the mega-clubs he managed, but even with the big budget at Manchester United he only managed 58%, and that included a lot of wins in the minor competitions to bolster his figures. At Spurs, after his team lost to Liverpool, it stood at just 48%, down on Pochettino's 54%, and that included the serious dip from the Argentine that was supposed to be arrested by the Portuguese. (By the time of lockdown, Mourinho's win percentage at Spurs was down to 41%; and he ended the season at 46%.)

I wrote in my first book, way back in 2005, that the best managers of the early part of the previous decade – George Graham, Kenny Dalglish and Howard Wilkinson, who between them won all the league titles between 1987/88 and 1991/92 – were out of work; as was Howard Kendall, who was the only other manager to win the title between 1985 and 1992, with his two successes with Everton. Dalglish obviously later made a comeback at Liverpool, and won another trophy, although he was no longer a cutting-edge boss (albeit someone who lifted our spirits after the dark days of Roy Hodgson).

Fifteen years on, if you looked back at the best managers in 2005, then Alex Ferguson – who successfully refreshed his staff and personnel to provide longevity – had retired; Wenger – after a period of almost a decade where his Arsenal team gradually declined, to the point where they finally lost their one saving grace (qualification every single season for the Champions League) was without work, at the age of 70; Benítez

– who won two incredible *La Liga* titles with Valencia and achieved the most incredible Champions League success with Liverpool – ended up in the second tier with Newcastle for a while, then after successfully getting them promoted and keeping them mid-table for a couple of years, now found himself in charge of Dalian Yifang in China; and Mourinho had gone from getting all the elite jobs to being given a "rescue us" role at the smallest of the established "Big Six". The most successful manager in the Champions League between 2003 and 2014 was Carlo Ancelotti, winning it three times (and if memory serves, losing another final, albeit the memories are a bit hazy), in addition to league titles with various clubs (albeit not as many as those big clubs expected); by early 2020 he was in charge of Everton, trying to steer them away from a potential relegation battle. Mourinho was at a club with no trophy in over a decade (albeit one that had been in a couple of recent title races, and reached the Champions League final), and Ancelotti was at a club that hadn't won anything since 1995, and qualified for the Champions League just once (in 2005), which they then exited at the pre-group stage. These were the 6th and 7th richest English clubs respectively. Unless Spurs could return to the miraculous levels seen under Pochettino, they weren't likely to even be challenging for league titles – especially while the bar for league titles was being set well above the 90-point mark.

Why weren't Mourinho, Ancelotti and Benítez still at the *biggest* clubs? Obviously Ferguson retired, and Wenger was perhaps too old to be given a job of note; although he also appeared to be out of touch with what was needed to succeed as the 2020s approached. They were all "winners".

When, in late December 2019, David Moyes was appointed as the West Ham manager for a second time, he said "I'm a winner, it's what I do". This was odd, from a man who had won zero trophies, and whose overall win percentage was nothing special. However, in the 2000s he was at least a *competitive* manager; Everton did pretty well, and his win rate was 42% – decent for a club of that size, if not utterly remarkable. But his season at Manchester United only saw him win 52% of games (losing a shocking 15 times), down massively on the win-rates they were accustomed to, as the reigning champions. He returned to West Ham in 2020 on the back of a 28.6% win rate at Real Sociedad (although kudos to him for at least going to Spain to try, however briefly), 18.6% at Sunderland and 29% in his previous brief spell with the Hammers. Admittedly not many of those clubs would be expecting even 50% win rates, but with those poor figures, by what definition was Moyes a *winner?* (He kept West Ham up in 2019/20, but his win percentage was 29% once again, and they ended in much the same position as they were when he returned.)

What marked out Wenger, Benítez, Mourinho – and even Moyes and Sam Allardyce, as plucky underdogs – was a distinct advantage that they later lost, when others copied their ideas, or supplanted their ideas with new ones. Wenger arrived in 1996 to take a big advantage by professionalising the culture: stopping the boozing by his players, and introducing modern diets. He also tapped into the opening up of the European market, bringing in outstanding players from France, in particular, at a time when France were becoming the best international team in the world, and had a crop of outstanding young players such as Patrick Vieira, Thierry Henry and Nicolas Anelka. Benítez utilised rotation and zonal marking, two things that are utterly commonplace now, and was part of the tactical tightening up in the mid-2000s, that saw a rise in the 4-2-3-1 formation, as two holding midfielders allowed games to be better controlled. Mourinho was also part of that tactical vanguard, and at that point had his youthful arrogance, his style and swagger, that diminished with age; once he started to *look* shabby, he projected less confidence and more paranoia. Moyes, when at Everton, signed a deal with Sports Interactive to use the immense Football Manager database to scout players, and gained an edge in the market. At Bolton, Allardyce was an early pioneer of Prozone; albeit Manchester United – driven by another bright young coach who is now seen as a has-been – had previously made use of their statistical insights, as explained in an article that appeared in *The Guardian* in 2015, having previously been published on *These Football Times:*

"Prozone was a young but growing sports analysis firm that had first made inroads into English football with Derby County, where a young Steve McClaren used it before he was brought to Manchester United by Alex Ferguson midway through the 1998/99 season. As assistant manager at Old Trafford, McClaren insisted the club use Prozone. In return Prozone insisted upon receiving a fee of £50,000 if Manchester United picked up a trophy that season. They won the treble."

In a sense, McClaren and Allardyce – as old-fashioned as they now seem – were at the heart of the data and player-tracking revolution.

Clearly, successful innovation buys you a period of improved results, but not a lifetime guarantee.

Allardyce, the article explains, "developed a system of play based around what he called 'the fantastic four'. These were tenets of the game he had found through data analysis that would serve Bolton well in their fight for Premier League survival and beyond. Bolton had to stop the opposition from scoring in at least 16 of their 38 league games to avoid relegation; if Bolton scored first they had a 70% chance of winning; set-pieces accounted for almost 33% of all goals scored; in-swinging crosses were more effective than out-swingers; and they had an 80% chance of avoiding defeat if they outran their opposition at speeds above 5.5m per second."

(Obviously such advantages also relied on referees ignoring fouls on goalkeepers.)

"… This knowledge was applied primarily to throw-ins, free-kicks and corners, where Allardyce placed great emphasis on something called POMO, or 'Position of Maximum Opportunity'. If a player failed to appear in the required position for one of Bolton's famed long throw-ins, he would not forget it in a hurry. Allardyce would make sure he knew a scoring opportunity had been passed up."

These advantages were largely *agricultural*; effective, but unattractive. Allardyce's brief advantage was lost when other Premier League teams began to use Prozone, or similar systems.

Allardyce moved from club to club, but in a way similar to Roy Hodgson (who was cutting edge in the *1970s*), seemed to win just a third of all games no matter the budget, nor the size of the club. (Newcastle United 33.3%; Blackburn Rovers 35.6%; West Ham United 37.6%; Sunderland 29.0%; Crystal Palace 37.5%; Everton 38.5%.) Sounding increasingly bitter, he came across as a man out of time, failing to understand that with the prices of tickets and television subscriptions now much higher than a decade earlier, some kind of *joy* was necessary from the football, too; winning a third of games wasn't enough if watching them made fans want to poke out their eyeballs. He once claimed to be good enough to manage Real Madrid, but in the end, only smaller-to-mid-level English clubs ever wanted him, and the fans of Newcastle, West Ham and Everton – who craved at least *some* flamboyance – found his football unpalatable. That said, what he achieved at Bolton, with the aid of Prozone, briefly put him at the cutting edge, before his dinosaur tendencies took hold, and he retreated to TalkSport, and regular appearances with his brethren, Andy Gray and Richard Keys, on Middle-Eastern TV.

Imperial Phase

In 2018, with the help of an interactive graphic from Tableau Zen Master Robert Radburn, I mapped out the career trajectories of 50 of the most prominent European football managers of the previous five decades – every European Cup/Champions League winner, plus those who mopped up most of the English, Spanish, Italian and German league titles. While there is no identical template – some managers were late developers, others youthful prodigies – the general trend was "ten years at the top". Even those who managed for decades tended to have just a small window of game-changing impact. The Pet Shop Boys' Neil Tennant dubbed it – in relation to the period of time when his band couldn't fail to produce hits (rather than a foray into football management) – their *imperial phase*.

While many of these managers had periods of brilliant over-performance with smaller clubs or in backwater leagues, those achievements – away from the spotlight – are much harder to quantify. Even winning the major trophies can be easier for some managers than others, given the resources at their disposal – but it seemed logical to focus on the main leagues, and the *big* European trophy.

Even managers like Brian Clough and Arsène Wenger, who seemed to be around for decades, won all their major prizes in under a decade. Both stayed on at the clubs with which they are now synonymous (Nottingham Forest and Arsenal respectively) for more than a decade after their imperial phase, and as seems a common theme, they then won only the smaller trophies: domestic cups. All of Wenger's great achievements happened between 1997/98 and 2003/04, with a near-miss in the 2006 Champions League final, until ultimately he was sacked 12 years later; while Clough won the title with Derby, then again with Forest, both in the 1970s, followed immediately by back-to-back European Cups, all in the space of nine years, before 13 more years that landed him only League Cups and, in his final season, relegation. Both managers strike at the paradox that is giving a manager time (such as with Alex Ferguson), but not just letting him steer the ship long after his vision has ceased to work. No manager becomes useless overnight – but like carbon monoxide poisoning, the effects can gradually take hold, whilst owners struggle to act, and pundits struggle to acknowledge the steady decline. On average, managers take around 7-8 years to enter their imperial phase, which then lasts another 7-8 years, followed by 11-12 years falling to the periphery, with the occasional burst of brilliance.

And while most managers have all their major success within the span of a decade-or-so, it can often be distilled down into an even shorter period, albeit sometimes with one or two late 'hurrahs'. Mourinho's eight major honours – two Champions League successes and six league titles – occurred between 2003/04 and 2014/15, but six of the eight came in just seven seasons, from 2003 to 2010. That was his imperial phase, and it was now over a decade ago. The frequency of winning league titles dropped, and then, suddenly, he was one of those managers in the hunt for the League Cup.

To go back a little further, Fabio Capello is an interesting example – five major trophies with AC Milan and one with Real Madrid in his first proper six years as a boss (starting in 1991), then one more title with Roma a few years later. His 2005 and 2006 titles with Juventus were revoked due to the *Calciopoli* scandal (which involved influencing the selection of favourable referees, and as such, you cannot ignore the advantage that might have given them). Then, another title with Real Madrid in 2007 that was still regarded as underwhelming in part due to an early Champions League exit and some dour football, and after only one "failure" in his first six seasons as a manager (with one of those five successful seasons including simultaneously winning *Serie A and* the Champions League), he had just two major successes in the next nine years, once Juve's back-to-back titles were expunged. And that dismissal from Madrid was the end of his success, with stints as the boss of England, Russia and Chinese side Jiangsu Suning all ending without glory. Had he forgotten everything he knew? Or did what you needed to know, to some degree, change? Even a compatriot like Roberto Mancini, who won league titles with Inter Milan (three times) and Manchester City (once) up to 2013, only won the Turkish Cup thereafter – in five seasons spent with Galatasaray, Inter Milan and Zenit Saint Petersburg – and, like Capello, was next found in the retirement home that is now international football.

Indeed, both these managers returned to their respective Milanese clubs later in their careers – in the phenomenon the Italians call "reheated soup" – with Capello winning games roughly half as frequently as he did the first time (excluding an initial six-game period as caretaker several years before he took the job on a permanent basis), and Mancini's second spell at Inter seeing his stats fall from 62% of games won to 47% – not quite as dramatic a decline, but a sense of falling from elite to "decent". (In these cases it was more like *gazpacho*.)

The craving to go back to a manager, because it worked in the past, is understandable, and some skills remain constant; but as the ancient saying from Heraclitus has it, no man ever steps in the same river twice, for it is not the same river and he is not the same man.

The tides of football move fast. Radomir "Raddy" Antić (who passed away in 2020) managed Atlético Madrid three times between 1995 and 2000, and his win rate fell from 51% to 28% to 13%; either side of which he managed Real Oviedo twice, but won 20% fewer games second time around. The list of almost 50 über-successful managers is full of homecoming heroes with diminishing returns: Howard Kendall at Everton, from 54% down to 37%, then down to 26% in his third and final stint. The hugely influential Arrigo Sacchi – whose back-four and pressing work was an inspiration for Klopp, Benítez, Mourinho and others – won the *Serie A* title followed by back-to-back European Cups in the late '80s, but when he returned to Milan in 1996 they finished 11th and suffered their heaviest ever top-flight defeat. Louis van Gaal won two *La Liga* titles with Barcelona in the late '90s – as part of his imperial phase that began with Ajax winning the Champions League in 1995 – but after returning to Catalonia in the summer of 2002 he was sacked in January 2003, with the club in 12th place, just three points above the relegation zone. In the final 16 years of his career he won just two league titles – and only one in the elite leagues – plus two domestic cups.

While there are examples of managers having successful returns to clubs, they are much fewer and farther between; their careers tailing off in a similar way to those who – unlike Bob Paisley – failed to get out while the going was good.

Perhaps it's just not the same river, but more likely, they are not, by that stage, the same manager.

If managerial talent was a constant, then careers at the very top should last longer, and they would not resort to taking lesser jobs as their stock falls; and returning to a club years later would more frequently rekindle the magic. While we can all continue to learn and improve – and gaining wisdom is one of the rewards of ageing – the same is true of managers as it is with players: the hunger to do so has to be there. Whereas players start losing their physical edge, it cannot be as easy for a man in his fifties to have the energy of twenty years earlier. Another maxim here would be about teaching old dogs new tricks: do older managers remain as open-minded as they were when first developing their skills? Presumably so many fall into the trap of "if it worked before …", but strategies have to keep pace with developments driven by a new generation with a totally different approach.

It's all just part of the natural process of ageing, and no longer being cutting-edge. To move with the times takes a complex approach to personal development, and a relaxing of the ego; and tactics evolve and develop all the time. Relating to players may become harder due to an increasing age gap; whilst *everyone* gets older at the same rate, teams are kept an average age of about 25-27, and once a manager becomes a pensioner, can he relate to the youngest ones in particular, and can they relate to him? Being a "winner" is not, in and of itself, enough. Time turns all winners into losers, sooner or later.

How Does Jürgen Klopp Fit In?

Back in 2018, Jürgen Klopp's imperial phase – counting only trophies as the criteria – seemed limited to just two seasons at Borussia Dortmund, where he won the German title in consecutive seasons, and added a domestic cup; starting in 2010/11 and over by the end of 2011/12. The parameters of the study excluded the prior overachievement at Mainz, whom he got promoted to the top flight on a tiny budget, as it did not fit the criteria; and as such, a closer look at his record was required, to see if he was a busted flush, or simply the victim of circumstance.

To help his case, if the imperial phase definition was widened to include reaching European finals, he would suddenly have appeared much more vividly on the radar, with the blank "major honours" gap between 2012 and 2018 being not an end to the imperial phase, but a constant line of achievement; reaching the Champions League final with Dortmund in 2013, then again with Liverpool in 2018 – both huge examples of overachievement based on spending and what he inherited – as well as finishing runners-up in the Europa League with the Reds in 2016. That barren spell was full of progression and near-misses.

Due to the league position at the time he took over at Liverpool in 2015/16, he didn't even compete in Europe in 2016/17. And so, between 2013 and 2019 he reached no fewer than four European finals, finally winning one in 2019.

Klopp had taken over a Liverpool team that wasn't *expected* to win league titles and Champions Leagues, not least because in the previous 25 years they'd won just one of the latter and none of the former. It was a club – initially, at least – merely looking to break back into the top four, after spending most of the decade excluded. Also, Klopp was fairly unique in that, when his stock was at its highest, he turned down the chance to join various clubs already geared up for mega-success; his rationale being that he'd rather start pushing than just jump on the moving train. And Liverpool were in dire need of a push.

But two years on from the study, his imperial phase can be seen to stretch clearly from 2010 to 2020, now that there are major trophies at either end of those "nearly" years.

However, where does he go from here? Will he be an Alex Ferguson, defying the 'manager melt', or is this – a decade in – the end of his imperial phase? The clue could be in the team around him …

Manchester Dis-United

Under a glowing red sunset at Anfield – the low clouds puffy and pink over the packed stands – Manchester United were all but taken apart. Liverpool FC were steadily making a mockery of the concept of *hyperbole*, as they absolutely overran the visitors. The scoreline – 2-0 – did not reflect the chances, the near-misses and the (dubiously) disallowed goals. Victory made for a 30th win in 31 league games, dating back to March 2019. The goals continued to flow, but the club also equalled its best run of consecutive clean sheets (seven) since December 2006.

The Reds' victory meant they ended the day some 30 points clear of United, and it was hard to recall any time since the mid-'70s (when United were relegated) that either club had trailed the other by such a margin so relatively early in the season. Converted to three points for a win, the gap was a whopping 37 in Liverpool's favour when they finished 2nd in 1974, as United were sent down to the second tier, in 21st place; but that was after 42 games, not 22. Obviously there was then an entire division between the two sides in 1975, and that's a gulf that's hard to top. After the Reds had played 22 games in 2010/11 – the nadir under Roy Hodgson (for the first 20 games, at least, before he was sacked) – the Reds were 13th, with 26 points; but United – the eventual champions – were 'only' 21 points ahead, albeit with a game in hand. Klopp's Liverpool were 30 points ahead *with a game in hand*.

Power

Liverpool took the lead with their first 1st-phase corner goal since Virgil van Dijk, against Brighton, powered home not one but two directly from Trent Alexander-Arnold crosses in November, which led to the "Liverpool *only* score set-pieces narrative". Here there were the same protagonists, with the same results: corner, van Dijk's head, goal. For all the open-play goals scored in the meantime – no fewer than 24 – the Reds retained that set-piece hammer, and used it with power against a United side who, despite paying a fortune for a giant defender, and having had a variety of 6'3" and 6'4" central midfielders as well as a tall goalkeeper, joined two relegation-zone teams in having conceded the joint-most goals from corners (eight). Height is important, but so is *coaching*.

It was about as simple as a goal can get, but it was interesting to see Harry Maguire suffer so badly in the air against his slightly cheaper counterpart, who not only matches him for size, but massively outranks him for skill, passing ability and pace; and, of course, goal threat. In 124 Premier League games up to this point Maguire had eight goals, but none yet for United; van Dijk had scored 50% more (12) from nine fewer appearances in the English top flight. (Maguire later scored his first United goal at Chelsea, having escaped a red card for kicking Willian in the groin. His previous goal was for Leicester against Liverpool, when he should have already been sent off for a last-man foul. In United's game against Chelsea, the referee was from Manchester, as was the VAR; it just needed Sir Alex Ferguson as the 4th official and it was almost a nap hand.)

It was van Dijk's 11th Liverpool goal in all competitions in 103 appearances, but ten had come in a span of just over 12 months. The Dutchman also had four international goals – all since March 2018 – from 33 caps overall, while Maguire had just one goal from 26 caps. While Maguire should logically be a goal threat for United, the evidence supports Liverpool's centre-back as having a clear edge in the attacking sense, too (before you start looking into their passing).

When van Dijk signed I asserted that he could be worth a 20-goal swing for Liverpool, by knocking ten off at one end and adding ten at the other (the latter based more on his goal output in Scotland, in a dominant team, where he reached double figures in one of his two seasons with Celtic), but only the defensive side of that equation seemed to be falling into place in the first year. But when including assists, he started to become worth that ten-goal swing in an attacking sense; but if anything, 20 goals were chalked off the 'against' column. Prior to his arrival, Liverpool were regularly shipping around 50 league goals a season; it dipped to 38 in his first half-season at the club, then way down to just 22 in 2018/19, with 21 conceded in 31 games at the point when the title was sewn up. Such figures are not purely down to him alone, obviously – the arrival of Alisson and Fabinho, and the improvement of Joe Gomez, have also played a role – but the goals-against column highlights the overall impact van Dijk has provided.

After the early headed goal, Liverpool sensed blood and went for the throat, but were denied a second that the referee (*not* from Greater Manchester) deemed perfectly acceptable, but that the video assistant referee (Paul Tierney – one of at least three referees from the Manchester area) ruled out. United players surrounded and jostled the referee – as if it was still the 1990s, and Roy Keane would pop up any moment – after David de Gea dropped a high ball under pressure from van Dijk, whose arms were at his side. Tierney claimed van Dijk was "not playing the ball", which suggests he doesn't understand how football works – if you jump *for* the ball, with your eyes *on* the ball, and try to connect *with* the ball, *you are playing the ball*. It was ruled out, when even *after* the incident Manchester United had a chance to clear, but messed up. The ball fell to Roberto Firmino to score his first Anfield goal of the season. But no, it was VARRED out.

Liverpool then scored another goal – a sumptuous work of precision and beauty – that was more swiftly disallowed. Firmino's flick found Alex Oxlade-Chamberlain, who arrowed a low pass into the path of Gini Wijnaldum, running beyond the defence, who then curled the ball into the far post past the sprawling de Gea. The Dutchman was fractionally offside, so there could be no arguments on this one.

The disallowed goals, plus saves from the United keeper, kept the visitors in the game. United had just two good chances in the entire match, both of which they failed to put on target.

It appeared that Mo Salah – who worked hard without finding his touch in the final third – forgot to pack his shooting boots, as he awkwardly kicked a glorious chance from one foot onto his other with the goal at his mercy, but then – thankfully! – seemed to change into David N'gog's boots in the 93rd minute, to replicate a famous last-minute goal from 11 years earlier, also to seal a 2-0 win (which incidentally, came just 72 hours after I spent the day with Rafa Benítez at Melwood; I hereby take credit for: "Give it to N'gog, and he will score". I take no blame whatsoever for the rest of N'gog's career.) In a weirdly fitting parallel with that game, the Liverpool goalkeeper – then Pepe Reina, now Alisson Becker – was the first to reach the goalscorer. In this instance it was Alisson's assist, as he hit a dropped clearance with the outside of his boot to Salah on the halfway line, as two United players chased to get back. However, let's go back a few seconds: before the move could even start, van Dijk was yet again involved – winning the header from United's late, late corner, and clearing the box; the resultant shot from a United player was tame, and Alisson was ready to start a counterattack. The backspin on his drop-kick meant Daniel James – capable of matching Salah for pace – was able to catch up to the Egyptian, but in three attempts to win the ball he just bounced off the Reds' no.11. After tucking his shot through de Gea's legs Salah removed his shirt to show the ripped upper-body musculature that had left James, 22, resembling a mere schoolboy trying to tackle his dad.

Such was Liverpool's domination in this game that even without two wonderful disallowed finishes adding to the xG – neither is included – they still got close to 3.0 – with *FiveThirtyEight* ranking Liverpool's shot xG as 2.5 and the non-shot xG (which, as "dangerous possession", could be seen most clearly when Mané was through on goal but got his touch wrong, and Luke Shaw cleared) as worth a further 2.3 goals.

By contrast, United's figures were about 1.3 and 1.0, even though they had almost as many shots in the match, because many of them were mere hopeful punts at goal. In terms of dangerous moments, United had one scrappy close-range miss, and one pretty decent chance for Anthony Martial that he sent high and wide. Martial and Fred aside, they had no one on the pitch who looked equipped for football from 1999, let alone 2020. David de Gea proved that he's still a great *foot*-stopper (although he also tipped a wonderful Jordan Henderson shot onto the post with a rare use of his hands), but Alisson – clearly his superior over the past 12-24 months – showed the more creative side of his game with the ball to set Salah free, to wrap up the points. De Gea was lucky to get away with bad handling for the disallowed Firmino goal, and due to his preference to save with his feet – to use them to get low shots to his left or to his right – he perhaps wasn't properly set to deal with Salah's shot, which the Egyptian didn't quite catch cleanly, but which still went through the keeper's legs. De Gea showed he is still capable of world-class saves, but for a couple of years had been making mistakes at a rate that Liverpool were used to in the 1990s. Had he become the new David James? The parallel seemed fitting when considering that United's league title drought now stretched back seven years; in 1997, seven years after the Reds' last title, James was in his final season as the undisputed no.1 at the club. (Brad Friedel replaced him for the final eleven games of the following season.)

Manchester United's success in the 1990s was partly down to the mighty Peter Schmeichel, and their success in the late 2000s owed a lot to Edwin van der Sar. In between they'd had more than a few goalkeeping aberrations, with goalkeeper the one position where a loss of confidence can affect the entire team. By contrast, Alisson had not conceded in the league since November, and his only other appearance since Napoli on 27th November – a 1-1 draw, the last time he conceded a goal in any competition – was the 120-minute shut-out of South American champions Flamengo.

While save-percentages don't take into account the *difficulty* of shots faced (and that requires looking at more detailed xG data that also includes where the shot was *heading*), Adrián had up to this point racked up 62.5% in his ten appearances during the understudy's stint in the team, which put him third-bottom of the 23 keepers to play over 400 minutes in the league. But this was not far behind some major names around the mid-60% mark: Ederson and Jordan Pickford; while de Gea was hardly miles ahead, at 70.1%. The most expensive goalkeeper in the world, *sans* inflation, Kepa Arrizabalaga, ranked bottom, at 54.3%, considerably worse than Liverpool's bargain back-up from the same country. (Arrizabalaga was later dropped, but then, as the reserve keeper, had a 'worldie' in the FA Cup game at Stamford Bridge in early March 2020, in which Chelsea beat an understrength Liverpool side 2-0.)

As with Harry Maguire and Virgil van Dijk, it seems that Liverpool, in buying Alisson for a (non-inflation adjusted) record that was then smashed by Chelsea shelling out more for Arrizabalaga, got it absolutely spot-on. Only one Premier League keeper had a save percentage better than 74.3%, and that was Alisson, in a world of his own at 85.7%. In Opta stats from the halfway point of the previous season Alisson was also top. What's remarkable is that it was also 85.7%.

And, of course, Alisson was also adding assists to his game – although his quick throws had already contributed to several goals, with many the Reds scored starting from the back. When he slid on his knees to hug Mo Salah, the Kop finally sang – with full gusto – "Now you're gonna believe us, we're gonna win the league".

The Kop's public show of belief, which had up to that point been kept in check, came after Leicester lost earlier in the day at Burnley.

More importantly, Manchester City had started the weekend in perfect style – *for Liverpool* – by coming from a goal down to apparently "win" the game at home to Crystal Palace in the 88th minute – cue Etihad-based euphoria – only to concede an equaliser in the 90th (as an error-prone expensive centre-back got exposed yet again). It felt like the Reds had too much for anyone to stop them. The advantage was 16 points over Man City, and 19 over Leicester, with a game in hand on both.

Writing in *The Guardian* the day after the Reds despatched United, Jonathan Wilson noted: "This was 2-0 going on 5-1. Liverpool's opening goal may have come slightly against the run of play but, in the 20 minutes that followed, United were overwhelmed. It was the same story in the 12 minutes of the second half from kick-off to Fred's chance. In both spells Liverpool were quicker, sharper, stronger and cleverer. In both they could have scored two or three times without it seeming outrageous. There were goals ruled out for marginal decisions, the woodwork was struck and Salah somehow scuffed wide from eight yards with the whole goal at which to aim. Without being anything like the best football they have played this season, that was the level Liverpool can reach when they put their foot down – and it was a level high above United's capacity."

Storm Brewing

At this stage, the novel coronavirus was just that: all pretty novel, and few outside China were taking it too seriously. The day after the Reds' victory over United, China reported a third death and more than 200 infections, with additional cases reported outside Hubei province including in the capital Beijing, Shanghai and Shenzhen. When Liverpool fans finally sang "now you're gonna believe us…", virtually no one in the west – bar some epidemiologists – was paying too much attention. When United brought in Odion Ighalo from Shanghai Greenland Shenhua F.C. almost two weeks later, some wags joked about how United were importing the virus to derail Liverpool's title bid. In the end it didn't need Ighalo to spread Covid-19 across Britain.

Out Come the Wolves

Jordan Henderson, Mackem warrior with a war-cry – a *Wear*-cry, if you will (with maybe a bit of *Why-aye man* borrowed from his native neighbours) – ran down the Wolves wing as if his life depended on it; chest out, legs pumping like pistons, albeit from those strange hips that made Alex Ferguson spend £16m on Phil Jones when he had the chance to get Henderson for the same price in 2011. (Nine years on, over 350 games for Liverpool for Henderson, barely 200 for the hapless gurning machine Jones at Manchester United.)

The best Henderson could hope for was to run like Forrest Gump and perhaps win a throw-in, but he chased it down all the same. Liverpool had not long been been pegged back to 1-1, and both sides were creating and missing good chances in the insanity that followed. With just six minutes left, another cutting Wolves break, should one arrive, would almost certainly have sealed the Reds' first league defeat in 40 games, and only the 2nd in 62; but more tellingly, *the first of the season*. However, Henderson was having none of that. Even if Wolves had dropped rugby-style flyer Adama Traoré into their left-back position then Henderson would still have chased him and won a throw. If Wolves had thrown on Mike Tyson with a baseball bat, and Conor McGregor with a set of nunchucks, the Reds captain would have been undeterred. First he'd have punched out Tyson, then spun a roundhouse kick into McGregor's mush that would have seen him hit the deck.

In short, the Liverpool captain *really wanted* this throw. A throw! It was one of the most indicative moments of the season: how something as apparently meaningless as a throw-in becomes another thing to fight for; in addition to how well Liverpool now dealt with such situations.

Thirty seconds later, thanks to Roberto Firmino, the ball was in the back of the Wolves' net, with just five minutes left on the clock.

That's why.

"He played an unbelievable game tonight," said Jürgen Klopp of his captain, who had also scored the opening goal. "He was really shouting at everybody, keeping everybody on their toes, but it's not just about shouting, it's about what you say and he only asks for things he expects from himself." Henderson's goal was the first time in five years that he'd reached double figures in a season – *when those figures are just 1+1*.

And, of course, Henderson then won the throw-in that led to the winner. By then Wolves had equalised, having created four clear-cut chances on the night – Alisson saving one, and with the other two put wide and over. Raúl Jiménez was the exception, heading Traoré's cross powerfully into the corner of the net after a fast break that would have made Liverpool proud. (As someone on *The Anfield Wrap* noted, dealing with Traoré was like trying to tackle an armoured bear.) Alisson had saved the previous 33 on-target shots he had faced, then added two more stops after the goal (on the start of a run that would morph into three more clean sheets). He kept the Reds in the game until Henderson's charge of the light brigade.

Klopp was a relieved man, knowing how hard his team had to fight to win, especially after Sadio Mané went off with an early injury. Takumi Minamino, who arrived at Liverpool after a month of inaction due to the Austrian league's winter break, was thrust into the action, for a Premier League baptism of fire 33 minutes into a helter-skelter game, that later resulted with him lying exhausted on the treatment table.

Klopp was a relieved man. "We changed the system two or three times, we calmed it down. We had incredible chances in the first half and then at the end it was a magic moment from Bobby … The boys are human. It was a little bit up and down. We had discussion on the pitch, there was stuff to improve but set-pieces can bring us back in the game, a good bit of skill can bring us back in the game."

Liverpool, scoring in their 33rd successive match, had amassed 67 points from a possible 69 in the season; a staggering *five* more than any side in English top-flight history had managed after 23 games.

At the two-thirds stage of the season – during the first ever midseason break – the Reds' probable best XI of Alisson Becker, Trent Alexander-Arnold, Virgil van Dijk, Joe Gomez, Andy Robertson, Fabinho, Jordan Henderson, Gini Wijnaldum, Mo Salah, Roberto Firmino and Sadio Mané had started precisely *zero* games together. (They finally did so in a league game *in June*.)

If you were to argue that Joël Matip was in fact the first-choice partner for van Dijk (certainly in the calendar year of 2019), then that XI had started … precisely *zero* games together. With all the fuss about a couple of injuries at Manchester City, that was a reminder that Liverpool hadn't had it easy, either.

What Records Next?
The Reds went into the midseason break on the back of two more wins, achieved away at West Ham and at home to Southampton.

The 2-0 win at the London Stadium took Liverpool to 106 points on a rolling 38-game basis, beating the all-time English league record of 104, that they themselves had only just recently set; before which, 102 was the best any team had posted.

Concurrent with this 12-month rolling league record, the Reds – in Europe – also beat Bayern Munich 3-1 (away), Barcelona 4-0, Spurs 2-0, and defeated Chelsea and Flamengo in the finals of the European Super Cup and World Club Championship, whilst topping the group stages of the Champions League in 2019. Going into the game in

London, the Reds were five points better off than any League team had ever managed in the top flight, and this applied across all the major European leagues.

As with the win a week earlier at Wolves, the win at the London Stadium was achieved without the prodigious powers of Sadio Mané (how could Liverpool ever cope without him? *etc.*) who limped out of that previous league game early on. Mané joined Xherdan Shaqiri, James Milner, Adam Lallana and Nathaniel Clyne on the sidelines, while Naby Keïta, Dejan Lovren, Joël Matip and Fabinho were all seeking match fitness after returning from long layoffs; all of the latter three looked woefully off the pace at Shrewsbury in the previous weekend's slightly ignominious 2-2 FA Cup draw, having been 2-0 up. But this rustiness was only as one might expect.

Liverpool also became the 13th team in English history to beat every other team in the top division, albeit it was the first time the Reds had achieved the feat. As Graeme Riley explained, the "…previous earliest by date it was achieved by was Preston on 9th Feb 1889". (Obviously there were only eleven other teams back then, as opposed to 19 now, and the season *finished* on 9th February 1889.) A further fact from Graeme made the Reds' achievement a bit clearer: "Earliest by percentage of games played was Manchester City in 2017/18 after 81.6%. LFC have played just 63.2%. Unlikely ever to be bettered."

Of course, this record could have been achieved *even earlier* had the game not been put back by a little over a month due to the Club World Cup. (Had that been the case, then, with the Reds only drawing away at Manchester United in October – the only team out of the other 19 to deny the Reds a win – the victory over Ole Gunnar-Solskjær's men in January would have moved the record achievement from league game 24 to game 22.)

Liverpool were totally dominant against David Moyes' West Ham, who looked bereft of ideas and direction. After Andy Robertson had twice put a ball dangerously across the Hammers' goal to see it not quite go in (his dinked shot trickled along the line – his fourth big-chance of the season – and a ferocious cross just missed the outstretched boot of Divock Origi), the Reds finally broke through, with ten minutes of the first half remaining.

Moyes' men were on a rare break, sending a ball across the edge of Liverpool's box. It didn't quite make it to Robert Snodgrass on the right flank, in part because Robertson was sharper, and cut it out. The speed of the transition could be seen when the Liverpool left-back charged into the midfield space, heading infield, left to right, as Snodgrass stood and watched. This was *totaalvoetbal*, where anyone can move into any area of the pitch with confidence, where positions are not restrictive.

With four West Ham players out of the game – it's very hard to catch fast players when they break, and harder still if you're not even prepared to *sprint* – the ball was fed to the right touchline and Trent Alexander-Arnold, who was bursting into the Hammers' half. But Robertson hadn't stopped – he was now a de facto attacking central midfielder, as the cross went into Roberto Firmino.

Firmino, in the area, twisted and turned near the byline, before squaring the ball to Origi, through the eye of a needle. The Belgian's first touch was equally superb, deftly taking him in between two Hammers' defenders in the tightest space on the edge of the six-yard box. With just the keeper to beat, those two defenders lunged in on him; the first missing, the second – Issa Diop – ploughing his thigh into Origi's thigh, after boot touched boot. It was about as blatant a penalty as you will ever see, not least as Origi was 99% certain (give or take 0.01 xG) to score, and had no incentive to go down. The contact was obvious, yet even then, Don Goodman – channelling his inner surrealist on Sky's evening highlights package – called it "borderline", adding that it was "very, very soft", as if he was looking at a totally different incident.

Interestingly, had Origi not controlled the ball there was another Liverpool player on hand to score: Robertson, arriving in the inside-left channel, having been the one to win the ball and create the attack in the first place.

The penalty, awarded by Jon Moss, took Liverpool up to joint-third in the season's Premier League penalty rankings, with five, level with Watford and Manchester City (who soon moved on to six, only to miss that penalty against Spurs and lose the game), while Leicester were second, with six. (Manchester United still seemed to have their own penalty laws, as they were way out in front, on *nine*. They'd soon reach ten while Liverpool were still stuck on five.) None of the Reds' rivals in the five-or-more-penalties bracket had a higher than 80% conversion rate, with United on a rather pathetic 55%, but, on the night, Mo Salah joined James Milner in keeping the Reds at 100%.

The Reds' second came from their opponents' corner. Yet again West Ham made the rookie mistake – no matter how tentatively – of *trying to attack*. Even then, they weren't committing many men into the box, but they were lulled into the falsest sense of security any team faces against the Reds.

On 52 minutes, Virgil van Dijk miscued the ball to concede the corner (he seems to slice one clearance per game – rarely none, *never two* – just to prove he's mortal), which finally enticed the Hammers into throwing five players into the Liverpool box, with two more on the edge. As the corner curled into the six-yard box, van Dijk – almost as if he planned it all along – headed the ball 30 yards, into midfield.

Two backtracking West Ham players let the ball bounce over their heads, and at this exact point there were four of Moyes' players still in the Liverpool box, two of them walking back (one of them not quite breaking into a casual stroll), whilst the Reds (in white) had all the other nine outfield players bursting forward. When Salah tried to control the bouncing ball there were still West Ham players making no effort to get back and stop the unfolding breakaway; one (and it looked like one of their centre-backs) was loitering 30 yards offside when Mark Noble tried to halt the move with a desperate flicked interception. The proverbial blanket could have been thrown over the Liverpool team at this point, with all ten compact and compressing the space, against a team strung all over the pitch. When Jordan Henderson deliciously volleyed Noble's flick forward to Salah, West Ham had nine players ahead of the ball, as three Liverpool players broke against the one helpless defender. The ball got a bit stuck under Salah's feet, but he managed to curl a pass through to Alex Oxlade-Chamberlain with the outside of his left foot. (Although in truth it merited a *right-foot* pass, but if you can use the outside of your stronger foot instead, and get it right, then there can be no nitpicking). It was a beautiful pass, but perhaps a touch behind where Oxlade-Chamberlain wanted it in order to get it fully into his stride. Even so, he was in on goal. In a one-on-one with the keeper, he scored for the third successive time at the London Stadium (the first one being with Arsenal), slotting past the otherwise impressive Łukasz Fabiański. Liverpool survived a few minor scares, although Alexander-Arnold lashing a clearance against his own post would have been a strong contender for own-goal of the season, had it not bounced out.

Liverpool extended their run to 41 Premier League games without defeat, winning a staggering 36 (88%). It was the third-longest such run in English top-flight history behind Arsenal (49, up to October 2004) and Nottingham Forest (42, up to November 1978).

It Gets Better Still…
In beating Southampton 4-0 on February 1st, Liverpool opened up the biggest ever gap between 1st and 2nd in top-flight English football history: 22 points, having played a game more. With City subsequently losing to Spurs, the weekend ended at 22 points and the same number

of games played. (Liverpool would then extend this gap to 25 points later in February, but on that occasion City won their game in hand.)

And, of course, it was not even like Manchester City were having a historically bad season for a team in 2nd place; it's just that no one had ever won 24 of their first 25 games before. And City were supposed to be *the best side ever*.

Southampton actually gave Liverpool a stern test in the first-half at Anfield, making use of their excellent fitness, after Liverpool played a league game just a few days earlier. Both teams had chances to score, although Liverpool's were the clearer, as was their penalty shout. However, the second half was something of a rout, once Oxlade-Chamberlain opened the scoring, thanks to the first of a hat-trick of assists for teammates in the game for Firmino. The second of those assists was for Jordan Henderson, now up to the heady heights of *three* league goals for the season. Henderson then set up Mo Salah for the third, and Salah added the fourth in the last minute.

It was the 34th consecutive league game in which Liverpool had scored, which was the best run for any team in over a decade, while Mo Salah had won each and every one of his last 31 league matches. Liverpool also equalled Man City's record of 20 consecutive league wins at home.

After The Midseason Break

In difficult, stormy conditions in Norfolk – upon the return to action after the league's first midwinter break (in that hazy ancient era when two-weeks seemed like a *long time*) – the Reds utterly dominated against Norwich, with two-thirds of the possession and 17 shots, with six on target; missing a couple of big chances, but taking away the points thanks to substitute Sadio Mané's goal, allied to a 10th clean sheet in 11 games.

The goal started just inside Liverpool's half, with Joe Gomez calmly taking down a long clearance. He fed the ball to Henderson, who hit another one of those longer passes that land right at the perfect spot. Mané's turn and stretch – in one movement – to bring the ball down was breathtaking (part football, part kung fu), and in a heartbeat, as the fallen ball took a second bounce, he fired a low shot past Tim Krul, in a similar manner to the winning goal against Wolves at home in late December.

"The gap is so insane, I don't really understand it," Klopp told Sky Sports after the game. "I am not smart enough. I have not had that before. It is outstanding, so difficult. I go back into the changing room and we chat about the things, and then I am like 'Oh, but congratulations. We won the game, another three points.'"

The BBC match report noted that Liverpool "… have collected a remarkable 103 points from the past 105 available. … The result also means 76 points after 26 games is the best record at this juncture in the history of Europe's top five leagues – something even the continent's great sides including *La Liga*'s Barcelona, Juventus of *Serie A*, *Bundesliga*'s Bayern Munich and *Ligue 1*'s Paris St-Germain were unable to achieve."

Over-reliance?
With Mané only starting on the bench against Norwich, this was the 17th league game in less than two seasons that Liverpool had started without at least one of Mané, Roberto Firmino and Mo Salah – although only Burnley away in 2018/19 saw all three absent from the XI (but two came off the bench, and immediately changed the game). Victory made it 15 wins and two draws from those fixtures; hardly a crippling reliance on the trio. Mané clearly made the difference at Carrow Road as a lateish sub, but the Reds had just scored six times in the two games he missed.

Mané and Firmino were each either injured or on the bench in eight of the aforementioned 17 league games where one or more of the front three were absent; while Salah was absent from the XI on just four occasions. The standard of opposition was generally below average, with only one Big Six clash – away at Manchester United, which was one of the two draws (away at Everton in 2018/19 was the only other failure to win, and the only failure to score; Salah would later miss the same fixture in 2019/20, post-lockdown, and again Liverpool failed to win and failed to score). In those 17 games, the Reds scored 48 goals, at a rate of virtually three per game. However, a small number of those games saw one of the trio emerge from the bench to seal the points, as was the case against the Canaries. (This was, however, Mané's first goal in the Premier League for Liverpool as a substitute.)

With two games against Norwich and another two against Huddersfield in the 17-game sample, nearly a quarter of the fixtures were against teams set for relegation, although the majority were actually against mid-table sides. Divock Origi started only nine of 17, scoring five times and also winning the game-changing penalty at West Ham. In 2018/19 it was often Xherdan Shaqiri who stepped into the front three upon an injury or rotation to the one of the main strikers, and he scored once and assisted two goals that season when standing in; while a rare appearance in 2019/20, against Everton at home, saw him grab another goal, as Salah and Firmino started on the bench. In contrast, Oxlade-Chamberlain missed almost all of the previous season, but started to get more game-time as a front three deputy, with Shaqiri often injured, and he'd grabbed three goals in the five most recent league matches for the Reds where one of the key trident was absent.

Interestingly, Virgil van Dijk scored four in the 17 games, to prove more prolific than his usual rate of one league goal every ten games. A clutch of midfielders – Gini Wijnaldum, James Milner, Jordan Henderson, Adam Lallana and Naby Keïta (with two) – weighed in with six further goals. One of the qualities of Liverpool under Jürgen Klopp has been how, when a problem presents itself, a solution emerges *from somewhere*. (Albeit if the fixture is at Goodison Park, put your money on a 0-0.)

While Firmino scored just twice in the eight he started with one of his two fellow line-leaders absent, Salah and Mané were at their most prolific when not part of the trio. Mané bagged 11 from just nine starts, while Salah helped himself to 13 goals from 11. While the quality of the opposition will have played a part, the fact that either Mané or Salah would be moved to a central position – particularly if Firmino was out – meant that they actually scored *more* goals. Salah, in particular, seemed to be at his most prolific when either Firmino or Mané was missing; scoring eight times in the eight games in which the Senegalese did not start, and grabbing five in five in the games without the Brazilian. (Of course, Firmino's brilliance is perhaps the least easily measured in goals.)

As of the end of February 2020, the Reds had won 86% of all league matches since the start of 2018/19, and without one of the three main strikers it was actually higher, at 88% – albeit in fixtures that were below-average in terms of overall difficulty. While all teams are likely to struggle longer term without their best players – and the more you remove, the more those teams are liable to suffer – it certainly hadn't proved to be costly for Liverpool.

Indeed, Salah and Firmino had each only missed one Champions League game since the start of 2017/18, and that was the 4-0 thumping of Barcelona. In that game, Origi scored twice, while Wijnaldum, who only arrived as a second-half sub (to play the more attacking role he'd been used to in Holland) also bagged a brace. Problems, solutions.

It Had To Happen Sometime …
Liverpool Finally Lose A League Game

Forty-four league games unbeaten, and in the process, equalling the country's all-time top-flight record winning sequence of 18. Plus, taking an unprecedented 110 points from the last 114 on offer, whilst scoring in 36 league games in a row – which had only once been bettered. And not having tasted defeat for 422 days. Those sequences all came to a crashing halt at a windy Vicarage Road. No goals scored, three conceded. *Ouch.*

With just five unbeaten games needed to equal Arsenal's record, the Reds fell short, but even so, the season's record still read 26 wins, one draw and one defeat.

"I see it [the defeat] as rather positive," Jürgen Klopp said. "From now on we can play free football again, we don't have to defend to try to get records. We can just try to win football games again."

Most teams tend to find this; many Arsenal players have subsequently admitted that during their 49-game run – which stretched out from their Invincible season – they ended up looking to avoid defeat, rather than gambling on the win. The phenomenon of 'loss aversion' kicks in. Indeed, they drew 12 times in the Invincible season, winning the same number in 38 games that Liverpool had in 28.

Klopp's team hadn't been two goals behind in over 70 league games; and at Watford they were three down, and it could have been four. The Reds created absolutely nothing – an utter rarity under Klopp – and with half a dozen players out injured, the bench didn't provide a solution; Klopp threw on more and more attackers, but as sometimes happens, that just left fewer players to actually create something, with the team shape torn apart. (While the players he threw on were not the first-choices.) That said, the players who started the game hadn't even looked like creating anything, and that was continuing into the second half, so it was possibly worth the gamble.

The points gap at the top remained 22 – the same as the number of confirmed UK cases of the coronavirus on the day of the game. But if a 22-point cushion looked unlikely to be overturned, the season itself was suddenly in jeopardy as the government published contingency plans that could include cancelling all big events, as the number of known cases rose by 50% in 24 hours, with many more undiagnosed people suspected to be carrying the virus. For the time being, it was only Italy that had seen its top division games postponed due to

Covid-19, and so the focus remained on the Premier League title race, and Liverpool's first serious slip-up.

Any knee-jerk thoughts of eclipsing Newcastle with the most calamitous collapse in history could still be soothed by the fact that results during the Geordies' demise in 1995/96 – which started in late February – still garnered them enough points (1.15 per game) to successfully take Liverpool over the line from the lead they had established, even if it wasn't good enough for Kevin Keegan's men to keep their narrower lead over Manchester United. After the defeat at Watford, Liverpool needed just 12 points from 10 games, assuming Manchester City won all their matches; while victory for the Reds against City, should it occur when the two sides were due to meet at the Etihad, would mean that Klopp's men could wrap up the title without winning another game, as long as they drew six.

Let's Get Physical

At Vicarage Road it seemed as if there were a number of physical problems, that were exemplified by how a rusty Dejan Lovren, as is his wont, tried to make it a physical battle with a burly forward (on this occasion, Troy Deeney) and, when losing, *tried even harder;* which, as can be the case, included being dragged deep and wide. This, when stepping away, to focus on the space behind, and the second balls, could have been far wiser. Since his arrival – and despite general improvements during Jürgen Klopp's tenure – this had proved Lovren's Achilles heel: the desire to win every ball, even when it could only result in conceding a foul, or being pulled out of position. Whereas the super-quick Virgil van Dijk and Joe Gomez remain able to follow a striker into deeper or wider areas and still get back to protect the danger area, the much slower Lovren has always been more likely to remain isolated. Gomez and van Dijk also seem more judicious regarding *when* they track their man into deeper areas, whereas Lovren sees the ball as a red rag, and he's the bull.

While Lovren was not the only bad performer on the day – and he won all three of his tackles, and played two of the game's best forward passes – his constant problems with Deeney set the tone, and disrupted Liverpool's shape. As such, it reminded me of the aerial duels analysis I'd undertaken when writing the chapter on the Reds' festive period, to show how Liverpool were much less likely to be physically bullied. The problem was, at Watford, being bullied is exactly what happened. It seemed that *this* side would not lose 3-0 against the big, powerful Hornets in the way that a much smaller, limper Liverpool side had in 2015. But then, due to injuries, this wasn't really the Liverpool that had come to be – if not bulletproof – then at least *bully*-proof. For the first time in eons, Liverpool looked a bit of a soft touch, and it was in no small part to the absent players – such as Jordan Henderson and James Milner – who usually provided much of the steel; and Joël Matip and Joe Gomez, who provided a lot of the aerial solidity. (Matip was on the bench, but still not fully fit after long-term injury.)

This was also the third consecutive league game Liverpool played in the midst of a named storm ('Jorge', following 'Dennis' and 'Ciara'), and as experienced at a blustery Goodison Park in March 2019 – where Klopp admitted his team struggled with the elements – the wind can wreak havoc and play into the hands of taller sides; aerial football being more effective in the winter, when the ball carries more on the wind. (Which, presumably, is why long-ball football was historically more prevalent in northern European countries, while warmer, drier climates proved more conducive to energy conservation through skill and passing.) Liverpool's own use of long passing generally tends to need accuracy, and in blustery conditions, the long switches of play could see the ball sail into touch.

The Bournemouth Bounce-back

Liverpool, still lacking the leadership of Jordan Henderson, and now without Alisson and Andy Robertson, bounced back to winning ways against Bournemouth – a 27th league win from 29 games. That said, it was achieved only after yet more catastrophic officiating, that set the Reds back after nine minutes of total dominance. *Everyone* could see that Joe Gomez was pushed by Callum Wilson – the commentators on every TV station covering it, for example, all called it as a blatant foul. Wilson shoved Gomez in the back so hard that Gomez went flying forwards, off-balance, but trying to stay on his feet. One of the Mancunian triad of referees – Paul Tierney – seemed to be the only person in the ground who didn't see it. Burnley manager Sean Dyche even used it as an example for an incident that happened in his own team's draw with Spurs. "I think football has to be careful, personally. We saw it today with Gomez in the Liverpool-Bournemouth game. It's a definite foul but he tries to stay on his feet and because he doesn't flail his arms out and go sliding on his face nothing is given, and then they go through and score."

Even at this stage of the season the myth that VAR was helping Liverpool to win the league abided, whereas in truth, the Reds were now, statistically, more sinned against than beneficiaries. And this was not the system, nor the concept, that was working against them, but the flawed individuals and Professional Game Match Officials Limited's attitudes in *implementing* the technology. Yet again Liverpool rendered the decision moot with a comeback, but it was yet another uphill climb based on bad decisions by the officials.

To further solidify Liverpool's "luck", this was the 11th league game in which the reserve goalkeeper Adrián had featured for the Reds, and despite clearly being inferior to the main man Alisson (the best in the league), it was his 11th win.

The game was turned on its head by two fast counter-pressing goals, with Jack Simpson – on as a sub, just as he was in the game at Dean Court – gifting the Reds a gilt-edged chance which they gladly took. Back in December it was Nathan Aké limping off with a hamstring pull, and here Steve Cook had a similar problem, after trying to foul Roberto Firmino when he shot at goal. That day, Simpson passed the ball straight to a Liverpool player, whereas at Anfield, in the 25th minute, he tried to dribble past Sadio Mané, who tackled him for a perfect 'final-third regain'. Mané drove into the box but played a truly terrible pass to Mo Salah, that was so misplaced it ended up behind the Egyptian; but Salah, who looked exceptionally bright all afternoon (albeit in another of those underwhelming lunchtime kickoffs), turned and fired a low shot into the corner from sixteen yards, using the defender as a shield to unsight the goalkeeper.

It was Salah's 70th Premier League goal for the Reds in his league 100th appearance – not quite maintaining the stupendous strike-rate of his first season, but yet again he projected himself into the hunt for the golden boot and, more importantly, *major trophies.*

That vital second goal came just after the half-hour mark, as Virgil van Dijk intercepted a Bournemouth pass on the halfway line, with the game so condensed that there were seven other Reds more-or-less within the centre-circle. But one player who was already looking to run in behind was Mané, and van Dijk played him in perfectly; helped by Aké, on the far side, being five yards behind the rest of his team. Mané gained twenty yards with just two touches, then produced the increasingly familiar hard-curl finish into the far corner. It proved the winning goal.

The man of the match award went to Milner, just edging out Mané, and Milner's influence could be seen all over the pitch – including having a word with the referee after his obvious mistake on the Bournemouth goal. Not only did he secure the win with a vital goal-line clearance, but he won both of his aerial duels and both of his tackles. While the quantity of two apiece was not especially noteworthy, he exuded the authority and leadership that had not been as obvious in the recent games where neither he nor Henderson featured. For all

Liverpool's qualities, those two perhaps still personify the unflinching desire to win every tackle and win every game.

A week after various Liverpool records came crashing to a halt, another all-time English top-flight high-water mark was set: overtaking the number of consecutive home league wins, set by Bill Shankly's Reds in 1972. Taking it up to 22 in a row, it was one more than the Reds of 48 years earlier, and two more than the Manchester City side of 2012, plus two other teams: Newcastle in 1907, and Preston in 1892, the year of Liverpool's founding.

The run lasted until July 11th, when Burnley snatched a point against the run of play to curtail the record at 24, after further wins against Crystal Palace (4-0) and Aston Villa (2-0). However, the home record in all competitions ended four days after the Bournemouth match, when the Reds faced Atlético Madrid. By this point Covid-19 was becoming an omnipresent threat; particularly in Madrid, which was an infection hotspot.

The game went ahead – to a packed house – and Liverpool were *outstanding*. Jan Oblak had an incredible game in the visitors' goal, but he could not keep out Gini Wijnaldum's 43rd-minute opener – a fantastic header from a perfect Alex Oxlade-Chamberlain cross – which levelled the tie at 1-1. A second goal, however, could not be found in normal time, despite Herculean efforts, but Roberto Firmino finally ended his Anfield drought to make it 2-0 early in the first period of extra time.

But that goal seemed to trigger a skewing of reality, and, as Atlético finally emerged from their defensive shell, Adrián gave the ball away, and then lost his footing. Whilst still setting himself, the ball flew past him, into the corner – a saveable shot had he been where he was supposed to be. Two further breakaway goals followed, as the Reds, going out on away goals at 2-1 up on the night, threw everyone forward, and ended up losing 3-2; and 4-2 on aggregate. But this was not just the end of Liverpool's Champions League campaign – it also signalled the end of *football*.

Part Four

Game Zero, Game Over

In the end, Liverpool's Champions League match against Atlético Madrid not only cost the Reds participation in the next round, and was, for a good time, The Last Game Ever Played. More importantly, the game cost *at least* 41 people their lives in north-west hospitals, according to a *Sunday Times* investigation. Covid-19 had now spread all across the UK, and as English football discussed the idea of playing games behind closed doors, as they were doing in Spain and Italy, it quickly became clear that the sport had to be mothballed, and the country to go into lockdown. The game against Atlético was a huge mistake.

The Liverpool Echo reported on the study towards the end of May: "Edge Health, which analyses health data for the NHS, has conducted modelling and estimated that the Liverpool-Atlético match is linked to 41 extra deaths at local hospitals in our region between 25 and 35 days after the game.

"This number could of course be larger, with fans travelling further afield to their homes after attending Anfield."

Given that so many Liverpool fans come from far and wide, this seems inevitable. And so, having killed more than died at Heysel, it could be that the figure – when adding those who took the virus from Liverpool back to London, or the Midlands, or Yorkshire (or even those who fly in from Scandinavia and beyond), could take the tally above the number who died at Hillsborough, even if this was a lot more indirect and not necessarily those attending who were the ones to perish. Plus, possibly half of all UK Covid-19 deaths were occurring outside hospitals – in care homes, and people living alone in isolation; and as such, the figure of 41 is clearly a case of under-counting. At the time of the game, Spain had at least six times as many expected cases of Covid-19 than the UK (640,000 vs 100,000), and Madrid was a key hotspot. Spain had forced *La Liga* games behind closed doors, but 3,000 fans were allowed to fly to Liverpool by the UK government.

The Sunday Times' investigation quoted Chief Scientific Adviser Sir Patrick Vallance from mid-March, from when he downplayed the chance of infection: "There's only a certain number of people you can infect. So one person in a 70,000 seat stadium isn't going to infect the stadium … They will infect potentially a few people they've got very close contact with."

This obviously ignores the way people interact at a football match; all the pubs and bars and cafés frequented before and after the event, and how they congregate outside turnstiles. It ignores the close proximity of the seats, and how cheering, chanting and celebrating could send viral particles into the air. And it ignores the prevalence of super-spreaders, who somehow manage to infect dozens and dozens of others.

The *Echo* continued: "On the day of the Liverpool-Atlético game itself, Deputy Medical Adviser Jenny Harries was featured in an interview with Boris Johnson where she said she felt such events would not have a big impact on transmission of the virus. Liverpool Council's Public Health Team is currently working on an investigation into the impact the match had on the city's infection rates."

The BBC also reported in late May – with the government in the Dominic Cummings lockdown-breaking scandal (an utter clusterfuck unfortunately dubbed 'cum-gate') – that two major sporting events held in March "caused increased suffering and death", according to the scientist leading the UK's largest Covid-19 tracking project.

The BBC noted that data gathered from millions of volunteers found coronavirus 'hotspots' shortly after the Cheltenham Festival and the Reds' Champions League match against Atlético Madrid. Professor Tim Spector said rates of cases locally "increased several-fold".

In the article, based on BBC Radio 4's *File on 4*, Mick Tucker and Adrian Goldberg note that: "Sports governing bodies in the UK were taking their cue from Prime Minister Boris Johnson who declared in early March that people should 'as far as possible, go about business as usual'."

But even had Liverpool wanted to cancel the match, it was not within their remit. "That decision," the authors noted, "would have had to come from one of football's governing bodies, such as the competition's organiser Uefa."

They quote Professor Spector as saying: "I think sporting events should have been shut down at least a week earlier because they'll have caused increased suffering and death that wouldn't otherwise have occurred."

In May 2020 I spoke to long-time *Tomkins Times'* subscriber and occasional writer for the site Professor Mike Begon (B.Sc., Ph.D. Professor of Ecology Evolution, Ecology and Behaviour at the University of Liverpool), whose work over the years has brought him into close contact with many of the key players in the government's Scientific Advisory Group for Emergencies (SAGE).

Mike provided a fascinating insight into how even science can get overruled – to at least some degree – by the passions of football, even if his attendance at the game was made less risky by his increased knowledge and generally safer approach.

"As to the Atlético match," he said, "I was there, I didn't socialise with the away fans, I haven't had the virus, as far as I know, and we were all aware that this may indeed be the last game for a while.

"But my whole response and attitude – as a biologist if you like – were interesting, I think. As a biologist – indeed as a biologist working in this field – I should have known better than almost anyone that the match shouldn't have been played – and that I shouldn't be going. But I went. I wasn't going to miss one of the big European nights.

"So two things. First, this tempts me to give the Government *some* slack on their slowness to respond – if I was getting it so wrong, can I blame them? But I'm resisting that temptation. I'm only human and my heart ruled my head. Their job is to do the right thing. They didn't.

"But second, my own getting it wrong suggests something possibly quite profound. Before this lockdown, the situation we now find ourselves in was to almost all of us – *even me* – almost literally 'unimaginable'; or at least in the category of things we can imagine in principle, but have never happened before in our lifetimes, such that something inside us says – no, it can't possibly…

"So one lesson surely all of us should have learned from this is that the unimaginable – the thing that has never happened before and will turn our whole world upside down – may indeed happen if rational argument suggests it might. And my greatest hope is that, as the pandemic has tragically taken hundreds of thousands of lives, it may somehow save the world if people now understand that The Big Unimaginable – climate change catastrophe – is all too imaginable and *will* happen unless we do something urgently to prevent it."

And, of course, there are also *the even more deadly* pandemics that most epidemiologists say are in store. Plus, so many other types of *force majeure* incidents, including volcanic eruptions, one of which, coincidentally, affected Liverpool against Atlético Madrid a decade earlier. Iceland's Eyjafjallajökull, which erupted in 2010, meant the Reds had to travel by road and rail to Spain; and even though it was only a small eruption by global standards, the ash cloud – whose clusters of tiny rock-like particles can destroy airplane engines – still disrupted air travel across the northern hemisphere for a week. Go back through history and there have been several far bigger volcanic eruptions (Thera, Vesuvius, Tambora, and also Krakatoa in 1883, at a time when football was an established sport) whose ash clouds blocked out the sun for a year or more, causing crops to fail and animals to die due to the lack of sunlight permeating the pall and the massive drop in temperature, which in turn led to many human deaths. Such an event could theoretically happen at any time, even if it probably won't happen today or tomorrow. Many volcanic "big ones" are long overdue.

Then there was the geomagnetic storm of 1859, often called the Carrington event (Richard Carrington and a certain R. Hodgson independently made the first observations of a solar flare; my hunch is that it *could* have been Roy, as a young man in the 19th century, but this may just be a spurious and decidedly sly dig at how old he is, and how Victorian his methods still seem.) Were such a massive solar event to occur today, it would likely wipe out all electronic communications, which in turn would be catastrophic, given how phones, computers and a whole host of electrical technology are what keep pretty much everything in our lives functioning.

In the winter of 1946/47, coinciding with when Liverpool – complete with Bob Paisley in the side – won the club's fifth league title (but its last until the 1960s), temperatures got so low and snowbanks so high that coal, which at the time provided 90% of the country's power, could not be shifted, and as a result, power stations went offline. Crops had to be dug out of the ground with pneumatic drills, while farmers saw a quarter of their sheep die in the extreme cold. It got so serious that national emergency plans were drawn up to deal with a widespread famine, before the thaw finally arrived. (As noted earlier in the book, this was the only other season when the Reds last won the league on a day they didn't play, as well as being the only other time the league title was decided in June.)

None of these types of occurrence appear to have been planned for by the Premier League, which had no method in place for deciding on the outcome of curtailed seasons. In June 2020, less than two weeks ahead of the planned resumption of football – Project Restart – clubs sat down (or rather, logged on) to discuss the methods to decide things like the title, European qualification and relegation, should a second wave of Covid-19 terminally curtail the campaign. Presumably such methods will be kept in place, for future unexpected events.

Jürgen Klopp gave his take, early on in the outbreak, when the country entered lockdown: "We said it now often enough, and I think everybody knows, football is not the most important thing in the world. One hundred per cent not. In this moment it's clear what is. But the only way to get football back as soon as possible, if that's what the people want, the more disciplined we are now the earlier we will get, piece by piece by piece, our life back. That's how it is. There is no other solution in the moment, nobody has another solution. We have to be disciplined by ourselves, we have to keep the distance to other people. We can still do some things, not a lot, but we have to just calm down a little bit with things. Yes, outside the economy has to carry on, that will start again. But the lower the number will be when we go out again, the number of people infected, that's what I understand, the better it is. It will not be like nobody anymore after the next few weeks but the curve will flatten, that's the most important thing. We have to give our people in the hospitals, our doctors, the chance to treat the people with serious issues with full concentration. We have to give people time to build ventilators, we have to give people time to find solutions. There will be a moment when other smart people find a vaccine for the virus. But until then, we have to make sure we do the best possible for all the people out there. You hear now more and more it's not only the elderly and weaker – it's not only that, there are younger people involved who can die of it as well. It's not about that, it's about just, show heart and a bit of sensibility and do the right thing: stay at home as long as we have to. And then at one point we will play football again as well, 100 per cent. I couldn't wish more for it because of a few really good reasons, how you can imagine. I can't wait actually, but even I have to be disciplined and I try to be as much as I can."

Kenny Dalglish was the only known high-profile person connected with Liverpool FC to have tested positive, albeit whilst asymptomatic and in hospital for another issue. The club itself was at the centre of a backlash when it furloughed its non-playing staff in line with the government offer, as gate receipts crashed to zero, and television money had to be repaid. Unlike those at many other clubs, Liverpool players had not offered to take a pay cut, nor had they deferred their wages. As such, the debate centred around whether the owners should cover the massive unexpected revenue shortfall, when their ethos was about not taking money *out* of the club, but also, not pumping it in, either; the idea of making the club self-sufficient was eminently sensible. However, out of nowhere, all the revenue streams they had helped build up over time were suddenly drying up. The compromise (as it still stands as of late July, with this book going to press) appeared to be that the club would not now spend money on player transfers – so the planned move for Timo Werner was suddenly off – in order that the existing players could continue to receive their full pay packets, which in turn would mean greater contributions to the NHS via taxes.

The first XI was certainly not in need of any major surgery, and rather than go all-out to try and win all the remaining league games (and set a points record) after the title was belatedly sealed, Klopp opted to start players like Neco Williams and Curtis Jones, to get them up to speed even more quickly, ahead of the impending 2020/21, whenever that should start (given that there would not be much of a gap between the end of the current season and the start of the new one). Rhian Brewster, scoring goals on loan at Swansea, would be another option upon his return, as would some others sent out to gain valuable experience. (Marko Grujić has been superb in two seasons in Germany, and at 24 may now be ready for the Reds, although as with Harry Wilson, being kept on could be more of a question of playing styles knitting with the existing midfield, and the difficult task of ousting highly-accomplished players from the XI. That said, it's likely that these decisions will have been decided by the time you are reading this.)

The three-month hiatus gave players like Alisson, Matip and Fabinho time either to get fit again, or to leave their indifferent form behind (Fabinho never looked the same after an ankle injury sustained in November, but rediscovered his mojo after the lockdown, and Matip also looked shaky after injury). Equally, while players looked after themselves, no one had the chance to get *ultra*-fit, with little time to prepare, and no time to do a proper preseason, despite the lockdown lasting longer than any normal closed season. Manchester City also benefitted from the rest, with various stars now free from injury. Perhaps importantly for Liverpool in the longer term, many of their international stars *finally* had a proper break.

Football resumed with Liverpool 25 points ahead, although City's game in hand was played three days before all the other matches, and they easily despatched Arsenal, to reduce the deficit to 22 points, with both clubs having nine to play. It was still surely too much of a bridge to gap – even if the Reds fielded their 1990 title-winning side, now in their fifties and sixties. But nothing could be taken for granted.

Woo-Hoo!

After three months of inactivity, and no chance for the kind of essential preseason training that helps Jürgen Klopp make his teams so hard to beat, Liverpool's Project Restart limped out of the starting blocks, with a dull 0-0 draw played out at a deserted Goodison Park. The Reds bossed the game until, late on, the introduction of Dejan Lovren for the injured Joël Matip gave the hosts a weak link to attack; as at Watford, and as can often happen when he hasn't had a run of games, the Croat was all over the place. (In fairness, the horror show at Vicarage Road aside, the other nine league games he started were all won, in what were some of the biggest tests: Leicester, Tottenham, Aston Villa, Manchester City, Crystal Palace, Brighton, Everton and Bournemouth.)

Manchester City's two convincing wins – including their game in hand – meant that the Reds could not secure the title when Roy Hodgson brought his troops to Anfield a few days after the derby draw. (City were due to play Chelsea the next day.) A mixture of Hodgson's lack of ambition and Liverpool's coruscating football meant that it was about as one-sided a game as you will see; not that many got to see it in the flesh, with the stands awash with iconic flags rather than fans. With the scoreline still level a quarter of the way into the match, Trent Alexander-Arnold, from 25 yards, curled a beautiful free-kick into the top corner, and from that moment on it looked like a Reds victory was a mere formality. However, the hunger to achieve it – and to not take that outcome for granted – never waned. Jürgen Klopp's men went at the visitors with a ferocious intensity that belied months of inactivity. There was no crowd to cheer, but the *Woo-hoo!* refrain from Blur's *Song 2* blared from the PA system as the players celebrated Alexander-Arnold's goal. Soon after, Jordan Henderson, still in the mood for goals (having already scored three in the league), hit the post with a fine shot. (As an aside here, while Henderson is not noted for his goals, with four matches to play – when his season was ended by a knee injury – he had four non-penalty goals, having added another fine strike away at Brighton, while Virgil van Dijk also had four; Alexander-Arnold had three and Andy Robertson had two, as did Fabinho, while Gini Wijnaldum, whose job is more about covering the space box-to-box and less about getting *into* the box, had five in all competitions. Across all competitions there were 19 different goalscorers for the Reds, as centre-backs, full-backs and holding midfielders weighed in with vital strikes that were not the odds-on chances of a penalty taker, which largely helped James Milner to his four goals.)

A move from the back, on the brink of half time, saw Fabinho curl a delightful ball – reminiscent of his pass to Sadio Mané against Manchester United the season before, also at the Anfield Road end – over the opposition defence, and this time it was Salah controlling and smashing it home. *Woo-hoo!*

(It was a pass Fabinho reprised yet again for Andy Robertson's goal in the unlucky 1-1 draw at home to Burnley in mid-July that ended the club's astonishing run of Anfield league wins.)

Salah's strike was the Reds' 100th goal in all competitions, a feat the club had achieved for three consecutive seasons for the first time since the 1980s. Fabinho, totally reborn after the hiatus (having been poor when returning from injury in January) then threw the xG rulebook out the window by hitting a shot from so far out it was almost in Goodison Park, and, like his critical goal against Man City in the autumn, it nearly took the net off. *Woo-hoo!*

The game was rounded off when Palace, in possession by the corner flag on a rare foray forward, gifted the ball to Mané, and his first-time spin-and-pass put Roberto Firmino in possession near the centre-circle. The Brazilian likewise turned and found Mo Salah, still in his own half, and Salah's ridiculous first-time wrong-foot pass was so glorious it had Mané in on goal on the opposite flank in a split second. As so often happened in 2019/20, it was from one end to the other – and often, one *side* to another – in the blink of an eye, with clever turns and inch-perfect incisive passes. As he also did so often, Mané curled the ball with power into the far corner. *Woo-hoo!*

Day of Destiny
On a personal level, having managed to get to sleep at about 2am as the adrenaline from watching the match slowly ebbed away, I woke a couple of hours later, suddenly aware that it was a day that Liverpool, without even playing, could win the title. The only times in my life since my late teens that such a day existed (I was 19 when the Reds were last crowned champions) were the end-of-season games I attended at Anfield against Newcastle in 2014 and Wolves in 2019, although both times Liverpool were hostage to the fortunes of games elsewhere, and each time the day ended with Manchester City winning their respective fixture, and thus the title too. In total, a staggering 11,000-or-so days had passed since goals from Ian Rush and John Barnes secured a win against QPR; and this was only the third day where any of us woke up when another title could be confirmed.

Unlike 2014 and 2019, City *had* to win – a draw would not suffice – to stop Liverpool being crowned title winners for the first time since 1990. And even if City beat Chelsea, Liverpool still had six more bites at the cherry, including a game at the Etihad (which, my faultless memory tells me, did not actually take place).

As the two blues lined up at Stamford Bridge, the Liverpool squad and some of the backroom staff were gathered at the golf club in Formby, watching on various television screens situated on the outside patio, where the players, vaguely socially distanced, sat in plastic chairs, arranged in semicircular rows, while others stood at the French windows. Glowing lanterns hung in the dusk, mixing with the bluer light from the TV screens, to give the scene a slightly eerie feel. As the game drew towards its dramatic conclusion, City, on top for a long period – having pegged Chelsea back to 1-1 – were suddenly scrambling chances off their own line, as they had done against Liverpool 18 months earlier. Goal-line technology again came to their rescue, as it had in January 2019, to prove that the whole ball hadn't crossed the line. Kyle Walker slid in as Christian Pulisic – a former tyro under Klopp at Dortmund – looked to have scored his second of the game (the first coming after some calamitous defending – indeed, a slip – from City's defenders sent Pulisic in on goal), but even though it looked a goal in real-time, the replays showed that it was not *quite* a goal. Next, an almighty scramble in the City box, and against all belief, *still* the ball wouldn't go in; only this time the goal-line technology – which again came to City's rescue, by not beeping the signal 'goal' to the referee's watch – couldn't entirely save Pep Guardiola's men, as the VAR spotted Fernandinho punching the ball clear. He was sent off, and it was a penalty to Chelsea.

Willian – compatriot of two of the Reds' Brazilian regulars – set himself for the spot-kick, as another national teammate of theirs trudged off. "Come on!" the Liverpool players shouted as the Chelsea man approached the ball. One by one the players (now spectators) took to their feet – Joe Gomez in his usual on-field spot next to Virgil van Dijk, who leant forward onto the backrest of the chair in front – as the commentator on BT Sports could be heard saying "Everyone on Merseyside is holding their breath…" and … up went the roar! Alisson, in cutoff jeans and a khaki t-shirt, removed his baseball cap to jump up and down with the other members of the back four who had been seated in front of him (no change there), before turning to throw, in delight, his cap into the chair behind. A couple of players hugged – Andy Robertson and Adam Lallana, Gini Wijnaldum and Naby Keïta, after Wijnaldum had looked to the heavens with clenched fists – but most just put a sensible arm around one another, such as Alisson around Firmino, in his black t-shirt and white baseball cap, as they whooped and hollered. Ever the sartorialist, Firmino adjusted his cap, which had gone slightly askew.

Woo-hoo!

There were still 12 minutes to play, plus ample added time after the various VAR delays and the drinks break, but it *felt* won. City needed to score twice with just ten men, and no Sergio Agüero. The Liverpool players returned to their seats for the remainder of the match, before, at the final whistle, they could genuinely go wild. Video from Alex Oxlade-Chamberlain showed the players counting down the final seconds of the game, and between the end of the countdown and the ref blowing his whistle the Liverpool players held the Jordan Henderson pose, jogging on the spot with arms held out in front, until finally rising up, as one, as the whistle went. Then they all grouped together, jumping up and down, singing "champione" with the bastardisation of champion and *campione* that is now too much a part of English culture to correct. (It's just a shame that the grammar police were not there to set them straight; perhaps even to disperse the party, as such crimes are unforgivable.)

In the crepuscular tableau at Anfield, fans lit flares and fireworks to the sound of honking car horns.

For all the waiting, the end was slightly anticlimactic in that Liverpool were not playing, and there could be no mass congregation due to the coronavirus (not that it stopped everyone). There would be no parade to prepare for. And for once, there was no great *drama* – at least not on Liverpool's part. The greatest single night in the club's history remains Istanbul, while the 2019 Champions League – the club's hitherto only other *really major* honour since 1990 – had the Barcelona semifinal, that will have a chapter all of its own in the folklore. Even the 2001 and 2006 FA Cup finals had late incredible drama, and many of the trophies the Reds won in the 30 years were on the nerve-shredding knife-edge of penalties. There was even the new rule of the golden goal in extra time in 2001, and while it was later replaced with a return to playing the full 30 additional minutes, the Reds grabbed a 117th-minute game-ender in the 2001 Uefa Cup final; as soon as the ball hit the back of the net, that was it – Gérard Houllier's men had completed their cup treble. So many of the Reds' trophies during what were – only by the club's own standards – three fallow decades, were won in some remarkable way; although in 2020, the entire situation was surreal and unique. It had its own drama – the global pandemic – that was much larger than anything in previous seasons, but that drama was not visible at the denouement, other than in the absence of fans, and the normal celebrations.

Thinking back, the successful league season – the first in 30 years – also had plenty of those high-drama on-field moments too; but it was almost July 2020 when the title was sealed, and many of them happened back in late 2019 – Aston Villa at Halloween being perhaps the most remarkable; but even after that, once Manchester City were beaten in the following game, even the comebacks and the late winners were achieved with a points lead that seemed increasingly unassailable. (Of course, not that we, as Liverpool fans, could ever quite relax.) The fact that the league could have been null-and-voided added further intrigue, while more than 50,000 dead in England from Covid-19 as part of a worldwide total that stood at half a million, and the global Black Lives Matter protests (mostly peaceful), made football feel a little more trivial; and yet, at the same time – as the paradox that is part of its enduring appeal – an even more important form of escapism from the descending darkness.

Now inside the golf clubhouse, Virgil van Dijk was mobbed by his teammates during his live interview on BT Sports, which followed a FaceTime interview with a champagne-drinking Kenny Dalglish whose phone – which had not been switched to silent mode – was receiving so many messages he ended up sounding like R2D2. Over on Sky (after BT failed to get an audio connection with him), Klopp – already red-faced – was soon reduced to tears; excusing himself from the Zoom interview, which included Dalglish, Graeme Souness and Phil Thompson, after eight minutes, when no longer able to speak, his voice tremulous, his throat constricted, the emotion just overwhelming him. Souness had just expressed how remarkable he found the current team's consistency; something, he said, that even the teams he played in could not match. (Such glowing, unrelenting praise from Souness is enough to reduce anyone to tears; this is not a man who is prone to eulogising. Add the illusion that Souness was also actually making *eye contact*, and anyone would melt.)

To better express himself, the next day Klopp wrote an open letter to the fans via *The Liverpool Echo*, "As well as the current players, I would like to pay special tribute to two of our former players who set many of the standards that all of us have to follow. Sir Kenny Dalglish is the soul of this club. His understanding of what Liverpool is and what it means to the people is vital to everything that we do. I saw how happy he was after we were confirmed as champions on Thursday and his smile meant so much to me that I can't put it into words.

"Steven Gerrard is the legs. He carried the club in so many ways as a player and there is no one who deserves this title more than he does. Along with Kenny, Steven is a symbol of this club and it is important that at a moment like this that we remember everything that all of our former players and former managers did to help put us in the position that we are in today.

"These are the people who built Liverpool. The same goes for our owners and I cannot speak highly enough of them or what they have done. In modern football you have to have a vision, a strategy and an unshakeable commitment to the cause to stand any chance of being successful. On all three fronts, Fenway Sports Group have shown to me that they are leaders in the field. My appreciation for them is absolute."

"You have to respect the things he does," Trent Alexander-Arnold told BBC Radio 5 Live. "To change the whole club, to change everyone from doubters to believers, to get everybody thinking the same way, believing the same way and having the same dreams... He just embodies the whole club. Even without being from the city, the country and being local, he just clicks with the club. He does it with every person - the fans, the staff and the players."

Barney Ronay of *The Guardian* wrote: "No asterisks. No caveats. And let's face it, no contest. For the last few months a theory has been doing the rounds that the ersatz nature of the Premier League endgame, five weeks of press-ganged summerghost-ball, would drain the colour from Liverpool's first league title in 30 years.

"Fat chance. Death, plague and economic collapse may have stalked the land, puncturing sport's ability to pretend the rest of the world is simply a subplot. But sport has many functions beyond simply flag-waving and Liverpool's success will be deeply felt at a club where, as with every other club, football has always been a bit more than just football.

"Not least for the players, a group of athletes who have achieved a kind of personal ultimacy in each other's company, reaching out into the very limits of their own powers, and playing these last 18 months through a kind of fury.

"Make no mistake, this was an annihilation. Liverpool didn't just outrun the rest of the field. From late summer into spring they seemed to be operating to a different set of physical laws, marching the Premier League around in a headlock, ruffling its hair, flicking its ears."

Just before the restart, the *London Evening Standard* reported that "Almost a third of football fans would sacrifice their own clubs' prospects for the remainder of the season in order to see Liverpool miss out on the title, a survey has found...", with the anti-Liverpool results even more marked in the capital amongst fans of Arsenal, Chelsea and Spurs, at well over 40%. Thankfully those fans – whose own clubs were at that point largely too mediocre to be in contention for *anything* – ending up chewing bitter pills and eating humble pie.

A week after being crowned champions, Liverpool went to Manchester City, and Pep Guardiola's players gave the Reds a half-hearted guard of honour, with Bernardo Silva (who just seems generally antagonistic) refusing to even lend his applause. City thrashed Liverpool, who looked like they'd been on the beer all week; but it was surely mainly the emotional release of not only their own efforts, but the 30 years of history they were carrying on their shoulders. City labelled the win as part of *next* season having already started, and then promptly lost 1-0 at Southampton.
Woo-hoo!

At Long Last…

The final games of the season saw Liverpool play a lot of extremely good football but, with nothing at stake, the cutting edge wasn't always there, and the defending was not as ruthless as it had been, with mistakes creeping in. The Reds were below par against Aston Villa but grabbed two late goals, and won 3-1 in an open game at Brighton. The run of 24 consecutive league home wins ended when Burnley inexplicably grabbed a draw against the run of play, before, four days later, the Reds had an astonishing 24 shots at Arsenal, while the hosts mustered just three, but the game ended 2-1 to the Gunners. (These kinds of games – with the shot count so wildly in favour of the losing team – are not "tactical masterclasses" by the victorious managers, but often swing purely on the randomness of finishing and whose goalkeeper had the better game.)

There were thirteen different goalscorers in the Reds' nine post-lockdown games, with the usual trio of Mo Salah, Sadio Mané and Roberto Firmino joined by Fabinho, Trent Alexander-Arnold (with two stunning 25-yard free-kicks), Curtis Jones, Jordan Henderson, Andy Robertson, Naby Keïta, Alex Oxlade-Chamberlain, Gini Wijnaldum, Virgil van Dijk and Divock Origi. With the exception of Jones, who only played a handful of games, everyone on that list ended the season with at least two league goals; as did James Milner. Add the helpful scorer Own Goal (who had transferred to Liverpool from Manchester United), and it made 14 players who racked up at least two Premier League goals. The midfield was *still* criticised for a lack of goals, even though its job was to balance the shape of the side, but Oxlade-Chamberlain, Wijnaldum and Henderson shared 18 goals across all competitions (Keïta added four more), while the defenders as a collective were well into double figures. The two full-backs, meanwhile, shared 25 league assists between them. (As an addendum, Firmino's goal against Chelsea – his first in the league at Anfield all season – involved a 20-pass move that started from … a *throw-in*; while Origi's goal against Newcastle, which involved an 18-pass move, also emanated from a throw-in.)

Boom!

July 22nd finally signalled the moment the Reds got their hands on the trophy, after the home game against Chelsea.

"It was for sure the most exceptional and successful year of my career," Klopp said, on the eve of the trophy presentation. "Being champion of Europe, England and the world doesn't happen too often. I think it makes sense that we take a picture with all four trophies [including the European Super Cup] because I don't think there are a lot of pictures in existence where a club has all four of these trophies. We will do that 100% and rightly so."

It's not just this was a rare achievement: *no one* had ever held all four at the same time before. Suddenly being ranked the 4th-best team *of all time* in the Elo rankings made a lot more sense.

Liverpool ended their home campaign with fireworks on and off the pitch, as they ran out 5-3 winners over Chelsea, with the celebrations outside the stadium starting well before the one planned for after the game; whip-cracks and bangs exploding in the night air and echoing around the empty stadium as the players tried to concentrate, with big chances arriving at either end of the pitch. Chelsea ideally needed something from the game to help cement their top four position, but even with that added requirement they fell short of a team essentially playing an exhibition match. The victory meant the trophy was lifted on the Kop with the Reds on the incredibly poignant figure of 96 points, some 31 years after Hillsborough, and 30 years after Kenny Dalglish lifted the club's previous title trophy. Unlike the Champions League, the Premier League format remained the same after its early '90s reboot; but also unlike the Champions League, the trophy was new.

In a virtually empty stadium – to swirling lasers and the kind of pyrotechnics often seen at Leicester and Wolves (before games) – Kenny Dalglish and the Premier League chief executive Richard Masters, their faces shrouded by masks, carried the trophy out onto the

Kop as if in some arcane religious ceremony in a post-apocalyptic landscape. One by one the members of the coaching and playing staff came up to accept their medals, doing a dance, taking a selfie with the trophy and waving into the dark void, where sat their families and some club staff, and no one else. Jordan Henderson – injured for the last few games of the campaign, after essentially leading the title charge all season – accepted the trophy, and lifted it with his trademark shuffle. Soon the *official* fireworks were going off inside the stadium, as everyone bar the cleaners marvelled at the millions of sparkling flickers of confetti that fired into the night sky.

The players and coaching staff did their best to enjoy themselves – lining up to sing *You'll Never Walk Alone* – and they were clearly having fun; but it was an even stranger sight than seeing games with no fans. And yet it was about the best that could be done in such unusual circumstances; something that seemed almost unthinkable just months earlier, as intensive care units across the land were overwhelmed with dying patients, and football seemed irrelevant.

A *real* celebration, Klopp promised, would be had once everything was back to normal. He would soon pick up the LMA Manager of the Year award, and his captain was voted the Football Writers' Association Footballer of the Year. But as nice as they are, the club is all about trophies, not individual honours.

Back in 2017, Anthony Stanley's *Tomkins Times* columns on each season of the Premier League were turned into a book: *A Banquet Without Wine: A Quarter-Century of Liverpool FC in the Premier League Era*. Well, that book can now be updated – the feast complete with added vino (*champagne*, even). The cover graphic depicted every trophy the club had won in that 25-year period – which was pretty much every one possible, bar the ghosted-out image of the Premier League trophy. Well, it's time to fill that image in, with the gleaming prize we have all been waiting for.

The wait was over and Jürgen Klopp, just like Bill Shankly all those decades ago, had made the people happy. Indeed, to circle back to the issue of the *perch*, Klopp – drunk on lager, and more than a little happy – phoned Alex Ferguson on the night of the title triumph. "I'll forgive you," Ferguson said upon presenting the Liverpool manager with his LMA award, "for waking me up at half past three in the morning to tell me that you'd won the league. Thank you! But anyway, you've thoroughly deserved it, well done."

Thirty years on, the liver bird was finally back on its perch.

Praise for Paul Tomkins and The Tomkins Times

"[Paul Tomkins' work is] … phenomenal. Absolutely quintessential reading for Liverpool fans."
The Redmen TV

"The Tomkins Times is an indispensable website whose diagnosis of all things Liverpool is beyond compare."
LFCHistory.net

"The best Liverpool FC writer, bar none."
Vic Gill, Bill Shankly's son-in-law and former LFC trainee.

"Perhaps the most intelligent guide to LFC available on the internet."
The Independent on Sunday

"Gold-dust analysis"
John Sinnott, BBC

"[Football analysis] is best left to the professionals, like the admirable Mr Tomkins."
The Daily Telegraph

"An ingenious and intelligent look beneath the surface to reveal what the headlines too often don't tell us. Fascinating."
Jonathan Wilson

"Another triumph of impeccable research, Pay As You Play brings much-needed factual insight to a discussion previously dominated by half-truths."
Oliver Kay, The Times

"Liverpool do happen to be blessed with supporters whose statistical analysis provides a lucid interpretation of where the club's strengths and weaknesses lie, accessible through the Tomkins Times website."
The Independent

A BIG THANK-YOU TO OUR BENEFACTOR SUBSCRIBERS

A Coles
Abraham Marret
Agnar Lavik
Aiden Halloran
Alan (Delta Driver)
Alan Hughes
Alan Ormrod
Alan Raleigh
Alex Merrifield
Alexander Tsachev
Allen Baynes
Alkesh Dudhaiya
Allan Høy-Simonsen
Allan Morris
Amer Mushtaq
Andrew Argyle
Andrew Arrojo
Andrew Chow
Andrew McAdam
Andy Coles
Angus Cheong
Anthony O'Brien
Anthony Partridge
Anthony Rodenhurst
Anton Black
Arjun Aiyar
Arjun Panchapagesan
Arun Butcher
Ashok Kelshiker
Asim Sarwar
B D Atherton
B Wright
Benjamin Freestone
Benjamin Howell
Bijin Benesh
Bjørnar Mikkelsen
Boerge Bolme
Boon Khai Tan
Booya BBQ
Bradley Knight
Brian Dolphin
Bryan Paisley
Callum Wilson
Ceri Glen
Chin Yet Ong
Chris Bracebridge
Chris Williams

Christine F Andrade
Ch. Christodoulakis
Christoph Tung
Christopher Bruno
Christopher Poh
Christopher Sewards
D Rock
Dan Jamieson
Daniel Zambartas
Danielle Warren
Darren Eyles
Darren Hanevy
David Evans
David F
David Hayward
David Kerr
David Miller
David O'Reilly
David Perkins
David Ryan
Declan McGill
Deena Naidoo
Dennis Lindsey Laurie
Donny Gow
Eamonn Turbitt
Edward Denton
Edward Robinson
Elbek Dalimov
Elisabeth Uggerloese
Emlyn Conlon
Eric Tan
Erin McCloskey
Fung Han Lim
George Bevan
George Ebbs
Gina Hoagland
Glenn Perris
Gøran Schytte
Greg Dickson
Greg Vinikoor
Guðjón Teitur Sigurðarson
Guohao Li
haluk arpacioglu
HongAik Yew
Ian Hopkinson
Ian Wilson
Ilan Shaw
Ingimar Bjarni Sverrisson
Ingvar Juliusson
Iyad Zahlan

J F Nolan
Jakra Srinaganand
Jamal Soliman
James Fleming
James Kelly
James Melvin
James O'Beirne
James Russell Johnston
Jan Ove Knudseth
Jared Faidley
Jason Ng
Jeff Orme
Jesper Marcussen
Jesse Wilde
Joe Power
John Clarke
John Goldie
John Gordon
John Hewitson
Jonas Luul
Jonathan Sowler
Justin Choong
Karapiah Tamilarasan
Kelley McDowell
Kevin Gibbons
Kinsley Ransom
Kostadin Galabov
Kris Barber
Krish Detter
Laurent Sampers
Lee Hammond
Leon Aghazarian
Leon Snoei
Leon Snoei
Lindsey Smith
Lodve Berre
M R Dancey
Marco Yeung
Mark Jeffcoat
Mark Jefferson
Mark Wise
Markus Topp
Martin Cooke
Martin McLaughlin
Matthew Beardmore
Matthew Duffey
Matthew Sewell
Matthew Willson
Michael Cheyne
M Gordon
Michael Sum

Michael Thomas
Michael Walston
Michael Williams
Mike Begon
Mohammad Al Sager
Mohd Farid Ibrahim
Murtaza Khan
N C O' Harte
Naomi Wilkie
Neil Brien
Neil Gold
Nick Hall
Nigel Ward
Noa Galili
Norman Hope
Ørnulf Schømer
Owen Kavanagh
Oyvind Henriksen
Padraic Leader
Patricia Jill Adamiecki
Paul Gottshall
Paul McCormack
Paul Morgan
Paulus Adhisabda
Peter Barber
Peter Danes
Peter Doyle
Peter Griffiths
Peter J Robinson
Peter Short
Phillip Collins
Philip Lindsay
Philip Tormey
Phillip Blanshard
Quinn Emmett
Raffi Hanneyan
Richard Harrington
Robert McHugh
Robert Sangster
Rolf Hoel
Ronny Knutsen
Rune Sollie
Sadiq Ahmadu-Suka
Sam McMaster
Santhanakrishna n Periathiruvadi
Saugato Banerjee
Sebastian Llabres
Sergio Trevino
Shawki Jounes
Shawn Warswick

Simon Barrington
Stephen Anderton
Stephen Benbow
Stephen Rigby
Stephen Robertson
Stephen Rowland
Stephen Sheils
Stephen Troake
Steve McCarthy
Steven Tan Stratoe Koutsouridis
Stuart Lloyd
Sujit Dasgupta
Suzanne Wiseman
Sze King Chong
T P Stringer
Taskin Ismet
Thomas Cannon
Thomas McCool
Tim Collins
Tomaz Racic
Torbjørn Eriksen
Waleed Alsager
Wally Gowing
Waqas Kaiser
Western Ivey
William Teck Sin Sim
Yasser Zayni
Yau Choi Yeung
Yoshiaki Izawa